Together We Fight

Together We Fight

Surviving Peru's Campaign
of Coercive Sterilizations

Ñusta Carranza Ko

UNIVERSITY OF CALIFORNIA PRESS

University of California Press
Oakland, California

Cataloging-in-Publication data is on file at the Library of Congress.

ISBN 978-0-520-39663-0 (cloth)
ISBN 978-0-520-39664-7 (pbk.)
ISBN 978-0-520-39665-4 (ebook)

GPSR Authorized Representative: Easy Access System Europe, Mustamäe tee 50, 10621 Tallinn, Estonia, gpsr.requests@easproject.com

35   34   33   32   31   30   29   28   27   26
10   9   8   7   6   5   4   3   2   1

CONTENTS

ABBREVIATIONS

AMAEF	Asociación de Mujeres Afectadas por Esterilizaciones Forzadas (Association of Women Affected by Forced Sterilizations of Anta)
AMPAEF	Asociación Nacional del Mujeres Afectadas por las Esterilizaciones Forzadas (Association of Peruvian Women Affected by Forced Sterilizations)
APRODEH	Asociación Pro Derechos Humanos (Association for Human Rights)
CAT	Convention Against Torture and Other Cruel, Inhuman or Degrading Treatment or Punishment
CEDAW	Convention on the Elimination of All Forms of Discrimination Against Women
CEJIL	Centro por la Justicia y el Derecho Internacional (Center for Justice and International Law)
CESCR	Committee on Economic, Social and Cultural Rights
CLADEM	Comité Latinoamericano y del Caribe para la Defensa de los Derechos de la Mujer (Committee for Latin America and the Caribbean for the Defense of Women's Rights)

CNDDHH	Coordinadora Nacional de Derechos Humanos (National Coordination of Human Rights)
CRC	Convention on the Rights of the Child
CRLP	Center for Reproductive Law and Policy (known today as the Center for Reproductive Rights)
DEMUS	Estudio para la Defensa de los Derechos de la Mujer (Study for the Defense of Women's Rights)
IACHR	Inter-American Commission of Human Rights
IACtHR	Inter-American Court of Human Rights
ICCPR	International Covenant on Civil and Political Rights
ICESCR	International Covenant on Economic, Social, and Cultural Rights
IDEH-PUCP	Instituto de Democracia y Derechos Humanos de la Pontificia Universidad Católica del Perú (Institute for Democracy and Human Rights)
IDL	Instituto de Defensa Legal (Institute for Legal Defense)
IWGIA	International Work Group for Indigenous Affairs
LUM	Lugar de la Memoria, La Tolerancia y la Inclusión Social (Place of Memory, Tolerance, and Social Inclusion)
MRTA	Movimiento Revolucionario Tupac Amaru (Revolutionary Movement of Tupac Amaru)
ONAMIAP	Organización Nacional de Mujeres Indígenas Andinas y Amazónicas del Perú (National Organization of Andean and Amazonian Women of Peru).
PIR	Plan Integral de Reparaciones (Comprehensive Reparations Plan)
PSRPF	Programa de Salud Reproductiva y Planificación Familiar (Program of Reproductive Health and Family Planning)
PUCP	Pontificia Universidad Católica del Perú (Pontifical Catholic University of Peru)

REVIESFO	Registro de Víctimas de Esterilizaciones Forzadas (Registry of Victims of Forced Sterilization
RUV	Registro Único de Víctimas (Registry of Victims)
UN	United Nations
USAID	US Agency for International Development

ACKNOWLEDGMENTS

This book has been a long time in the making, and I have incurred innumerable debts along the way.

For sparking my curiosity in this research, I thank Francisco (Pancho) Soberón. Pancho was a human rights activist and founder of the Asociación Pro Derechos Humanos (APRODEH). I am particularly grateful for the mentorship that I received from him. He was an extraordinary human being who, when I asked how I could repay him for all the help and mentorship he had given me in my research, simply told me to write, not give up on writing, and publish this book. This book is dedicated to the memory of Pancho.

For the development of ideas and feedback on the cases that I present in the book, I especially want to thank Rocío Silva Santisteban, Thomas Ward, Marie-Christine Doran, Harry Targ, Clifford Bob, Christy Thornton, and students and colleagues from Johns Hopkins University's Latin America in a Globalizing World (LAGW) forum. I am also grateful for the comments on parts of the research from the speaking invitations I received at the University of Pennsylvania's Center for Latin American Latinx Studies, University of Delaware, Center for Advanced Genocide Research at the University of Southern California, Johns Hopkins University's LAGW forum, and the University of Baltimore-School of Law.

Others who contributed insights and encouragement include Francisco Carranza Romero, Pascha Bueno-Hansen, Margaret Stetz, Sarah Federman, Ronald Niezen, Matt S. Weinert, Nienke Grossman, Elizabeth Salmón, Salomón Lerner, Licho López López, Gioconda Coello, Elizabeth O'Brien, Alejandra Ballón, Victoria Vigo, Hilaria Supa Huamán, Lucía Stavig, María Ysabel Cedano, Eduardo González, Charles E. Scheidt, and Sarita.

For critical financial and academic support, I thank the College of Public Affairs at the University of Baltimore, particularly Dean Roger Hartley. I am also thankful to my colleagues, whose assistance in my scholarship and teaching during this project has been crucial. This includes Ivan Sascha Sheehan, Jennica Larrison, Yunzi (Rae) Tan, Laura Wilson-Gentry, and Shelly Clay-Robinson. I am also thankful to the State University of New York–Binghamton's Institute of Genocide and Mass Atrocity Prevention's Charles E. Sheidt Faculty Fellow Program; Small Grants Program at the Women, Gender and Politics Research Section of the American Political Science Association; and the University of Maryland Women's Forum Faculty Research Award.

At the University of California Press, I would like to also express my most sincere appreciation to acquisitions editor Enrique Ochoa-Kaup, whose patience, sound advice, and eagerness to assist made my task easier. In addition, I greatly appreciated the dedicated copyediting help from Catherine Znamirowski and Aleksandra Kasztalska.

My thankfulness to my friends and family is greatest. A special note of thanks to my friends Junheui Lee, Hyowon Lee, Aleksandra Kasztalska, Bharathi Radhakrishnan, Erica Stern, Andra Nicolescu, Christina W, Georgia S, and Kelly Stallard for their years of friendship and care. Most importantly, I thank my family. My husband Fernando, who has patiently waited for me to complete this project, and my daughter Marie, who has at times been frustrated that her best playmate is busy working. My parents Francisco and Hye Sun, who endured my numerous calls of complaints and helped me in better understanding the Andean Quechua world; my in-laws Luiz and Maria Angélica, who remained supportive; my sister Ayra and brother-in law Eric, who continued to encourage me; my niece and nephew Zoe and Alex, who cheered for me; and Nathalia, who has been an ally from afar. Your encouragement, support, and understanding made this whole thing possible. Gracias, Qam Kallarchi, Gomawoyo, Obrigada.

Introduction

Racialized Gender-Based Violence in Peru

It was a cold and wintry day in Lima, Peru, that June in 2017. The event was held in the Hotel Wyndham Costa del Sol in the middle-class neighborhood of Magdalena del Mar, more commonly referred to as Lima Moderna (Modern Lima). The passageway leading to the event was filled with the low chatter of people speaking in languages distinct from Spanish that sounded familiar to my ear. Farther inside, past the corridors of placards displaying names of nongovernmental organizations, intergovernmental organizations, and the embassy that sponsored the event (e.g., United Nations, Organización Nacional de Mujeres Indígenas Andinas y Amazónicas del Perú [ONAMIAP; National Organization of Andean and Amazonian Women of Peru], and the Embassy of Canada), was the room that had been converted into a conference space for the "Conversatorio—Esterilizaciones forzadas: Mujeres indígenas en búsqueda de verdad, justicia y reparación" (Discussion—forced sterilizations: Indigenous women in search for truth, justice, and reparation). Facing the main podium, dozens of women wearing colorful attire that symbolized the various Indigenous communities of Peru sat and talked among themselves in Indigenous languages native to their places of residence, such as Asháninka from the Amazonian areas and Quechua dialects from the Northern and Southern Andean regions of Peru.[1] There were also women in the audience who spoke Spanish. These women had traveled to Lima from their hometowns—some traveling for days—to witness what the event's discussion would reveal about the coercive sterilization of thousands of women during the second term of President Alberto Fujimori's government (1995–2000).

From 1996 to 2000, the coercive sterilization campaign was disguised as a family planning program under the name Programa de Salud Reproductiva y Planificación Familiar (PSRPF; Program of Reproductive Health and Family Planning).[2] The program resulted in the sterilization of 294,032 people. Most of this population consisted of women (and some men) of poor, rural, and Indigenous-language-speaking backgrounds who were sterilized without consent, misinformed about the practice, and forced to undergo surgery. Initially, members of the human rights community, particularly women's rights organizations, were split: Some raised concerns about PSRPF, while those who supported it believed that the family planning policy reflected a progressive women's rights discourse initiated by President Alberto Fujimori at the 1995 Beijing Conference on Women.[3] Their position, however, quickly shifted against the policy after reports of irregularities in the application of PSRPF began circulating in newspapers, and human rights activists began sounding the alarm about the program. Human rights lawyer Giulia Tamayo's investigative report on sterilization practices from 1996 to 1998 and the Human Rights Ombudsman's Office reports on tubal ligations added more weight to the concerns being raised about PSRPF.[4]

With time, this family planning program and its genocidal policies became a driving force in mobilizing nongovernmental organizations in defense of women's rights (e.g., Estudio para la Defensa de los Derechos de la Mujer (DEMUS; Study for the Defense of Women's Rights). This program also received greater attention in the

Inter-American Commission on Human Rights (IACHR) (i.e., *María Mamérita Mestanza Chávez v. Peru*) and the Inter-American Court on Human Rights (IACtHR) (i.e., *Celia Ramos v. Peru*), and even became prominently discussed during Peru's 2016 presidential elections.[5] Some artistic movements committed to defending women's rights, such as Alfombra Roja, made media headlines with their performance art about PSRPF. In one popular series of interventions, participants wore red clothing to symbolize the gender-based violence inflicted upon women who were sterilized against their will. Throughout 2013 and 2014, Alfombra Roja's activism and gatherings were organized in the Palace of Justice, the Ministry of Women and Vulnerable Populations, the Cathedral of Huancayo, and other local government buildings and spaces, and during press conferences of nongovernmental organizations and political party gatherings.[6] These forms of activism, however, were unsuccessful in their attempts to bring the case of coercive sterilization into mainstream political, social, and legal discourse. In fact, one could argue that coercive sterilizations had been marginalized, even in the broader human rights discussions, since they were excluded from Peru's Truth and Reconciliation Commission (TRC) report, which investigated and summarized its findings on human rights violations from the internal armed conflict period (1980–2000).[7] As scholars note, the exclusion of this crime from the TRC report presented an even greater obstacle for victim-survivors to seek criminal accountability, let alone to receive reparations.

Against this backdrop, the Conversatorio I attended in June 2017 was organized by ONAMIAP in collaboration with the United Nations in Lima to discuss the case of coercive sterilization. It was a timely event, as interest in studying coercive sterilization had decreased after the 2016 presidential elections, and in July 2016 the Public Prosecutor's Office refused to consider cases of forced sterilization against Fujimori and his government personnel, explaining that there was insufficient proof of the crime.[8] Unfortunately, coercive sterilizations were—and to some extent still are—not considered a pressing matter within the broader discourse of the human rights violations that occurred during the internal armed conflict period. In fact, while some scholars and human rights activists consider the case to be a modern-day genocide of Indigenous women and, more broadly, a case of discrimination against socioeconomic and gendered minorities in Peru, it is a story that remains sidelined.[9] Yet despite the government's and scholars' waning interest in this topic, the Conversatorio attracted an array of participants with firsthand experience in coercive sterilization, including numerous Indigenous women who were directly affected as a result of forced sterilization; personnel from organizations for reproductive rights, including those from intergovernmental organizations; and people generally interested in human rights. Thus, the public Conversatorio was a step forward in amplifying visibility and generating more interest in the case from the public.

After the initial welcome remarks by Ketty Marcelo López, president of ONAMIAP, everyone observed a moment of silence to watch the documentary produced by ONAMIAP and the International Work Group for Indigenous Affairs (IWGIA) on coercive sterilizations. The documentary, *Esterilizaciones forzadas: Un camino a la justicia* (Forced sterilizations: A road towards justice), included testimony from women of Indigenous descent, from the Amazonian areas to the central Andes region of Ayacucho. The people in the audience gasped and exhaled, and some, including myself, shed tears while watching and listening to the stories being told on screen. The documentary served as a reminder that the violence inflicted against the women took place throughout many different parts of Peru. After the screening, two Indigenous women shared their experiences as victim-survivors of coercive sterilization. One victim-survivor had been forcibly taken from her Indigenous community in the Amazons, coercively given anesthesia, and subjected to tubal ligation surgery. The other had had a similar experience in the Southern Andean region, having been discharged without a proper postoperative consultation. Their stories resonated with audience members, some of whom shared their own experiences with forced sterilization, thus creating a sense of camaraderie among event participants. Following these personal accounts, personnel from nongovernmental organizations discussed the need to fight against this injustice. At one point, United Nations Special Rapporteur on the Rights of Indigenous Peoples Victoria Tauli-Copuz expressed her deep concern over the impunity surrounding the case. Many participants also noted the various types of coercion that women endured during the sterilization process and the enduring effects of these forced procedures on their physical and mental health. At times, the physical and mental health effects of coercive sterilization threatened the victim-survivors' lives. Yet the suffering of thousands of these women had not been enough to ensure legal accountability, let alone reparations.

Attendees of part Indigenous descent, like myself, understood that coercive sterilizations and the stories about them that the survivors shared—both in the documentary and during the public event—could have easily happened to a member of our own extended family, such as an aunt or cousin who resides in the Northern Andean community. A sense of anger, anguish, and despair that this case evoked in me, as a person who shared something with the Kichwa (Quechua)-speaking Indigenous communities, as a woman, and now as a mother, made this research personal. How did the government get away with the genocidal act of sterilizing thousands of women predominantly of Indigenous descent? What conditions and contexts made it possible for the stories of these women (of both Indigenous and non-Indigenous descent) to be lost, overlooked, and ignored? Who are the people that support these victim-survivors, and what motivates their activism?

In *Together We Fight: Surviving Peru's Campaign of Coercive Sterilizations*, I engage with these questions by centering the voices of the victim-survivors and their allies. This deliberate focus on the victim-survivors brings to the forefront what the coercive sterilization campaign meant for Peru's Indigenous communities, Peru's women (Indigenous and non-Indigenous), and Peruvian society as whole. The main objective is twofold: (1) to present the perspectives of actors who were and are involved in the significant, yet often overlooked, reproductive rights violations associated with this case; and (2) to amplify and strengthen the collective voices of victim-survivors of Indigenous and non-Indigenous descent as well as their allies. This is to ensure that this case is not forgotten, some form of justice is rendered, and these actions are never again repeated. In writing this book, I have pieced together how the coercive sterilization case unfolded and the context (including societal reactions) in which the women's struggles for justice took place. The context extends to the period after the death of former President Alberto Fujimori on September 11, 2024, during the resurgence of Fujimorism (a largely right-wing movement centered around the legacy of the former president and his family's political party), which threatens human rights movements seeking justice from Fujimori's administration. This book thus comes at a critical moment and adds to the pressing need to confront, think, and respond to those that challenge the collective voices of victim-survivors and allies.

CASE AND METHODS

I first encountered the case of coercive sterilization of women in Peru in 2014. I was concluding my research on cross-regional comparative transitional justice processes, which covered several countries. This transitional justice project focused on norms of reparations, truth seeking, and criminal accountability and compliance with norms as policies in three countries, Peru, Uruguay, and South Korea. While conducting fieldwork and interviews with human rights activists and scholars abroad, I was positioned in Peru's Institute for Human Rights and Democracy (Instituto de Democracia y Derechos Humanos de la Pontificia Universidad Católica del Perú; IDEH-PUCP) as a visiting researcher. There, my work focused on Peru's TRC, with an emphasis on the results of the findings and policy outcomes that were generated. At that point, I became more aware of women's rights violations that had occurred during Peru's period of internal armed conflict, including those that were missing from the final report of the TRC. The focus on gender-based violence and the stories that were missing from the truth-seeking processes led to many conversations with human rights scholars and activists. For instance, I had one discussion with the founder of Asociación Pro Derechos Humanos (APRODEH; Association for Human Rights), Francisco Soberón, about the limitations of truth-seeking processes. Our discussion revolved around the framing of Peru's TRC: Because the commission had a mandate to explore human rights violations that occurred during the country's internal armed conflict period and that involved the state and subversive leftist guerrilla forces, this framing left out other human rights violations committed by the state that did not fall within those parameters. Our conversation led to a continuing relationship with Soberón, who provided me with the opportunity to interview other human rights activists and scholars. This in turn allowed me to further engage with larger ally movements that formed in defense of women's rights, namely related to the forced sterilization cases. The stories of many of the individuals I met during my research on transitional justice are included in this book.

Regarding methodology, I have used a combination of methods. First, the empirical chapters are predominantly based on archival research. This includes the usage and analysis of primary documents from many entities: the final report from Peru's TRC; legislative records and special committee reports generated by governments (i.e., Peru and the United States); memos, publications, and notes from nongovernmental organizations; and legal treaty documents and related reports from intergovernmental organizations.[10] In some cases I have used newspaper records, particularly to identify the most up-to-date developments regarding coercive sterilization cases within the criminal justice system of Peru.

Second, archival research–related findings are complemented by seven stories of women victim-survivors of coercive sterilization, human rights activists, and scholars. Of the seven women whose stories are present in this book, two are victim-survivors. One of the victim-survivors is Sarita, who is a Kichwa-speaking woman of Indigenous descent, and the other is Victoria, of non-Indigenous descent. Each brings her own breadth of experience about coercive sterilizations. Sarita's case has not been heard previously, neither in public hearings nor among victims' cases reported in media outlets. She suffered the crime as an underage minor in a rural area of Peru, where she currently still resides. On the other hand, Victoria's case is widely known, yet little attention has been given to the death of her prematurely born child as a result of her coercive sterilization. She was forcibly sterilized in Piura, the eight largest city in Peru.[11] In addition to the two victim-survivors, I have also included the voices of five human rights activists, also women. They are of Indigenous and non-Indigenous descent, some being scholar-activists whose involvement in their search for justice on behalf of victims began at diverse points of the family planning program implementation. They include Rocío Silva Santisteban, current leader of the nongovernmental organization DEMUS, a human rights activist, scholar, and former congresswoman; María Ysabel Cedano, a human rights activist, lawyer, and former leader of DEMUS; Alejandra Ballón Gutiérrez, a human rights activist, scholar, and artist; Ketty Marcelo López, Indigenous human rights activist and president of ONAMIAP; and Hilaria Supa Huamán, Indigenous human rights activist, former parliamentarian, and community leader. Some of these women joined at the onset of the report of coercive sterilizations, while others became involved because of what other activists were reporting, and together they now represent the key allies contributing to the movement in defense of victim-survivors. As a whole, victim-survivors' and allies' voices represent both Indigenous and non-Indigenous women's voices in defense of women's rights, Indigenous rights, and reproductive rights.

Along with these stories, there are two additional voices of Kichwa (Quechua) scholars in this book. One is Francisco Carranza Romero, an Indigenous scholar, community leader, and linguist from the Northern Andes of Peru whose work is deeply engaged with Indigenous communities. The other scholar is Lucía Stavig, a longtime collaborator of

Hilaria Supa Huamán, whose work in anthropology involves women who were coercively sterilized. These voices are included throughout various parts of the book to provide more context to the legal, sociopolitical, and cultural discussions.

Admittedly, my selection of those whose stories are told means that I will not be engaging in discussions that involve all victim-survivors of coercive sterilization or all activists and organizations that were involved in the movement against impunity for this case in Peru. In fact, this book does not purport to represent all the individual experiences of Indigenous and non-Indigenous victim-survivors and activists. However, there is merit in exploring the understudied stories from victim-survivors, analyzing normative angles that have not been discussed, and reflecting upon the allies and allyship that helped call attention to this case. Their stories will bring to light how coercive sterilization can be understood within the framework of genocide; highlight the victimhood of Indigenous children who have yet to be acknowledged; draw attention to non-Indigenous victim-survivors who have been at the forefront of activism; and explore the role of human rights nongovernmental organizations and activists. Particularly, on the basis of speaker selection, each story, including those of victim-survivors and allies, includes the individual's own experiences associated with coercive sterilization and shares their meaning of justice associated with this case.

Indigenous Methods

Research, primarily that which centers on Indigenous stories, such as this case, where the majority of victim-survivors are of Indigenous descent, embeds Indigenous values and beliefs.[12] For this reason, when engaging with the stories of Indigenous women I draw on methodologies that have Indigenous roots. As Indigenous scholar Shawn Wilson notes, the "use of an Indigenous research paradigm when studying Indigenous peoples requires the holistic use and transmission of information," where what is more "culturally appropriate for Indigenous people" is for the researcher to take on the role of a storyteller who serves to retell the stories and listen to Indigenous peoples' experiences.[13] This is somewhat emic for people of Indigenous descent or those who are a part of Indigenous communities. As Wilson explains, when "outsiders [are] researching Indigenous peoples" a problem arises: "There is always a comparison made between the culture of the studied and that of the studier." Indigenous scholars may be able to avoid the imposition and comparison with dominant cultures and systems, given their unique positionality and by recognizing the "holistic approach to oppression that is evident in all of the ways that Indigenous peoples are held down by research."[14] I follow Wilson's methodological recommendations in my study, both in my style of writing and my approach to engaging with Indigenous women.

First, there is a conscious effort in this book to not refer to Indigenous peoples as *pueblos originarios* (original peoples). This, in part, follows the conception of Bolivian sociologist Silvia Rivera Cusicanqui, who explains how the label of "origin" in effect "denies the contemporaneity" of Indigenous populations and "excludes them from the struggles of modernity." By referring to peoples as *pueblos originarios*, one is assigning a "residual status," which converts Indigenous peoples into "minorities, ensnaring them in indigenist stereotypes of the noble savage and as guardians of nature."[15] Additionally, as this term carries the stereotype of a group of peoples with a designated territory who live in rural areas with particular ethnic and cultural identifiers, it excludes the presence of Indigenous peoples who reside elsewhere (e.g., in cities). For this reason, Cusicanqui argues that the terminology reflects a strategy of "depriving indigenous peoples of their potentially hegemonic status and their capacity to affect the state."[16] Given that these ideas are associated with *pueblos originarios*, this book conscientiously uses the term "Indigenous peoples."

Relatedly, within the Peruvian legal lexicon, the wording *comunidad nativa* (native community) has been used interchangeably with *comunidades campesinas* (agricultural communities) in place of Indigenous peoples.

These terms emerged with the 1979 Peruvian Constitution, where under Article 161 the state recognized the "legal existence" and right to "autonomy" of land/territory for the *comunidades campesinas* and *comunidades nativas*.[17] The same norms and terminology were reiterated in the subsequent Constitution of Peru in 1993, under Article 89.[18] Similar language of referring to Indigenous peoples as *comunidades nativas* emerged with the 1969 Ley de Reforma Agraria (Agrarian Law Reform) and the 1978 Ley de Comunidades Nativas y de Desarrollo Agraria de la Selva y de Ceja de Selva (Law of Native Communities and Agrarian Development of the Amazon and Outer Edges of the Amazon [Jungle Areas]).[19] Particularly, the Ley de Reforma Agraria replaced the denomination of *comunidades indígenas* (Indigenous communities) with *comunidades campesinas* (agrarian communities).[20] National holidays, such as June 24, named the *día del indio* (day of the Indigenous) also was replaced by a new name—the day of the *campesino* (those associated with agricultural work).[21] The agrarian reform and the *campesino* thus created a new class identity, which "rather than overlapping with ethnicity, instead replaced the ethnic identity of individuals."[22] As some scholars note, the introduction of the term *campesino* was a form of assimilationist policy used by the government to displace Indigenous peoples.[23] This rhetorical erasure reflected the efforts to make Indigenous peoples invisible in official, public, societal, and even educational discourse. While this identity did not erase the practice of Indigenous languages or customs, it did create an additional class-based identity for Indigenous peoples, who now self-identified as *campesinos* who spoke Kichwa (Quechua), Aymara, or some other form of Indigenous language.

The *campesino* identity also facilitated expansion of Peruvian government and private sector mining interests into Indigenous peoples' lands, as according to the government these were *campesino*-residing areas.[24] Indigenous lands are protected by the International Labor Organization's Indigenous and Tribal Peoples Convention from 1989 (commonly referred to as ILO Convention 169), which binds governments to engage in "prior consultation" with Indigenous peoples if there were ever to be any intrusion into Indigenous peoples' lands. According to the Peruvian government, *campesinos* were distinct from Indigenous peoples and for that reason were not protected by ILO Convention 169. Indigenous communities, supported by intergovernmental organizations (e.g., the Committee of Experts on the Application of the Conventions and Recommendations of the ILO), pushed back, explaining their dual identity as *campesino* and Indigenous communities.[25] Furthermore, as not all individuals of Indigenous descent dedicate themselves to agricultural work, referring to Indigenous peoples as *campesinos* was also exclusionary to certain Indigenous peoples. I challenge the use of the term *campesino*, an artificial class-based identity imposed upon Indigenous peoples since 1969 with the Agrarian Reform and used in mainstream discourse. Instead, in this chapter and throughout the book I purposefully use the term "Indigenous" or "Indigenous peoples" to discuss experiences and identities of Indigenous persons.

Second, along with using the term "Indigenous persons/peoples," I use the capital "I" when referring to Indigenous peoples. This is built in part on the literature in Indigenous methods and my own positionality.[26] Specifically, capitalizing the "I" represents a decolonizing effort to restructure unequal power relations through changing terminologies. It is a conscious choice to recognize and emphasize the agency and sovereignty of Indigenous peoples in Peru and push back against pejorative traits linked to these peoples. Scholars explain that the term *indígena* (Indigenous) has been used in association with colonialist discourses that characterize this group of peoples in discriminatory ways.[27] For instance, the notion of the Indigenous person as a "brute, ignorant, lazy" reflects "cultural discrimination" within the Peruvian context which has a colonialist undertone.[28] In my choice to capitalize the letter "I," I am challenging and deconstructing the power dynamics manifested in colonialism, where to be Indigenous was to simply be a person who did not partake in European cultures. In fact, there was no "intent to define what is Indigenous culture," except in contrast with the European.[29] This contrasted identity of the Indigenous person to those of European origin involved a colonial power dynamic, in which Indigenous peoples are assumed to have characteristics that are "taken to be of distinctly lower value than the colonizer's own cultural repertoire."[30] Such comparisons were and are shared globally in non–Latin American contexts in which Indigenous populations also faced the violent arrival of Europeans. By capitalizing the "I," I acknowledge the agency of Indigenous peoples and their equal "human rights" status to that of "nations, ethnic groups, and other named political entities," not restricted to a contrasted frame with others (i.e., European).[31] In essence, "Indigenous" represents something that is above and beyond a term linked with politico-cultural and historical legacies.

As Colombian scholar Ligia López López and Ecuadorian scholar Gioconda Coello explain, "Indigenous" can be understood as a "genre" separate from only being understood in relation to the "stories of empires and kingdoms which overdetermined their own existence as the norm and in doing so justified the use of their power to displace people, narrate them as backward, and change their destinies."[32] It is a representation that is not limited to this relation and in fact goes beyond the confines of the colonial past. From a similar perspective, "Indigenous" as used in this book also embeds a sense of futures, a transformative agency of Indigenous peoples that are not objects of control but are self-determined and self-empowered. It is my hope this epistemological engagement will contribute to rewriting Indigenous experiences, recognizing the space and place of Indigenous peoples as equal contributors to society.

One thing that is important to clarify is that in referring to Indigenous peoples, this book does not aim to represent all Indigenous peoples and experiences in Peru. In fact, there is a concerted effort, from the introduction to each of the chapters that deals with victim-survivors' or allies' stories, to specify everyone's origin, including their linguistic capacities in specific Indigenous or non-Indigenous languages. For instance, in chapter 3, which narrates the story of one Indigenous victim-survivor, I specify the Kichwa (Quechua) mother tongue of the person, along with their region of residence. However, forced sterilization processes were unfortunately not quite unique or distinct for Indigenous women either from the Amazons or the Andes. As evidenced in the Quipu Project, which records anonymous testimonies of victim-survivors, and discussed further in the testimonies of Amazonian and Andean women and genocide in chapter 2, Indigenous women's experiences of forced sterilization were similar in the type of coercion they suffered, including the mistreatment by medical personnel.[33]

Ultimately, what matters more for this book than these terminological debates are the identities that victim-survivors of coercive sterilization use in reference to themselves. From the stories victim-survivors have told in person and the testimonies accessible via the Quipu Project, victim-survivors of coercive sterilizations who are of Quechua-speaking or Asháninka-speaking descent prefer to self-identify as "Indigenous persons" or "Indigenous peoples" in Spanish. As a result, "Indigenous" is the term that has been used and will be extensively used in discussing victim-survivors' identities. Related to these terminological debates and following the decolonial praxis and reflection of Cusicanqui, there is also a concerted effort in this book to use Indigenous scholars, feminist scholars, and scholarship originating from Latin America. As we are dealing with a genocidal health policy that impacted the majority of Indigenous peoples in Peru in addition to some non-Indigenous peoples—like Victoria Vigo, who is also discussed in this book—I use ideas from Indigenous scholars, feminist scholars, and intellectuals from Latin America to discuss context-specific matters, such as colonialism, ethnic discrimination, social class stratification, and gendered relations in Peru.

Positionality and Engagement with Women

To restate my engagement with various individual speakers in Indigenous terms, I am listening to and retelling the stories of the women in the form of storytelling. Listening allows for "open dialog between researcher and participant," and it "affectively implies accountability, as well as a commitment to growth and space for becoming."[34] This is somewhat similar to *testimonios* or testimonials, often referred to as a "verbal representation" or a "written representation of voice."[35] *Testimonios* have been used as "narratives of collective memories" and as a political narrative of oppression.[36] In these *testimonios*, the writer uses the "I" form to directly narrate their experiences, as evidenced in Guatemalan Indigenous activist and leader Rigoberta Menchú's narratives about her family's struggles, the pain of her people and their modes of resistance, and the atrocities and losses she and her Indigenous community suffered.[37] The person who narrated Menchú's stories (Venezuelan anthropologist Elizabeth Burgos-Debray) fulfilled the role of the transmitter of the stories, similar to the ways in which Indigenous storytelling, in this book, communicates the experiences of the Indigenous person, peoples, and the community. Hence, one can think of the usage of Indigenous methods of storytelling as overlapping with *testimonios* in that storytelling also contributes to a collective story, similar to how *testimonios* have been used to make sense of histories and shape a collective memory.

At this point, it is also important to emphasize my position in relation to the women whose stories I have listened to. I represent the union of two cultures, one Northern Andean Indigenous background from my father's side and the other Korean ancestry from my mother's side. As a person of part Indigenous descent, namely of Kichwa (Quechua)-speaking peoples, my language, tone, and focus of research reflect my positionality. As such, I have an advantage, as I am working with peoples' cultures that I am already a part of. I am, however, aware that I am part of Indigenous communities by relation and not necessarily through my day-to-day experiences over a long period of time. I also recognize that my linguistic ability in Kichwa is basic, while Spanish and Korean are my native tongues. Therefore, I have put an even greater emphasis on "relational accountability," which requires that I, as the listener, storyteller, and researcher, "form reciprocal and respectful relationships within the communities" whose stories I am transmitting.[38] To do so, I have continuously asked for input from Indigenous scholars about my style of writing, tone, and reproduction of stories that I am retelling.

Additionally, in explaining Indigenous peoples' views and thought processes, I center the current discussion on the importance of relations in Indigenous cultures. In Indigenous cultures, relationships are fundamental to the "Indigenous way of living and working in the world," in which the individual represents the relationships that one holds and is part of.[39] It is a cyclical, nonlinear worldview, wherein the present is part of the past, the past is part of the present, and there is "no forward or backward, no isolation."[40] Within this view, the individual and their experience is not compartmentalized as a separate entity from their surroundings but is considered integral to the whole. This view of relationships, which is fundamental in Indigenous communities, establishes the basis for my discussion of Indigenous women's stories and takes into consideration the needs of the Indigenous peoples. The development of this relational approach to research—one that is based on Indigenous cultures—leads to a better understanding of the unique challenges facing Indigenous peoples.

My approach to discussing the stories of women of Indigenous and non-Indigenous descent is also strongly influenced by decolonial feminists' ideas. Decolonial feminism, as gender studies and political science scholar Pascha Bueno-Hansen explains, studies the "ways that colonial relations of exploitation and domination function and persist to the present day."[41] This framework aims to reconceptualize former colonial states and necessitates the overcoming of colonial relations of economic power, territorial boundaries, and materialism based on patriarchal norms. To do so, it is important to engage in a feminist praxis that is inclusive of women who have been excluded by society marked by colonial traits. As notes Bolivian sociologist Silvia Rivera Cusicanqui, women's identities resemble a *tejido* (woven fabric), in that they weave in the theme of "interculturality through its practice: as producers, merchants, weavers, ritualist, creator of languages and symbols that attract the other, and ones who establish pacts of reciprocity and co-living among different peoples."[42] The feminist praxis is more grounded, organic, and far truer to the culture and origins of the space whence it emerges, helping the researcher to be aware of the power relations that have continued from the colonial period and to propose a vision of a world that is multicultural, is decolonizing, and rejects patriarchal roots of society (even within Indigenous communities). Similar ideas are noted by Mexican anthropologist Márgara Millán, who discusses the "capacity of feminism," more specifically one that engages in decolonial practices, to recognize its own "condition" of being colonized, engage with those who are at the margins of society (i.e., Indigenous populations and other minorities), strategize the deconstruction of racism and coloniality, and construct a future that is inclusive of Indigenous women and others in society.[43] From this vantage point, I intentionally engage with Indigenous and non-Indigenous women who are victim-survivors and activists/allies, understanding their positionality in an exclusionist society dominated by colonialist norms and reflecting upon their ideas about rights and justice.

I find these methodological approaches with Indigenous roots and grounded in decolonial feminist praxis to be also useful in communicating and transmitting the stories of non-Indigenous victim-survivors of coercive sterilization or allies of this movement. Despite the different ethnic backgrounds between the Indigenous and non-Indigenous victim-survivors presented in this book, both women's identities coincide in representing the intersection of marginalized sectors of societal class and gender. Indigenous research approaches (i.e., storytelling) are also more holistic and critically aware of the hegemonic or dominant systems of societal construction, emphasizing the excluded position of victim-survivor groups and excluding peoples, which helps to better understand victim-survivors' and allies' needs and experiences. Listening, which is at the core of Indigenous methods of storytelling, is in fact a "symbol for healing wounds of colonialism as a demonstration of resistance" and is considered an important part of decolonial methodology.[44] Drawing on these methodological approaches with heavy Indigenous, decolonial, and consequently feminist praxis, I also take on the role of a listener and storyteller in my engagement with the women.

ARGUMENT

In many scholarly accounts, the coercive sterilizations of a majority of Indigenous women from 1996 to 2000 have been linked with terms such as "eugenics," "socioeconomic differences," and "discrimination" built on ethnic and gendered grounds.[45] It is important to acknowledge the importance of discrimination as a violation tied to coercive sterilization, since marginalized populations are more vulnerable to discrimination in health-care settings than nonmarginalized populations. Studies have shown how forced sterilizations primarily target "women who are perceived as inferior or unworthy of procreation."[46] Related specifically to the treatment of Indigenous peoples in Latin America, this is a point that Eduardo Galeano raises when decrying the policies that were focused on killing the "beggar" or "beggars-to-be" before they were born—a population control policy that would eliminate those who are believed to later become a part of the future generations of poor classes in society.[47] These attempts to restructure society reflected colonial legacies of hierarchies that established race relations based on the concepts of "superiority"—linked with Europe and those of European descent—and "inferiority," linked with Indigenous and non-European peoples.[48] Such societal approaches, intensified by Malthusian beliefs of population control, targeted Indigenous communities who were part of the socioeconomically marginalized groups of peoples and were used as justification for the killing of the future generations of those who would reproduce poverty—a form of genocide. These explanations, in large part, frame the conversation about coercive sterilization as a normalized outcome for Indigenous women.

This book highlights the understudied voices of victim-survivors, both of Indigenous and non-Indigenous descent, within the coercive sterilization discourse and reveals the problems associated with not using an actor-centric approach to address this particular human rights violation. By focusing on the actors who were involved, either as victim-survivors or as allies, in the coercive sterilization case, this book lays the groundwork for a much-needed deeper conversation. Specifically, this book focuses on victim-survivors' visions of justice operating in an Indigenous and non-Indigenous context, allies' roles in challenging impunity, the intersections of these different actors' objectives, and the challenges of political interests that remain on the ground. I draw on stories from victim-survivors, experiences shared by human rights advocates and scholars of Indigenous cultures and studies, observations from public hearings, and over five years of in-person and virtual fieldwork as well as archival research, to trace the connections between victim-survivors' experiences, the violence that was perpetrated, and the current state of affairs related to the case. In addition, I focus on a new victim-survivor group—young girls (under the age of eighteen) who were forcibly sterilized—that has remained overlooked in existing research and legal petitions. Throughout the book, I focus on coercive sterilization as a violation of reproductive rights, noting its connections to human rights norms from various angles. By reproductive rights, I refer to the rights set forth by international legal norms that protect women's rights to privacy, education, freedom from discrimination, and protection from torture, all of which are interrelated with women's rights to health and access to reproductive health-care services and goods.[49] The other rights violations include women's rights, Indigenous peoples' rights, and children's rights norms, in addition to specific rights violations related to torture and genocide. Such collective rights violations have developed from a relational practice, with the state supporting the violence against groups of peoples through the family planning health program.

The PSRPF, which some scholars have noted was a genocidal policy that intentionally aimed to destroy either in whole or in part a specific population within Peru, grew to be the largest and most visible violation of women's reproductive justice rights.[50] Founded on the grounds of progressive reproductive rights, the program deceptively claimed to provide services to "promote, prevent, cure, and rehabilitate reproductive health to the highest quality."[51] Admittedly, in terms of maternity-related services, PSRPF did play a central role in providing women's access to contraceptive methods and education on family planning. Notable program objectives included the reduction of maternal and infant mortality rates, in addition to increased national use of contraceptive methods to reach the global average fertility rate of 2.5 children per woman.[52] Given these objectives, it seemed unlikely that any acts that violated women's rights would occur in Peru. However, from the onset of the program, the state prioritized sterilization campaigns and publicized them widely, targeting eight nonmetropolitan rural areas with majority Quechua-speaking populations.[53]

In this book, I argue that the PSRPF strategy was rooted in post-colonial perspectives of Peruvian society, mirroring the intersections of ethnicity, socioeconomic class, and gender. Together, these elements produced a discriminatory and genocidal policy targeting women of poor, rural, and Indigenous backgrounds. I use the term "postcolonial" to describe the survival of colonial visions of ethnicity, class, and power discrimination that subjugated nonwhite and noncolonial groups of power, namely the Indigenous population.[54] As Aníbal Quijano writes, post-colonial perspectives in governance were manifested in the form of most violent forms of repression, in which Indigenous peoples were deprived of opportunities, access to resources, and cultural heritage, and as "non-Europeans" or "colonized peoples," labeled as "inferior" to Europeans.[55] On the one hand, the Peruvian government launched a policy that was supposed to expand women's rights by providing access to family planning options. This was a controversial move in a country with a 76 percent Catholic majority.[56] Despite the Catholic Church's opposition to state-led family planning policies, the government embedded catchphrases of women's rights in its original policy mandates, emphasizing women's "freedom" and "autonomy" about decisions involving their bodies.[57] With this progressive-rights-based language, the Peruvian government was even able to garner support from feminist and women's rights non-governmental organizations, such as Manuela Ramos, which was one of the agents that implemented the program ReproSalud alongside PSRPF. Funded by the United States Agency for International Development (USAID), ReproSalud was an "innovative reproductive health and rights initiative" focused on "promoting better reproductive health."[58] Manuela Ramos advanced the ReproSalud program, which aimed to empower individual women to "advocate on their own behalf for improvements in available health services." This included educating women on sexual and reproductive health rights. However, in contrast to these women's rights objectives, the Peruvian government, through the implementation of ReproSalud and PSRPF, engaged in what I call genocidal policy by forcing massive numbers of women (and girls) from low-income and ethnically marginalized backgrounds to undergo sterilization procedures without their knowledge or consent.

The challenges that emerged after the culmination of the sterilization campaign served as confirmation that the government had intended to commit these wrongs against Indigenous women (and girls) and other women whom the state perceived were not a part of the dominant classes of society. Nongovernmental organizations' reports on coercive sterilizations went unnoticed. Calls to address irregularities in the family planning program by human rights activists were pushed aside, and any efforts to achieve criminal accountability were readily dismissed by the government. This case reflected the unequal system of societal relations: the dominant classes of society—defined predominantly by their ethnic and economic background—were the former colonial power holders who descended from Europe and thus could neglect, ignore, and push aside the horrific experiences of women of lower economic classes and Indigenous ethnic groups. This was the case because there were no consequences for the government's actions, and the victim-survivor group was—and still is—a minority (i.e., not part of Peru's dominant classes).

The subjugation or suppression of minorities—namely the socioeconomic minorities whose class status aligns with Indigenous communities who have been deprived of opportunities for power, economic gain, and education—is not a new phenomenon. It is a continuation of colonial visions about Indigenous peoples and Indigenous lands, from the very first encounters between European and Indigenous peoples. Walter Mignolo writes that the tale of "discovery" of the Americas was an imperialist "invention" from the European side.[59] For the Indigenous civilizations that were already established in the Americas, there was no "discovery" happening. Rather, it was an encounter shaped by "colonization" that generated the idea that "certain peoples" such as those of non-European descent "do not form a part of history" and are "not human beings."[60] As a result, from the early moments of conquest, Indigenous populations were annihilated to satisfy the "demand abroad for silver and gold."[61] Any form of violence inflicted against them, as detailed in *A Short Account of the Destruction of the Indies* in 1552, went unnoticed in the name of conquest, settlement, and capitalistic gains.[62] These realities reflected racial discrimination with long-standing roots in colonial legacies, something this book explores further in the ensuing chapters.

What was occurring in the late 1990s, and what were the experiences of victim-survivors? What were the positions of human rights defenders? How have their positions and views changed throughout the course of the aftermath of these policies? What has been each actor's conception of justice? These additional questions guide this book and illustrate the complexity of Peru's societal dynamics, political obstacles, and hurdles within the justice system that impede change. The human rights movement, however, has remained steadfast, producing a coordinated coalition of allies and victim-survivors represented through nongovernmental organizations, former politicians, activists, and scholars.

To understand how the victim-survivors and activists have continued their work and what their end goals are, it is necessary to understand and explore their stories, including how they became involved and why they have continued their work. This is the primary intention of this book: to provide a space for victim-survivors' and allies' stories to be represented. In essence, this book argues that the stories of the victim-survivors and allies need to be heard. In transmitting the voices and stories of victim-survivors and allies, this book also focuses on the contextual realities that each actor embodied. For instance, in recounting Indigenous victim-survivors' stories, consideration is needed in terms of what constitutes Indigenous beliefs and visions of reproductive rights, life, and community. The same is true for victim-survivors of non-Indigenous descent, whose economic and social contexts were influential in shaping their experiences. For allies, careful attention is paid to their positionalities, including their ethnic background and their journey of becoming involved as allies to the victim-survivors. If we want to understand the difficulties and struggles endured by the victim-survivors, we must grant them the opportunity to communicate and transmit their stories and allow them to explain what they experienced and how they perceived what was happening at the time. In short, this book draws from the personal experiences of Indigenous women, other victim-survivors of coercive sterilization, and allies to foreground the varied voices of this movement against impunity as well as their respective visions of justice.

GENDER-BASED VIOLENCE AND INDIGENOUS PEOPLES

The literature on racialized, gender-based violence against Indigenous peoples has historically been contextualized in research that examines colonial and postcolonial practices and policies that legitimized sexual violence.[63] They include studies that engage with the sexual exploitation of Aboriginal women in Australia and the government's policy of "unspoken reliance of biological absorption" channeled in practices of rape and sexual violence;[64] colonial reproductive politics in the United States that conditioned Native women's reproductive experiences in early reservation years with colonial policies that shrunk tribal lands, restricted the movement of Native peoples, and produced economic underdevelopment;[65] and genocidal policies of forced removal of children from Indigenous mothers who were forced to grow up as "white" either in white families or in off-reservation boarding schools in the United States, Australia, and Canada. Particularly, the removal of children can be seen as an extension of reproductive rights in terms of women's rights as mothers and their ability to care for their offspring.[66] Colonial genocidal violence against Indigenous women's reproductive rights thus did not stop once the woman was violently abused, but instead continued until the next generation was also traumatically impacted.

Other genocidal policies that normalized sexual violence against Indigenous women and impacted children and future generations of Indigenous peoples include settler-colonial governments' policies of coercive sterilization policies.[67] Scholars have documented various cases of coercive sterilization in the North American context.[68] As Sally J. Torpy and Myla Vicenti Carpio note, during the 1970s the Indian Health Service (IHS), an agency within the Department of Health and Human Services of the US federal government, was responsible for the involuntary sterilization of thousands of Native American women.[69] Similar sterilizations were also conducted in Canada. As Karen Stote explains, when discussing forced sterilizations in Canada, in Alberta alone more than 2,834 sterilizations were performed under the Sexual Sterilization Act, which was enacted in 1928 and remained in effect until 1982.[70] The act and its subsequent amendments allowed the state to categorize "any patient" who scored below the mandated IQ test category as "mentally defective," thus providing the legal grounds for sterilization. Given Aboriginal peoples' limited educational opportunities and lack of experience with Western European exam standard measurements, they were susceptible to being categorized as being "mentally defective." As a result, a disproportionate majority of Aboriginal peoples were sterilized, and the Canadian federal government "refused to make an incrimination declaration on the subject."[71] At times, forced sterilizations also took place within the context of Canada's residential schools. Annett documents how legislation permitting the "sterilization of any residential school inmate was passed in BC [British Columbia] in 1933, and in Alberta in 1928."[72] Aboriginal peoples were seldom given the chance to not be sterilized, and those who were proven "hostile to conversion and assimilation" into Western traditions and Christian practices were often targeted.[73] Similar sterilization practices also took place in Mexico. Scholars explain that sterilization practices were predominantly concentrated in impoverished rural and urban areas (places where Indigenous populations reside in disproportionate numbers).[74] Coercive sterilizations were primarily linked with Indigenous female populations, reflecting an often-ignored aspect of gendered policy that prioritized tubal ligations and not vasectomies. All of these governments shared the goal of/had the collective effect of violently unsettling Indigenous women, destabilizing Indigenous communities, diluting their biological ancestries and identities, and essentially wiping out Indigenous populations in one form or another, which scholars argue is a form of genocide that wiped out future Indigenous traditions, cultures, and peoples.[75]

Peru

Similar policies manifested in Peru, where the majority of the women who were sterilized by government policy were Indigenous. Before discussing research that examines this type of gender-based violence, however, there is merit to considering the literature on gendered violence in Peruvian society that contributed to laying the groundwork for this policy.

The TRC of Peru dedicated a part of its final report to addressing racialized gender-based violence from the internal armed conflict period (1980–2000). The TRC identified the profile of most victims of gender-based violence inflicted by the armed forces, security forces, and leftist guerrilla groups as being young Indigenous women. Jelke Boesten's work explores the impunity surrounding racialized gender-based violence from the internal armed conflict that further normalizes violence inflicted against Indigenous women. As Boesten explains, the identity of these victims unfortunately also overlaps with the profile of the majority of the victims of the conflict, particularly regarding the intersection of gender, race (a social construct), and class.[76] Class is extremely racialized, to the extent that "one cannot be middle class and Indigenous at the same time, because such 'acculturation' changes the race," as Boesten writes.[77] Race in Peru is tied to language, region, attire-related identifiers, education, and other physical characteristics (i.e., hair color and what not). Relatedly, gender helps define and stabilize the hierarchies based on race.

Bueno-Hansen points out a similar matter, noting how within the context of Peru, it is necessary to adopt an intersectional analytic sensibility that "reads for the factors, such as ethnicity, language, and gender, that interact to compound the effect of the internal armed conflict on certain people."[78] These certain people are the Indigenous peoples, more specifically Kichwa-speaking women whose identity represents the nexus of gender, class, and race. Relatedly, María Eugenia Ulfe also discusses the search for justice by victims of sexual violence from the internal armed conflict period, as well as contemporary issues of feminicide in Peru. She explains how, due to the fear of "societal shame and humiliation" and because they knew that "the state was not going to repair their suffering," Indigenous women found it difficult to come forward, let alone register as victims in the Registro Único de Víctimas (RUV; Registry of Victims)—a mechanism that allows victims of the internal armed conflict period to receive reparations from the state.[79] Ulfe further explains how the situation of sexual violence in the present day mirrors a similar victim dynamic, particularly the victims' identities—which represent a similar intersection of gender, race, ethnicity, and class. In other words, they represent victims who are from rural regions, of Indigenous descent, and from lower economic classes of society.[80]

Similar ideas are echoed in Cristina Alcalde's work on domestic violence. In her research on women who suffered domestic violence, she describes the regionalization of race in Peru and the "resulting association of various negative connotations with women from the highland region." *Sierra* (rural highland region) and *selva* (Amazonian jungle region) are associated with Indigenous cultures and languages, and thus, women who are from the *sierra* or *selva* are categorized as being of Indigenous identity. As Alcalde explains, both regions are "imagined as poor, backward, and racially inferior precisely because Lima ... is perceived as more powerful and white." The women of *sierra* and *selva* whom Alcalde interviews in her research are "perceived" commonly as embodying negative characteristics and are seen as passive, complicit in their suffering, and "enjoy[ing] violence because of their race and culture."[81] These ideas of racialized gender-based violence have colonial undertones and resonate with studies about the case of coercive sterilizations.

From 1996 to 2000, the Peruvian government used the disguise of a family planning policy to coercively sterilize thousands of women, the greater part of whom were of Indigenous descent, resided in rural areas, and were of poor economic background. Scholars and activists have analyzed the case of coercive sterilizations as a form of sexual violence, one embedded in deep-rooted racial discrimination resulting in the unequal treatment of Indigenous peoples. On the component of discrimination, Ernesto Vasquez del Aguila, Ñusta Carranza Ko, and Rosario De la Cruz Huamán have argued that the victim-survivor's identity related to this case was representative of the intersections of gender, ethnicity, and socioeconomic class dynamics in Peruvian society from the colonial period.[82] Indigenous peoples, particularly Indigenous women, represented the intersection of marginalized peoples in three distinct ways: (1) as a gender far from dominant power; (2) as an ethnic group subjugated by those claiming European heritage and thus assuming the colonizer role; and (3) as members of the lower economic class due to the structural inequalities that hampered Indigenous people's access to economic opportunities. Kimberly Theidon calls this campaign of forced sterilizations a war on reproductive rights derived from a discourse and ideology about the "war on poverty" and "economic development," which targeted Indigenous women and those of lower economic classes.[83] In short, as Melania Canales Poma writes, Indigenous peoples "always" have been treated as "inferiors, and as inferior beings they have enslaved us," an act so evident in this colonial imposition of so-called family planning directed only toward Indigenous women.[84]

Along with the intersectional analysis, this case of reproductive rights violations in Peru has also been presented as one that embodies multiple rights violations. Julissa Mantilla Falcón explains that the forced sterilization of thousands of Indigenous women represents the Peruvian state's violations of various international legal norms, including the right to life without discrimination and violence on the basis of gender.[85] As the state is party to international treaties that espouse and protect women's reproductive health rights, Mantilla Falcón calls on the state to recognize its international legal obligations and violations. Furthermore, this case has also been argued as a case of genocide. The outcome of the state's violence was the destruction of the reproductive health and rights of many Indigenous women and the destruction, in part or in whole, of a future generation of Indigenous peoples.[86] It was the *basurizacion* ("the act of becoming trash" or the act of "trashing") of a group of peoples, a reflection of a strategy of "us and "them," and a genocidal policy of "preventing" births, which Rocío Silva Santisteban calls a "silent and invisible genocide."[87]

This book presents and explores the stories of the women who participated in the reproductive rights movement against coercive sterilizations in Peru. The women in the movement include victim-survivors of coercive sterilizations, whose victimhood represents both Indigenous and non-Indigenous identities, and allies who help maintain the discourse on reproductive justice in Peruvian society. These allies are also of Indigenous and non-Indigenous identities, and their stories have never been presented in the literature before. This book's objective is to provide a comprehensive picture of the coercive sterilization atrocities and explore the meaning of justice, centering the stories and experiences of the actors—the victim-survivors and the allies who mobilized the movement against impunity from the beginning. After their stories have been presented, this book aims to unpack the ideas of justice that emerge from diverse perspectives and provide the space to engage in a dialogue about where the movement is headed next. In the process, this book engages with theoretical approaches about Indigenous women, racialized violence, and colonialism for thinking about coercive sterilization.

STRUCTURE OF THE BOOK

There are many interesting elements of Peru's coercive sterilization case and the politics of family planning specifically. However, most are beyond the scope of this book, which primarily aims to provide a space for victim-survivors' and allies' stories.

In chapter 1, "Gender, Class, and Ethnicity: The Politics of Victimhood," I reflect upon the intersectional theoretical lens of gender, class, and ethnicity that shaped the victimhood of the survivors. The intersectional victimhood was important in influencing the response from the state that impeded these women's struggles for criminal accountability. However, beyond considering this victimhood, the chapter also focuses on analyzing how the nexus of marginalized identities represented in coercive sterilization victim-survivors was at times politicized by political actors and by the victim-survivors themselves. The politicization of this victim-survivor group, particularly during political rallies, became a phenomenon that would occur every five years, coinciding with presidential election cycles in Peru. In this chapter, I explain how intersectional victimhood has offered opportunities for victim-survivors to push for administrations whose interests are more aligned with theirs. These include leftist administrations, namely that of President Ollanta Humala (2011–2016), whose government promulgated a supreme decree to create the Registry of Victims of Forced

Sterilizations (Registro de Víctimas de Esterilizaciones Forzadas; REVIESFO), and the administration of President Pedro Castillo (2021–2022), whose ministers held talks with leaders of victims' associations, such as the Association of Peruvian Women Affected by Forced Sterilizations (Asociación Nacional del Mujeres Afectadas por las Esterilizaciones Forzadas; AMPAEF).[88] Using these examples, I illustrate how victim-survivors in organized groups have also used their agency to set their agenda and mobilize for their own interests.

Chapter 2, "Indigenous Women and the Genocide: Peru's Coercive Sterilization of Indigenous Women," provides the first legal argument for considering the coercive sterilization case as an example of modern-day genocide against Indigenous peoples. It acknowledges that the literature remains theoretically useful in explaining the violence inflicted against a majority of Indigenous women, including a clear pattern of engagement in "crimes against humanity" by the Peruvian government under the leadership of President Alberto Fujimori.[89] Importantly, the normative analysis of the family planning program, which takes into consideration the human rights norms established in the international arena (e.g., prohibition of crimes against humanity), may be familiar to some readers. Yet it is the theorization of the case as a policy of genocide that provides the crucial backdrop and sets the tone for the rest of the book.

Furthermore, chapter 2 interweaves archival research and testimonies from victim-survivors in public forums to explain how and why the sterilization of Indigenous women ought to be understood within the framework of genocide. Critically unpacking this atrocity as genocide and using the normative standards from the United Nations Convention on the Prevention and Punishment of Crime of Genocide is crucial, for it reveals the gravity of the crimes committed against Indigenous women. My analysis elucidates, in short, the two main elements of genocide, pointing out the *mens rea* (guilty intent) and *actus reus* (material acts) of genocide that were evident from the planning phase of the PSRPF. Approaching this case as an atrocity that stripped

Indigenous women of their reproductive rights and jeopardized the futures of Indigenous communities is central to thinking further about questions that are not readily answered by the existing literature. The most important unanswered questions are: Why did a genocide against Indigenous peoples go unnoticed? Why has this case not been considered a form of genocide? Chapter 2 aims to provide the answers to these questions, which are central to understanding the stories of Indigenous women.

Chapter 3, "Then, There Were the Children . . . ," tells the first story of Sarita, a victim-survivor of coercive sterilization. It complements chapters 1 and 2 by retelling a personal story, out of which a new victim-survivor group is considered. While it is important to understand the coercive sterilization case as a history of atrocities committed against a majority of women who resided in rural areas, were of poor economic backgrounds, and were of Indigenous descent, it is also necessary to consider the possible victimhood of groups that may have been excluded in this history. The chapter uses Indigenous methods of storytelling to explore the story of Sarita, an Indigenous woman who was forcibly sterilized at the young age of seventeen. Her story is, in part, an account of how the victim-survivor experienced the process. At the same time, it is a story of how this victim-survivor and others like her in the community begin to identify and process the violence. This includes the question of what constitutes justice for the victim-survivor. Far from the stories that have been told in public forums and hearings, restated in legal briefings, or brought up in published academic literature, this chapter expands the scope of coercive sterilization as a violation of children's rights.

Chapter 4, "The Other Victims: Victoria Vigo's Story," provides space for another victim-survivor of coercive sterilization, Victoria, whose identity has not been a part of the dominant narratives of Indigenous women who were victimized. She, however, has been one of the most active leaders in the fight against impunity. Influenced by Indigenous methods of storytelling, we discover from her story that there were victim-survivors of the family planning program who were not of Indigenous descent and did not reside in rural areas. Her story, however, was similar to that of the other Spanish-speaking women who came from working-class backgrounds and were subject to coercive sterilization in urban city settings. With Victoria's story, this chapter explains and explores the broad reach of the family planning campaign and the victim-survivors who emerged from the violence against women's reproductive rights. The emphasis on Victoria's story also serves to provide the background on how initial attempts to seek justice, primarily criminal accountability, took off in Peru. As the first victim-survivor of coercive sterilization to sue the doctor who carried out the surgery, Victoria provides unique insight into the legal obstacles and the politics of reproductive rights that shaped the outcome. Some of Victoria's stories also center around the difficulties in generating among victim-survivors a cohesive human rights movement (inclusive of nongovernmental organizations and others alike) against impunity, notwithstanding the same type of crimes that they had suffered. What makes the cacophony interesting is how the perception of what constituted justice varied among victim-survivors. In 2001, the doctor in Victoria's case was found guilty of grievous bodily harm and sentenced to four years in prison; however, Victoria still felt dissatisfied with the case's outcome.[90] Victoria believed she had not been given true justice because the case failed to hold the entirety of the culprits—the government, health ministers, and those involved in the execution of the family planning policy—criminally accountable for their crimes. Victoria's experience navigating the process and searching for justice is important for understanding more clearly the complexities of the coercive sterilization experience in relation to victim-survivors. The stories Victoria shares in this chapter also further illuminate the history of international partners, such as USAID, that funded Peru's family planning program. Although actors like USAID backed out when irregularities (i.e., coercive sterilizations) were being reported at PSRPF's onset, the international organization's role as an initial program funder is arguably more important than the role of those organizations who were executing the program on the ground. This point is further explored in Victoria's story.

Chapter 5, "Together We Fight: Role of Activists and Allies in the Fight Against Impunity," provides a deeper examination of the allies that accompanied and formed the movement against forced sterilizations in Peru. This chapter narrates the formation of the movement in defense of women's rights and victim-survivors, emphasizing the processes through which each activist became aware of coercive sterilization cases and what prompted their involvement in the defense of victim-survivors. In essence, it is a chapter dedicated to recognizing activists and their various forms of work as artists, scholars, politicians, and nongovernmental organization personnel in advocating for victim-survivors' rights, especially from various positions of ethnic identity (i.e., Indigenous and non-Indigenous). I organize the chapter by focusing, first, on telling the stories of the allies, starting with the initial moments when they were exposed to the case of coercive sterilizations. When did they hear about this case, and why did it catch their attention? What were the early moments of advocacy like? And how did they become involved? This chapter explores the emergence of the movement against coercive sterilization, which later became an even more important political tool used to oppose Keiko Fujimori's bid for presidency. Keiko Fujimori is the daughter of former President Alberto Fujimori, the politician largely responsible for the coercive sterilization campaign that emanated from the family planning program he launched during his second presidential term. Allies were important in calling attention to coercive sterilizations and victim-survivors. As such, hearing their stories of the movement's early moments, including the behind-the-scenes moments of optimism, confusion, and tension, helps in creating a more comprehensive picture of what was taking place at the time.

After this chapter narrates the experience of each ally, it examines the relationship between the allies and the victim-survivors. Did it involve any struggles about reconciling differences in ethnic or class identity? Were there any growing pains associated with ally-driven objectives versus victim-survivor-driven goals? With these questions, this chapter examines the possible differences that were present in each group's understanding of justice and human rights and how they may have influenced the formation of priorities that have been put forward in the public realm. I highlight the complexities in navigating the needs of victim-survivors and advocates by helping readers gain a thorough understanding of how each group may have had different outlooks on the crime and different ideas about their final objective, including each groups' visions of justice.

The conclusion, "Justice, Reproductive Rights, and What Remains," brings back the stories of the victim-survivors, scholars, activists, and participants in the human rights movement, connecting them to broader normative discussions on Indigenous peoples' and women's rights, and hypothesizing the future of justice. In doing so, it takes a step back to analyze the broader context of human rights, focusing specifically on what remains of the efforts to seek justice and where reproductive rights stand within Peruvian society. In many respects, the fight has not changed significantly. After eighteen years of legal difficulties, on December 11, 2021, the Ministry of Justice opened official investigations into the coercive sterilization case against President Alberto Fujimori, his health ministers, and related persons from the Ministry of Health.[91] Despite this one step toward criminal accountability, there appears to be no end in sight regarding how much longer the process might take given the number of victim-survivors listed in the case—more than two thousand—and given the appeals that have been promised by the opposition. Furthermore, victim-survivors faced a controversial decision issued by the Constitutional Tribunal on March 17, 2022, which voted in favor of releasing Fujimori from jail, thus challenging the twenty-five-year sentence he had received in 2009 on charges of crimes against humanity, murder, aggravated kidnapping, and battery.[92] This decision eventually laid the groundwork for Fujimori's release on December 6, 2023. Nine months later, on September 11, 2024, Fujimori passed away, without having paid the civil reparations he owes since his conviction in 2009 and without being charged for forcibly sterilizing thousands of women—a case that is still in legal process in the judicial system. These developments indicated the difficulties in navigating Peru's criminal justice system in favor of victim-survivors of coercive sterilizations. Additionally, to date, reparations to victim-survivors of coercive sterilizations have yet to be distributed by the state, including those that were urged and obligated by the Inter-American Commission on Human Rights in two cases of coercive sterilizations (*Celia Ramos v. Peru* and *María Mamérita Mestanza Chávez v. Peru*), and it is questionable whether victim-survivors have been included in the conversations about the types of reparations they would like and want to receive.

Have Indigenous women and women who represent the intersection of marginalized identities been given a chance to be consulted and included in policy changes involving reparations? The gap between what victim-survivors want, namely what Indigenous women and other women who were victimized would like; what the allies are communicating as intermediaries; and what the government has determined is the adequate response, is a problem that still merits more discussion. The conclusion explores probable policies of symbolic reparations (i.e., memorialization initiatives) and truth seeking (i.e., truth commission) that generally accompany the aftermath of repressive authoritarian governance and human rights violations, which may serve as vehicles for the rapprochement of victim-survivors, allies, and government objectives.

In the end, there may be no adequate policy to address the atrocities that Indigenous women such as Sarita or others like Victoria have suffered. There may never be a perfect alliance that aligns everyone's interests, victim-survivors and allies alike. And yet there are several reasons to be hopeful about the search for justice: listening and calling attention to the stories of each victim-survivor, recognizing one's suffering and pain, creating a community of help that is based on one's *ayllu* (community that identifies as family per geography, bloodline, or shared objectives), and engaging in collective healing using Indigenous approaches to health. These reasons, combined with legal responses in criminal accountability, reparations, and truth seeking, may be just enough to start the search for justice.

CHAPTER ONE

Gender, Class, and Ethnicity

The Politics of Victimhood

According to 2015 census reports from Peru's National Institute of Statistics and Computing (Instituto Nacional de Estadística e Informática; INEI), 56.5 percent of the total population self-identified as *mestizo* (mixed Indigenous and European).[1] Smaller proportions of the population self-identified as Quechua (19.8 percent), Aymara (2.2. percent), and other "native" populations (1.4 percent). Those identifying as white constituted 5.2 percent of the total population in 2015. In terms of linguistic practices, according to INEI's 2017 census reports, approximately 17.4 percent of the total population declared having a mother tongue other than Spanish (i.e., Indigenous), of whom 13.9 percent were Quechua speaking, 1.7 percent were Aymara speaking, and 0.3 percent were Asháninka speaking and 0.5 spoke other Indigenous languages.[2] These numbers decreased in 2022, with about 12 percent of the population reporting speaking Indigenous languages in Peru.[3] It is clear from these estimates that while Indigenous peoples do not constitute a majority population in Peru, they form a sizable group, with an important presence in terms of their ethnic background and linguistic practices. Quechua-speaking peoples in particular have a significant presence—even among Indigenous populations—and are Peru's second largest group of peoples.

The significance of Indigenous peoples is also acknowledged in the 1993 Constitution of the Republic of Peru. Article 48 of the Constitution stipulates that the state's official languages are Spanish, Quechua, Aymara, and other "aboriginal languages" in "areas where they are predominant" or where they are most spoken.[4] The recognition of Indigenous languages as official languages of the state—in addition to the sizable population of Indigenous peoples—demonstrates, in part, the influence of Indigenous peoples in shaping Peruvian national identity and the nation-state. Notwithstanding these factors, Peru's Indigenous peoples, particularly Indigenous women, have been oppressed, deprived of rights, and marginalized in society.

This chapter heavily engages with the intersectional identity of Indigenous women as victim-survivors of the genocidal PSRPF, by unpacking theoretical discussions about Indigenous peoples, Indigenous women, and Indigenous children's identity connected one way or another with colonialist legacies. While not denying that some victim-survivors of PSRPF were of other ethnic backgrounds—as evidenced by Victoria Vigo's story in chapter 4—it is important to acknowledge and recognize that Indigenous women (and in certain instances girls, as evidenced in chapter 3) were the group most impacted by the coercive sterilization campaign, which was disguised as a family planning program. The identity of the majority of victims is in part why I argue in chapter 2 that this family planning program involved genocidal intent by the state that targeted Indigenous peoples.

Recognizing Indigenous women's victimhood, this chapter uses the intersectional lens of gender, class, and ethnicity to analyze the meaning of Indigenous peoples' and women's identities and the role of colonialism in shaping ethnicity, class, and gendered relations in Peruvian society. Rather than view this victim-survivor group as one that only represents the nexus of marginalized identities and is therefore unable to wield power, this chapter examines how such victimhood also offered a new political agency for Indigenous women. These women seized and used their identity to leave their enduring imprint on politics. They worked and mobilized to demand their rights, which under the broader umbrella of human rights included reproductive rights, women's rights, the right to life, and the right to freedom from discrimination. They became recognized as a group that had political agency and influence, and their protests resonated not only because masses of people believed they were doing the right thing for themselves, but because their efforts also opposed political candidacies that represented a common ill for society (e.g., that of Keiko Fujimori). Scholars note that "rights provide another abstract but critical end: recognition," and that "forcing those in power to grant such recognition may be as important to the rights proponent as attaining material aims."[5] Considering this point, Indigenous women, whose rights were conditioned by thought processes stemming from the colonial period, were no longer an invisible population. Now they were recognized by the state and political actors (e.g., presidential candidates) as effective campaigners for their own rights and interests.

ON COLONIALISM

Indigenous communities in Latin America have been deprived of opportunities for power, economic gain, and education since the arrival of the Spaniards, the establishment of colonies, and the imposition of colonial orders, which have carried on to the present day. As Argentine scholar Walter Mignolo writes, from the first encounter between European and Indigenous peoples, a falsehood or an "invention" framed this experience.[6] Europeans claimed "discovery" of a place that did not need to be discovered.[7] Their actions were framed as a discovery to suit the political objective of the Spaniards and the Portuguese, to "appropriate the continent" and to "integrate it in the Euro-Christian imaginary." By being called a discovery, the land became a place that was nonexistent and then "discovered" and appropriated, which justified Europe's plunder of the Americas for its own economic and political benefit.[8] As Mignolo explains, this was evident in the renaming of peoples. For instance, ethnic groups and civilizations of the "Tawantinsuyu"—an endonym for the Incan empire—were simply reduced to a category of *indios*. Through renaming, the colonial powers imposed control over the ethnic identity of peoples and in doing so established dominion over Indigenous populations.

This power took the form of discrimination and exploitation of Indigenous communities, disguised as the discourse of "salvation, progress, modernization, and common good."[9] This colonial positionality, based on the Spanish and Portuguese notion of "ethnic superiority," was shared by *criollos* (those of European descent born in the Americas).[10] This shared "colonial" perspective among those of European descent—from Europe or in the Americas—created the framework for postcolonial societies and reproduced discrimination against Indigenous peoples.

Argentine scholar Enrique Dussel describes this period as the birthdate of the "myth of modernity." This myth "came to birth in Europe's confrontation with the Other. By controlling, conquering, and violating the Other, Europe defined itself as the discoverer, conquistador, and colonizer of an alterity likewise constitutive of modernity."[11] Hence, Europe's modernity necessitated the identification of "the Other" and served to justify the violence against what was considered non-European. The myth of modernity concealed and rationalized Europe's violence toward Indigenous peoples; it was considered an essential step in civilizing peoples. Consequently, as Chilean scholar and poet Cecilia Vicuña notes, the destruction of "native cultures" was "never seen as a loss, only [as] a necessary by-product of progress—a view that persists today."[12] This insight is relevant in thinking further about the positionality of Indigenous peoples in the Americas today.

Peruvian sociologist Aníbal Quijano explains how "race," which he describes as an "invention," was a "way to authorize legitimacy to the relationships of dominations imposed by conquest."[13] This was evident in the relationships established in Latin America during the colonial period. The Europeans' belief in their racial domination pitted them against the non-Europeans, and it was a way to legitimize the "old ideas and practices of relations of superiority/inferiority among the dominated and dominating groups."[14] The ethnic composition of peoples played a central role in the social class structures constructed in postcolonial states. These ideas, as Quijano argues, were part of capitalist economics, where ethnicity influenced and dictated one's economic position. For instance, in the Americas unpaid work, whether in the form of enslavement or enforced labor, was associated with *indios, negros* (Indigenous peoples and black populations) and—in complex ways—the *mestizos* in the Americas. At the top of the labor chain stood the "colonizing" group or the white population.[15] This form of colonialism, control of labor, and power manifests globally in places where relationships between the colonizer and colonized populations remain prevalent.

Mestizaje and *mestizo* identity are central to understanding the complexities associated with colonialism, postcolonial societal structures, and the impacts of colonialism on Indigenous peoples. Quijano explains that *mestizaje* and *mestizos* became part of the social class structure and participated in work and activities previously dominated by Europeans of non-noble lineage.[16] On *mestizo* identity and *mestizaje*, Bolivian sociologist Silvia Rivera Cusicanqui offers a unique insight, specifically one that is much cruder about *mestizaje* (i.e., the process through which the *mestizo* identity is formed, or a violent union of European and Indigenous blood). Cusicanqui argues that "the world of mestizaje—marked by an inescapable ambivalence—becomes a critical space, in which one is as much the victimizer as the victim, both a subject and an object of oppression."[17] On the one hand, a *mestizo* is a victim in the sense that to be *mestizo* reflects a violent union between the European colonizer and the Indigenous person. As Cusicanqui explains, the origins of *mestizaje* were based on the "rape" of Indigenous women by the *encomenderos* (those who had the right to collect tribute of Indigenous peoples entrusted to them), priests, and Spanish soldiers.[18] Relatedly, because of the violence that *mestizaje* represented, *mestizo* has at times been regarded as a "derogatory name" and associated with words such as "cur-dog, mongrel, mixed blood." These words were hated by the "indigenes they were displacing and by the foreign rulers attempting to keep power."[19] In part, literary scholars Cristian Iglesia and Julio Schvartzman have described it as the "new fear . . . that is rewed with all might: that the mestizo is Spanish blood mixed with the different, with the enemy, with the demon."[20] As a result, this new hybrid identity disrupted the social order of the colonial system.

The *mestizo* is therefore discriminated against and rejected by dominant groups in power—those of Spanish lineage—due to the perceived challenge that the *mestizo* identity represented. In other words, *mestizo* is excluded from being part of the upper social class. On the other hand, being a *mestizo* reflects the status of a victimizer, as *mestizaje* further segregates the Indigenous population from the European and Spanish while creating a new social class that exerts dominance over Indigenous peoples. In *mestizaje,* Indigenous women were the most impacted because they were exploited for labor—particularly in the "tribute of textiles"—as well as abused and subjected to "sexual service." It is through the sexual violation of Indigenous women that the *mestizo* population was produced. These developments profoundly impacted the decimation of Indigenous women.[21]

When Spanish colonies in the Americas gained their independence after the region's wave of independence movements during the 1800s, changes seemed to begin taking place. Unfortunately, once former colonial areas gained independence, nothing much changed. The international structure remained the same, with dependent colonies (i.e., newly independent Latin American states) that continued to function under the power center of colonialism (i.e., the Spanish in Europe). Within these newly independent colonies, a similar situation manifested. Mexican sociologist Pablo González Casanova describes this as a form of "internal colonialism."[22] He notes that with independence there emerged the notion of "integral independence and a neocolonialism." This new colonialism was manifested in the creation of the nation-state. For instance, the disappearance of a "direct dominion" by the "foreign" power or the foreign colonizing power over "native" populations resulted in the emergence of a new "dominion and exploitation of the natives by the natives."[23] Specifically, the Spaniards were replaced by *criollos*, a new foreign power that continued to exploit Indigenous peoples. This situation, which can be understood as discrimination by a group of peoples against another based on ethnic background, is "essential for colonial exploitation of one group of peoples over others and influences all the configurations of development and colonial culture."[24] Such discrimination, in turn, is manifested by dehumanizing the oppressed population, which González Casanova explains is accompanied by the "perception" and treatment of the "colonized . . . as a thing" or a commodity.[25]

Mestizaje and the *mestizo* played a unique role in the postindependence period. This violent—and often coercive—Spanish and Indigenous union was considered an essential part of the nation-building project of many Latin American states. The focus was on bridging the differences between Indigenous peoples and those of European descent by creating a hybrid identity—*mestizo*—which would, in essence, move these new states toward "whitening" or "closer to the European heritage."[26] Underlying this process was the idea that "whitening" was the desired outcome of societies, as it would help "improve" states' ethnic composition and resolve problems associated with the non-European, which Dussel referred to as "the Other."[27] Such ideas associated class structures with ethnic identity: Those of European heritage occupied the upper classes, and those of non-European or Indigenous descent were relegated to the lower classes of society. This class structure divided the economic and political opportunities available to peoples and, in doing so, further relegated the person of Indigenous descent to a marginalized class in society. As political scientist and gender studies scholar Pascha Bueno-Hansen observes, "[T]hrough the nineteenth and twentieth centuries, the Peruvian nation-state adapted this social hierarchy to an understanding of what it means to be modern," as a

Peruvian's "distance from or proximity to the modern ideal determines their access to citizenship."[28] These ideas are mirrored in the 1823 Constitution of Peru. Article 17 stipulates that, to be considered a citizen of Peru, one had to have "ownership of a property, or have a profession, or working in art with a degree, or working in an industry."[29] Similar ideas were manifested in the 1826 Constitution, which restricted citizenship based on one's ability to "read and write" under Article 14.[30] From these standards, Indigenous peoples who had no access to property ownership, education, or means to learn the dominant Spanish language could not access citizenship.

Political power differences are also exhibited in geography. Geographic identifiers accompanied the restrictions and divisions imposed on Indigenous peoples. In practice, this means that Lima holds the "majority of the administrative decision-making power and Spanish-speaking, literate, educated, and wealthy population," while the rural areas have "high levels of poverty, illiteracy, and Quechua-speaking population."[31] Additionally, urban and coastal areas (e.g., Lima) are associated with *criollos* and *mestizos* and conflated with notions of "progress," whereas *sierra* (rural highland) and *selva* (Amazonian jungle region) are linked with Indigenous communities and seen as "retrograde."[32] Bueno-Hansen explains that this spatial configuration, "rooted in exclusions based on rurality, language, and ethnicity, is crucial for understanding the embedded layers of violence and their aftermath."[33] In essence, geography serves to demonstrate an underlying prejudice toward Indigenous peoples. This is most evident in the findings from the TRC, which was mandated to investigate the internal armed conflict (1980–2000) involving leftist guerrilla forces and the state's armed and security forces. The TRC determined that most of the violence occurred in rural areas, and *campesino* peoples (those dedicated to agriculture) were most impacted.[34] The areas of conflict and affected victims point to the ethnic undertones that accompanied the violence from this period.

These differences in class based on economic, geographic, and ethnic categories during the colonial period continue to the present day in

Peru. Marginalization is evidenced by the economic situation of Indigenous peoples, with 38.5 percent of the total indigenous population living in poverty in 2022.[35] Similarly, *sierra* and *selva* regions, which are majority Indigenous, record high poverty levels.[36]

The long-lasting impact that the Europeans' arrival in 1492 had on the Americas was unprecedented. And due to the hierarchy of power manifested in societal, economic, and political relations, Indigenous peoples largely accepted this reality. Despite the violence of colonization, rape, war, and enslavement of peoples, Indigenous cultures and peoples still survived and persisted in their own ways. Nevertheless, colonial structures of power, which transformed with the emergence of new groups of peoples (e.g., *mestizo*), remain largely the same today. Specifically, they subjugate Indigenous communities by subjecting them to similar mistreatment rooted in colonialist visions. For example, the rhetoric of modernity, which implies the existence of "the Other," continues in Andean states, where *mestizo* peoples now govern and monopolize local structures in the name of "civilizing" the "savage" societies of *ayllus* (Indigenous communities).[37] Anthropologist Jessaca Leinaweaver explains that elements of race are embedded in commentaries about modernization and modernity. The idea of *superarse* (to overcome or to be ahead or above) in Peru is tied to one's ethnic, socioeconomic, and geographic positioning. Specifically, the idea of progressing from a "negative state to the positive connotations of modernity" is infused with an ethnic and geographic element. As Leinaweaver notes, "[O]vercoming poverty—superando—means sloughing off the markers that might make others define you as indigenous."[38] To *superar* is to become "educated, speaking Spanish instead of Quechua, dressing in store-bought 'Western' clothing instead of woven skirts or felt hats or rubber-tire sandals ... living in the city instead of in the *campo*."[39] This is similar to what Peruvian anthropologist Carlos Iván Degregori has described about no one wanting to identify as Indigenous, or as Degregori has referred to it, as *indio*. Degregori explains that being Indigenous became synonymous with the "poor *campesino*" (poor rural agricultural worker/poor farmer) or with being "servile" or subservient to others of non-Indigenous or mainly white backgrounds.[40] Relatedly, given this racialized history in Peru, along with the negative ethnic and linguistic stigma (i.e., nonmodern) linked to Indigenous identity, most contemporary Peruvian peoples do not self-identify as Indigenous and prefer to identify as *mestizo*.

The reluctance to self-identity as Indigenous is traced by Guatemalan sociologist and community leader Avexnim Cojti Ren. She argues that this phenomenon reflects the low status associated with Indigenous identity. As Cojti Ren argues, there is "continued colonialist blaming" for the "lack of progress, poverty, and violence" among Indigenous peoples.[41] She explains that this type of colonialist blaming results in "low self-esteem, self-alienation . . . and the practice of discrimination against our fellow Indigenous people and their cultures."[42] Moreover, this discrimination against Indigenous peoples was used to justify "land expropriation and relocation and assimilation of Indigenous people" in Guatemala, a country with colonialist dynamics of class and ethnicity similar to those of Peru.[43] In Peru, similar ideas influenced how the internal armed conflict (1980–2000) unfolded and can help explain why most victims of the violence were of Indigenous origin.

Marisol de la Cadena explains that Indigenous peoples' high level of victimhood during the internal armed conflict in Peru "obliges us to at least begin to interrogate the history of modernity and see how it has legitimated inequality."[44] Ethnic discrimination against Indigenous peoples and a general disregard for their lives—rooted in historical colonialism—affected the outcome of victimhood from this period. Similar ideas were also present in the shaping of PSRPF. As a state-led health program (implemented from 1996 to 2000) that overlapped with the internal armed conflict period (1980–2000), the PSRPF targeted Indigenous peoples, as they were considered the cause of the "problem," namely the group that was holding back the state from economic progress.[45] Seen as a "problematic" population, they were targeted by a genocidal state policy, which was justified under the disguise of a progressive reproductive health and women's rights program. From victim-survivors' testimonies, it becomes clear that those impacted were chastised and made to feel ashamed. Moreover, these dynamics—which Cojti Ren has described in her work on Indigenous peoples as a form of colonialist blaming—hampered early efforts by Indigenous women and men to discuss their experiences openly. In this context, the identity of the Indigenous woman represented an additional layer of intersected identities of exclusion, one that incorporated gender as an element of subjugation and subaltern category in Peruvian society.

INDIGENOUS WOMEN

Gender is a social construct. Supporting this view, Judith Butler explains that gender is "real only to the extent that it is performed."[46] By this she means that the essence of "gender is manufactured through a sustained set of acts, posited through the gendered stylization of the body."[47] It is created through the repetition of certain bodily acts and is a social construction that can be challenged and changed. This construct, in turn, "intersects with racial, class, ethnic, sexual, and regional modalities of discursively constituted identities."[48] Therefore, it is "impossible to separate out gender from the political and cultural intersections in which it is invariably produced and maintained."[49] Because gender is impossible to separate from political and cultural intersections, it is only fair to assume that gender oppression in the form of patriarchy is also conditioned by the cultural and political context. Butler argues that despite its enduring effect on society, the traditional notion of gender is now increasingly being questioned. In particular, Butler shows that "universal patriarchy"—the notion that the oppression of women has "a singular form discernible in the universal or hegemonic structure of patriarchy"—has been widely criticized in recent years.[50] Particularly, the emerging criticism of universal patriarchy stems from "efforts to . . . appropriate non-Western cultures to support highly Western notions of oppression . . . to construct a 'Third World' or even an 'Orient' in which gender oppression is subtly explained as symptomatic of an essential, non-Western barbarism."[51] While these claims against universal patriarchy are welcome, the status and perception of women as a single group with a common identity of being subjugated and oppressed has been difficult to change.

Thinking about this view as it relates to colonialism in Latin America, it is indisputable that the new social class structure—which subjugated Indigenous peoples by making them an excluded class—carried a gendered element that targeted Indigenous women. After all, Indigenous women's identity represented the nexus of an oppressed ethnic group, marginalized class (politically, socially, and economically), and gendered subaltern entity, whose gendered position of subjugation was imposed on them through colonialism. Reflecting on Butler's criticism of universal patriarchy, I emphasize that the imposition of gendered oppression against Indigenous women—channeled through colonialist class structures—was not a completely foreign concept to Indigenous peoples. However, it is difficult to characterize what existed prior to the arrival of the Europeans (the period known as pre-*hispánico*) as solely representative of the oppression of gender. As Peruvian historian María Rostworowski explains, divisions of gender existed in Andean societies. In fact, "nunca existieron derechos iguales absolutos entre el sexo masculino y el femenino" (there never existed absolute equal rights between the male and female sexes).[52] By this, Rostworowski means that certain roles in society were associated more with men or women. These are evident in the accounts by Guaman Poma de Ayala, who wrote about and illustrated the lives of peoples in the Incan period in *El Primer Nueva Corónica y Buen Gobierno*, showing that women's and men's activities and functions in society differed greatly. For instance, women and girls (who were their helpers) were primary caretakers of children, cooked, and sewed, while men and boys (helping the men) hunted game, tended the livestock, and learned the ways of war.[53] However, in some work, men and women shared responsibilities, such as gathering wood. Hence, gendered defined roles existed that were not exclusive of men (and boys) and women. Instead, they existed complementary to and with one another and taking into consideration the needs of the *ayllu*, a community that identifies as family per geography, bloodline, or shared objectives.

During the pre-Hispanic or precolonial period, women were not totally cut off from civic life in their communities, and depending on the circumstances of one's social class (through lineage) and political circumstances, women (both from high classes and lower classes) participated actively in civic life. For instance, during moments of conflict and war, women of high-class lineage in Cuzco led armed groups. While not allowed to take on a leadership role, even women of lower classes, such as those who worked in agricultural sectors, also took part in "actividades guerreras. Se las incluía en el sector servicios, haciéndolas participar en las marchas, permanentemente a retaguardia, para cumplir tareas en provecho de la tropa" (warring activities. They were included in the service sectors, participating in marches, permanently in rearguard, to complete the tasks for the benefit of the troops).[54] Hence, while women's roles may not have been the same as men's, the magnitude of their repression as understood in discussions of gendered relations from Europe was significantly less and different than for European women.

Other scholars have gone as far as to argue that the system of patriarchy was foreign to the Andean region and was an import of the colonial system.[55] Peruvian sociologist Lucía Alvites Sosa engages with the work of Rostworowski in detailing the stories from precolonial periods that provide a glimpse into Indigenous society's gendered roles. For instance, in the origin myth of Incan society, the brothers Ayar Uchu, Ayar Cachi, Ayar Mango, and Ayar Auca and their sisters Mama Ocllo, Mama Huaco, Mama Ipacura, and Mama Rauca embarked on an expedition to find a settlement for their peoples. In their expeditions, Mama Huaco took on the role of a leader, commanding the armed forces in the conquest of Cusco and fighting alongside men of various ranks.[56] This myth, Alvites Sosa argues, demonstrates Indigenous women's positionality as being able to participate in politics, hold high-ranking positions, and lead military expeditions—which is difficult to achieve in Peru even in the twenty-first century.[57]

Alvites Sosa explains that through myth, we can better understand that the social reality and system of "sex gender" manifested in the Indigenous context (i.e., before the arrival of the Europeans) was distinct from what was present in the "West." According to Alvites Sosa, "during the same period in Europe there were religious discourses" critical of "the houses of witches." These witches comprised "women who practiced another type of knowledge," which at times took the form of midwifery and healer work that did not have any religious connections.[58] Relatedly, Alvites Sosa notes that the religious story of "the original woman, Eve," in the Christian West is associated with everything negative, and "everything negative emerges from her, the bad intention, the loss, and the guilt."[59] These examples from Europe are juxtaposed with examples from the period of the Incan Empire or the Tahuantinsuyo (or Tawantinsuyu). For instance, in the Tahuantinsuyo, any sons and daughters of the Curaca (chief or authority figure) could accede to power, and women and men were able to serve as priests.[60] And womanhood was not equated with sins or guilt.

In the myth about the settlement of the Incan empire, women also had an important role. It is said that Mama Huaco took two staffs of gold and threw each in a different direction. The first staff landed in Colcabamba but did not stick in the ground. The second one penetrated gently into the ground in a place called Guayanaypata (in the center of Cuzco). This myth of the magical staff indicated the settlement area for the Incan empire.[61] Rostworowski explains that Mama Huaco's myth represented the sociopolitical order of the Incas, in which Indigenous women occupied a central role in politics and society.[62] Likewise, chronicles tell of the legends of the battles in Cuzco and the story of a woman named Chañan Curi Coca. She was a warrior and chief of the *ayllus*, who fought alongside the Incas in the war against the Chancas in defending the Choco-Cachona neighborhood in Cuzco. The stories of both Mama Huaco and Chañan Curi Coca arguably represent the worldviews of this period, suggesting that the practice of war was not a "function of men only" and that women held considerable power and high political roles in society.[63]

And yet not all Indigenous women had access to these higher political roles. The "elite" women were the ones who held economic, social, and political roles, which disrupted European standards of gendered divisions. In contrast, the women of lower classes or *hatun runa* (common peoples) took part in agricultural activities, specifically in planting seeds and serving as caretakers.[64] However, even women of lower social class status held a unique position in Incan society. As historian Estefanía Sanz Romero explains, some of these women were involved in textile-related activities, which was empowering in its own ways.[65] This is largely because the *mundo textil* (textile world) was central in Incan society and the economy. As women carried the greater weight of this line of work, they played a greater economic role than their male counterparts.

What mattered most in societies during this period was that the role of each group relied more on the decision and needs of the *ayllu*. Within this context, women and men (of nonelite status) participated jointly in domestic and nondomestic, work and children (regardless of sex) were considered to merit protection in the *ayllu*.[66] At a more fundamental level, both sexes were considered simply as children of Pachamama (Mother Earth or Mother Nature).

Other work about the pre-Incan period also describes societies in which women yielded considerable power. Bolivian archaeologist Claudia Rivera Casanovas writes that toward the end of Moche society, which flourished on the Northern and North Central Peruvian coast, priestesses of elite lineage had a high status and possessed great riches due to the work they performed in incarnating Moche deities.[67] This is evident in the burial sites of these priestesses. These priestesses also participated in weaving for funerals, and textiles produced by these women were considered to have a supernatural meaning. These women were venerated in society.

Maya-Kaqchikel anthropologist Aura Estela Cumes offers similar observations. As she explains, in the Guatemalan context, the Mayan cosmovision is based on the principles of "duality, complementarity, and equilibrium," among other things. A complementary and interdependent relationship (of equals) involving shared responsibilities and work among Mayan men and women helped construct their livelihoods and society.[68] In the Andean context, Cusicanqui argues that women had more rights, and families reflected more balanced gender roles.[69] Men and women both participated in ritual celebrations, and women's voices were prominent in parenting structures within families. Women were "never segregated in all the normative production and the formation of the 'public opinion,' in the ayllu or in . . . the Indigenous community."[70] It was only in the early days of governance in Bolivia that Bolivian lawmakers adopted the European "Victorian model of family."[71] This included a strict representation of gender roles, with men in the public sphere and women in the private sphere without a voice or ability to make decisions on their own. Along with these gendered adaptations of the European model, the process of "modernization" in the Bolivian context contributed to "creating a materialized image of women, that resulted in devaluing their knowledge as shepherdesses, weavers, and ritualists."[72] Consequently, Westernization—or Europeanization—was accompanied by the "patriarchalization of the systems of gender," which effected significant changes to the more equal and egalitarian gendered roles that were present in Indigenous communities.

The system of gender, imported from Europe, was imposed parallel to the colonialist project that divided people based on ethnicity. The social class stratification from the colonial period pitted Indigenous peoples against those of European descent and imposed upon them a position in society in which they were excluded from diverse opportunities for economic, political, and social power. Embedded within both systems was the notion of power. Reproduced in colonial relations of economic and racial power, the system was profoundly patriarchal. In this context, the Indigenous women's place was made even more vulnerable within this already discriminatory class system due to their ethnic and gendered categories. Argentine scholar María Lugones discusses how, in the name of "civilizing," the colonial system dehumanized Indigenous women in the Americas and subjected them to sexual violence.[73] To this end, they were forced to become acculturated to European patriarchal norms that situated men and women on different pedestals in society and had to endure the brutalization and dehumanization imposed upon them by "gendered colonialism." In this context, the position of the Indigenous woman made her more susceptible to enduring recurrent and prolonged violence.

In colonial and postcolonialist societies, these ideas were reified and reproduced in such ways that the oppression of Indigenous women and their sufferings were not questioned. This included Indigenous peoples themselves. By not challenging or pushing back against this new system of oppression, Indigenous peoples also contributed to reaffirming the subaltern position of Indigenous women in the sociopolitical and economic class structure.[74] As Cumes notes, during the colonial period in Guatemala, Mayan women were thought of not as "beings that could think/reflect"; instead they were regarded as manual workers who worked, for instance, as "servants."[75] Cumes explains that this perspective was so deep-rooted, it was reproduced without question throughout the entire society. One way this notion was reproduced was through the colonial thought process that negated Indigenous women's individuality and their complex and diverse identities. In modern-day Guatemala, this is evident in the practice of referring to Indigenous women as "maria," which Cumes explains is a way to "negate Indigenous women of the right to be regarded as individuals with their own proper names."[76]

Another way colonial thought and oppression against Indigenous women was reproduced in contemporary society was by the social class stratification itself. Cumes argues that the stratification of class, embodying elements of ethnicity and gender, "impacts the knowledge (political-academic) that is generated."[77] According to Cumes, the "privileges that each group is assigned in the chain of power" and class do not "permit the questioning of one's own privileges and power."[78] In fact, "political identity (of gender, ethnicity or class) has been more important than the questioning of a system that has resulted in" the idea that "being different means being unequal." Indigenous women, like other minorities in Guatemala, have "become principal subjects in reasserting cultural, social, and biological characteristics" rather than regarding their own identity as a social construct impacted by colonial history.[79]

Other discourses of gender note the complexities of gender ideologies that are reproduced in Indigenous communities. Looking at the context of Peru, anthropologist Krista E. Van Vleet explains that the discourse of gender in Andean communities is more complicated. Although there are gender divisions of labor with women as the primary caregivers for children, women also "control the distribution of household resources (in a subsistence economy), travel independently, maintain individual relationships of exchange, and own property."[80] And, compared to "mestizo and urban" communities, in Andean communities, political, economic, and social authority are more "broadly distributed between men and women." These aspects, however, do not paint a perfectly egalitarian gender vision of the Andean context in Peru. In fact, as Van Vleet describes, the "culturally specific practices and concepts of gender in a Quechua-speaking native Andean collectivity are intertwined with national hegemonic gender and racial formations that reinforce a particular coloniality of power."[81] In other words, even Andean communities' gender dynamics cannot be completely free of the influence of the broader Peruvian society's perception of gender, still based on colonialist principles of power that intersect ethnicity, class, and gender.

During Peru's internal armed conflict period (1980–2000), Indigenous peoples made up the majority of the victims. According to the TRC, a total of 69,280 people were killed or disappeared during the internal armed conflict, and most of the victims resided in "poor rural areas and spoke Indigenous languages as their mother tongue."[82] This profile of the victim-survivors shows "deep-rooted inequality" within Peruvian society that played a central part in the violence. The nexus of gender and ethnicity was most evident during this period. As Bueno-Hansen notes, "ethnicity, language, and gender" similarly interacted to make the Andean Quechua-speaking women peasants into vulnerable targets of violence.[83] Gender studies scholar Jelke Boesten also explains that due to their ethnic- and class-related identifiers (i.e., occupation, education, and economic categories of class), Indigenous women were subject to more human rights violations than other women during the internal armed conflict. Interestingly, the human rights violations, at times, were committed by individuals of Indigenous descent. Perpetrators of violence included those identified as *cholo*, who are of Indigenous descent but speak Spanish, have work experience outside of the agricultural sectors, and are regarded as "external" to their Indigenous communities.[84] A number of *cholo* men, who had also suffered abuse and discrimination based on ethnicity and class in society, reproduced the violence they had experienced themselves by "following the same discriminatory premises" and sexually violating women of Indigenous descent.[85] This act of violence sometimes produces a feeling of superiority or a position of "social dominion" over the victim. Indigenous women were the most victimized in these events due to their ethnic and gendered backgrounds. Such ideas mirror the perspectives of critical race studies scholar Kimberly Crenshaw, who theorizes that the "experiences of women of color are frequently the product of intersecting patterns of racism and sexism," and their "intersectional identity as both women and of color" marginalizes them further.[86]

Coinciding with the internal armed conflict's latter period, Peru's Indigenous women were targeted with the launch of PSRPF from 1996. While the program originally set out to provide surgical interventions for men and women, in practice it prioritized female tubal ligation, as evidenced in the Human Rights Ombudsman's Office report. According to data on the number of tubal ligations in comparison to vasectomies performed by health personnel from 1996 to 2001—a year after the official end of PSRPF—a total of 272,028 tubal ligations and only 22,004 vasectomies were recorded.[87] Hence, there were twelve times more cases of tubal ligations than vasectomies or twelve times more cases of women impacted than men in terms of a surgical procedure that prevented future births. While it is true that in some cases women themselves sought sterilizations, these were a minority. Additionally, it is important to understand that while women had agency to exercise their decision, this decision likely was constrained by other societal and economic conditions. For example, in the context of sterilization of women in Puerto Rico, women who underwent the procedure may have expressed a desire to be sterilized, but this was not reflective of their "complete reproductive freedom," because "oppressive colonial population control policies and current poverty" restricted women's' ability to consider other options.[88] In similar ways, Indigenous women in Peru, particularly those who did consent to sterilization, were not necessarily consenting out of free choice, but often due to the socioeconomic factors (i.e., poverty and ethnic discrimination) that conditioned them.

For the most part, however, the majority of the women who were sterilized—most of whom were of Indigenous descent—were given false information about the outcome of sterilizations or even pressured with threats and forcibly sterilized. Of these thousands of women, the majority were of Indigenous descent. Government documents also attest to the family planning program's selective application aimed at women. According to congressional records, there was a "compulsive tendency" in the program's application—via threats and incentives—to achieve "programmatic objectives on the number of women that were to be sterilized."[89] The specification of women as a selected group is noted in Ministerial Resolution No. 089-98-SA/DM, which specified "women in fertile age" as the target group.[90] The resolution also noted the prevention of adolescent pregnancies, specifying, once again, adolescent women.[91] In chapter 2 I discuss how gender and ethnicity played a part in genocide.

As previously noted, however, not all women were selected for this program. The social construction of Peruvian society, which was shaped by colonialism and conditions modern-day experiences, affected Indigenous women more than other women (i.e., those of European descent or of *mestizo/a* identity). The identity of Indigenous women represented multiple layers of discriminated groups based on ethnicity, socio-economic class, and gender. As a result, these women became regarded as a dispensable population, whose bodies could be violated with the goal of preventing future generations of Indigenous peoples. To understand this process, it is helpful to consider the term "trashing," coined by Peruvian poet, feminist, and human rights activist Rocío Silva Santisteban. Trashing refers to "throwing away trash" or making someone equivalent to "trash," which involves a process of differentiating between things or people framed as "trash" and others who are not part of this group. Reflecting on the case of coercive sterilization, Santisteban asserts that the biopolitics of control over Indigenous women's bodies served as a "strategy of symbolic trashing," or more specifically, a trashing of peoples who were considered *sobrantes* (surplus or leftovers).[92] Furthermore, coercive sterilization of Indigenous women prevented not only future births of their children but also births of potential future "subversive" forces or peoples who would revolt or challenge the state. Embedded in these views was the legacy of colonialism that considered Indigenous peoples an unwanted and unneeded population.

Indigenous leader, activist, and former president of ONAMIAP Melania Canales Poma describes how the family planning program implemented in her Indigenous community was only directed at women. In noting this gendered aspect of the program, she points out how patriarchal norms in her community, where Indigenous women were considered "inferior," enabled the targeting of women.[93] This was shown in nongovernmental organization reports that documented cases of forced sterilizations in which the male partner (through marriage or civil union) was induced by health personnel to sign off on the sterilization of his female partner.[94] In fact, health practitioners encouraged this practice. They explained:

> Se acostumbra acreditar la autorización la firma del cónyuge, además nuestra zona es eminentemente rural donde impera el machismo, y la mujer después de someterse al bloqueo tubárico sin autorización del esposo corre el riesgo de recibir maltratos por parte de éste, para evitar esta situación era menester elaborar la constancia que debía ser firmada por el esposo. (It is customary to accredit authorization signature from the partner, as our region is eminently rural where *machismo* dominates, and the woman after submitting herself to tubal ligation without authorization from the husband runs the risk of being mistreated, so to avoid such situation it was necessary to prepare the certificate to be signed by the husband.)

Hence, to prevent Indigenous women from being mistreated, it was argued that the consent form had to come from the male partner. The health-care system and related paperwork mirrored these patriarchal societal norms—with colonial roots—that restricted Indigenous women from being able to make choices about their own reproductive health. Hence, even if Indigenous women had agency to decide their fate, they were conditioned institutionally and through their male partner's decisions not to exercise it.

INDIGENOUS CHILDREN

Similar to Indigenous women, the status and treatment of children, specifically Indigenous children, involved exclusionary and discriminatory dynamics of ethnicity, gender, and class. According to sociologist Jessica Taft, the forced removal of children from Indigenous communities during the colonial period, for instance, "traces the violent process of indigenous children's insertion into the colonial project."[95] In the name of solidifying colonial control over the Indigenous populations in Peru, colonialist governments understood that Indigenous children had to be converted and educated in their cultural ways. Central to the education of these children during the colonial period were the ideas of control, regulation, punishment, and the making of good Christians, which Indigenous children were seen as lacking.

Scholars explain how this colonialist vision of punishment and control over children continued into the modern state period and manifested in diverse ways.[96] Legal scholar and policy expert Mikaela Luttrell-Rowland refers to the "making of a child citizen," which involved education or schooling.[97] The education of the Indigenous child was tied to the ideas of modernity and progress, seen as distinct and different from Indigenous cultures and identities. Through education implemented by the state, Indigenous children would be turned from Indigenous beings into citizens of Peru, with identifiers and identities that separated them further from their ethnic and cultural roots. Hence, education served the colonialist project of the shedding of Indigenous identities, as had been the case with *mestizaje*, in which the violent mixing of blood forcibly changed peoples' identities. However, as Luttrell-Rowland explains, education is not an easily accessible path for children whose identities represent the intersection of an impoverished class and marginalized ethnic identities (of nonwhite and of Indigenous origin). Discussing her work with children and schooling, she explains how Peruvian society is infused with colonialist visions that equate being Indigenous with being not civilized or modern enough. However, the Indigenous child's condition of poverty and the financial stress of obtaining school supplies (including uniforms) prevent these children from being able to finish their education. As education is regarded as the primary way for Indigenous peoples to become "better" or real citizens of Peru, the inaccessibly of education presents an obstacle for these children to be seen as "somebody" or as legitimate peoples "in the eyes of the state."[98]

Taft also explains how in the modern state system, children were seen as needing to be controlled by way of discipline and hard work. For street children, in particular, who had not been "properly disciplined and raised by their families," their behaviors had to be "corrected by the controlling interventions of the state."[99] Embedded within this logic of an interventionist state was a racial undertone, whereby the "label of a bad parent" was "weaponized and used against primarily poor, working-class, and indigenous families." In faulting the caregiver, who due to their ethnic identity is not seen as capable of raising and educating their own children, the state had the excuse to become an active agent in intruding upon the development of the child. As Taft argues, "children, especially poor and nonwhite children, were understood by the colonial and early modern state as unruly subjects who need to be controlled, managed, and disciplined into appropriate behavior as part of a racialized project of civilization, modernization, and national development."[100]

These racialized beliefs about nonwhite children continue to the present day and are implicated even further when we consider Indigenous girls, particularly those who have become mothers at an early age. In her ethnographic work with young mothers, Van Vleet narrates the stories of young mothers living in Palomitáy, a secular independent orphanage run by a European nongovernmental organization in Cusco, Peru. The orphanage serves only "girls between twelve and eighteen years of age who choose to keep their babies."[101] While the young mothers come from diverse parts of the country, most are "born in rural highland communities or poor and working-class urban neighborhoods," and many speak Quechua as their first language.[102] And while many are young, during their "short life histories" they have already endured "structural" and "everyday" violence of "poverty and marginalization based on gender, age, class, race, and ethnicity."[103] In other words, due to their Indigenous ethnic background, rural residence, economic class, and even young age, these women continue to occupy a more vulnerable status than others in Peruvian society. This is noteworthy, as the factor of age adds another layer that marginalizes these young mothers from society. Despite the challenges associated with their gender, ethnicity, class, and age, these young mothers, Van Vleet finds, still make efforts to "imagine and enact themselves as mothers" and find their ways of "living well."[104] The idea of living well and making a better world for their children invokes the discussion of modernity, which anthropologist Leinaweaver explains is often equated with "overcoming poverty," becoming "educated," and "sloughing off the markers" that identify one as being Indigenous.[105] However, many young women at Palomitáy are unable to increase their educational access due to their circumstances of motherhood; as a result, it is unattainable for them to overcome economic hardships, let alone hold down jobs that necessitate education,. These young women's experiences provide a glimpse of how Indigenous young women's and girls' lives are also conditioned by colonialist discourses of modernity.

IDENTITY AS A POLITICAL TOOL

When did this marginalized, excluded, and subaltern Indigenous identity of victim-survivors (women and girls) become an important political tool? Coercively sterilized Indigenous women—and Victoria Vigo, a non-Indigenous victim whose story is covered in chapter 4—first emerged prominently in the public sphere during the 2011 presidential election period. Prior to this presidential election cycle, victim-survivors of coercive sterilization were less visible and exerted little influence on national elections.

The lower visibility of Indigenous peoples in Peruvian politics is not a new phenomenon. As scholars note, in terms of ethnic politics, Peru is considered an anomaly in the region. It has a sizable Indigenous population yet has no "national-level" Indigenous parties, "nor has any major presidential candidate self-identified as indigenous."[106] That is not to say that Indigenous identity was never used in the past to persuade Indigenous voters. For instance, consider the myth of Inkarri.[107] The invocation of the Inkarri is not "new to mainstream Peruvian politics," as Peru's Incaic roots have long been used in political discourses.[108] According to Quechua scholar Francisco Carranza Romero, the myth of the Inkarri is the rebirth of something that has disappeared.[109] Although there are debates over when this myth originally emerged, it is clear that this messianic myth is about the return of the

Inca.[110] Carranza Romero explains that the myth is often associated with Tupac Amaru II, who had a noble Incan lineage and organized a rebellion to overthrow Spanish colonial rule in Peru. It is said that when he was captured and quartered, his remains were hidden and sent to four cardinal points, with his head buried in Cuzco. According to the myth, these body parts will unite together and one day be reborn to save the Indigenous peoples.

The myth about the return of the Inca was invoked during the presidential candidacy of Alejandro Toledo (2001–2006). Toledo never openly declared his Indigenous identity, but he understood the advantage of using the ideas associated with Inkarri and successfully mobilized votes in favor of his presidency.[111] He invoked Indigenous symbols, embraced Indigenous demands, and presented himself as more "proximate" to the Indigenous populations than his "competitors, who represented the Lima elite."[112] Essentially, he was comparing his presidential candidacy to the return of the Inca or a prosperous period for Indigenous peoples. Interestingly, Alberto Fujimori in 1990—and later Ollanta Humala in 2006—used a similar approach during their candidacies to sway Indigenous voters, emphasizing their non-Lima, nonwhite, and nonelite identity and focusing their "campaigns and proposals on the poor."[113] As Indigenous peoples disproportionately represent the poor and politically marginalized groups, this ethnic appeal won Indigenous support for these candidates. And yet despite Indigenous peoples' voter turnout, Indigenous women impacted by coercive sterilizations did not mobilize en masse in public prior to the 2011 election period.

The year 2011 was a unique moment because it was a catalyst for human rights activists and the emergence of an anti-Fujimori movement, as discussed in greater depth in chapter 5. By 2011 Alberto Fujimori had been extradited from Chile, after fleeing from Peru to Japan in November 2000 and then arriving in Chile in 2005. In 2009 Fujimori was convicted and jailed for twenty-five years on charges of crimes against humanity, murder, aggravated kidnapping, and battery. Eleven candidates ran for the presidency during the first round of the

2011 presidential elections, and two candidates who received the highest number of votes competed in the runoff elections. The candidates included former Lieutenant Colonel Ollanta Humala and the daughter of Alberto Fujimori, Keiko Fujimori. Keiko—who had been the first lady during the implementation of the family planning campaign—had managed to secure enough votes to compete in the runoff against Ollanta Humala. It was against this political backdrop (i.e., the possibility of another period of human rights violations involving forced sterilization) that Indigenous victim-survivors joined the Fujimori Nunca Más (Fujimori never again) campaign. Victim-survivors of the internal armed conflict, nongovernmental organizations, and victim-survivor groups of coercive sterilizations collectively opposed the candidacy of Keiko Fujimori, who represented the return of "fujimorism," and found a common objective with Fujimori Nunca Más. For victims of coercive sterilization, this was a needed mobilization, one that would prevent another Fujimori family member from acquiring power and instituting another genocidal policy against their reproductive rights. The anti-Fujimori movement culminated in protests, which initially were limited to Lima and other urban settings but eventually spread throughout the country.

The mobilization of the coercive sterilization victim-survivor group differs from the more commonly acknowledged "rights proponents or activists," who "formulate, raise, or advance rights claims on behalf of themselves or other groups."[114] As political scientist Clifford Bob explains, activists or proponents often face "opponents" who fight against the proposed right and promote a "contrary set of rights."[115] However, this has not been the case for this group of victim-survivors in their political agency acquisition process. The opposition group did not put forward a set of rights; rather, the opposition represented a more traditional political opposition group, mobilized in favor of Keiko Fujimori or those who wanted the return to Alberto Fujimori's style of governance.

The mobilization of Indigenous women in 2011 thus aligned with their own interest in preventing a future genocide and seeing some form of justice. In a way, this development resembles the mobilization of the Mapuche community in Chile, where Mapuche peoples (as Indigenous peoples) took advantage of the human rights discourse and "appropriated" international human rights norms to appeal to the international community about their conflicts with the state regarding matters of land.[116] Similarly, Indigenous women in Peru used the 2011 period to push forward their cause and gain more media and societal attention. As newspapers reported throughout this period, victim-survivors of coercive sterilization marched with victims of internal armed conflict and other nongovernmental organizations because they believed "con Keiko, no habrá justicia para nosotras" (with Keiko, there would be no justice for us).[117] Furthermore, the Fujimori Nunca Más campaign also coincided with the work of the No a Keiko (No to Keiko) movement, which had begun on Facebook in 2009. Using the language of political memory to point to crimes of *fujimorism*, together, No a Keiko and Fujimori Nunca Más—aided by Indigenous victim-survivors of coercive sterilizations—successfully intervened in the 2011 presidential election and pushed for the election of Ollanta Humala.[118]

The Indigenous women's political agency helped them continue their demand for recognition and justice for their victimhood. This activism (including the related cause of justice) was also pushed by human rights organizations that continued pressuring Humala's government. Originally, "Humala . . . did not pursue any legal investigations into the coercive sterilization practice," which scholars have noted may have had to do with Humala's own political links to Alberto Fujimori, as Humala had served as a military attaché in South Korea during Fujimori's presidency.[119] However, a few years into his presidency, in 2015, Humala issued a supreme decree to establish REVIESFO. This could be interpreted as a step toward some level of reparative justice, as there was now a registry that identified the victim-survivors of coercive sterilization. Unfortunately, this action was not followed by any other concrete developments regarding retributive justice, including no requests to expand the extradition order for Alberto Fujimori. The absence of expansion of the extradition request was particularly critical for victim-survivors, as the principle of specialty governing extradition law—a principle of international law—"prohibits the prosecution for any offence other than that for which the extradition request is granted."[120] Hence, under this principle, the person being extradited can only be held accountable for the crimes committed under the extradition order. Because Fujimori had been extradited from Chile under seven cases that excluded forced sterilization, for him to be held legally accountable for these crimes a request had to be made by the Peruvian government to the Chilean Supreme Court to expand the terms of the original extradition request. However, this did not occur during Humala's presidency (2011–2016).[121]

Victim-survivors were once again at the forefront of political mobilization during the 2016 and 2021 presidential election periods. In 2016 the story surfaced as an "emblematic case of impunity against Indigenous people's rights," and questions were raised by presidential candidate Pedro Pablo Kuczynski (PPK) about candidate Keiko Fujimori's knowledge of this "crime against humanity."[122] During the following presidential election in 2021, presidential candidate Pedro Castillo again brought up the case of coercive sterilization and asked that candidate Keiko Fujimori, "for the first time in history, ask for forgiveness to the women who were sterilized."[123] Castillo even made efforts to meet with victim-survivors of coercive sterilization.[124] The political spotlight that Castillo and PPK brought to this issue of coercive sterilization emboldened victim-survivors and their activism. As a result, during both the 2016 and 2021 presidential election periods, victim-survivors of coercive sterilization effectively mobilized their efforts within the Keiko No Va and Fujimori Nunca Más campaigns and influenced the outcome of the elections. Following the vocal activist campaigns and the candidates' growing interest in the case of the coercive sterilizations, victim-survivors were hopeful after the elections in 2016 and 2021. Indeed, during this time there were efforts by both President PPK (2016–2018) and President Castillo (2021–2022) to open the registration process for victim-survivors in REVIESFO and arrange meetings with victim-survivors (i.e., AMPAEF). However, despite initial steps taken by both PPK and Castillo to seek justice for victim-survivors of coercive sterilization, no greater level of change ever materialized.

It is important to note here that both PPK and Castillo were elected to office in part as a result of the social movement led by Indigenous victim-survivors of coercive sterilizations. However, as previously explained, apart from one or two sporadic events of so-called justice for victim-survivors of coercive sterilization (i.e., REVIESFO and meetings with victim-survivors' organizations), there was no sustained change toward the advancement justice. Perhaps one could argue that the lack of changes made during these elected presidents' terms may be due to their short presidencies; PPK was impeached within two years of beginning his term, and Castillo was ousted from power within one year of beginning his. These are critical moments to consider, although there may have been something else at play. The real underlying reason for the delayed progress on the coercive sterilization case may have to do, once again, with Indigenous identity and the position of the majority of the victim-survivors of coercive sterilization in Peruvian society. While this group of people were initially important for voter turnout for PPK and Castillo, ultimately for both presidents, Indigenous women were not a group that mattered. These women, whose subaltern identity represents the nexus of marginalized class, ethnicity, and gender, did not hold socioeconomic power in Peruvian society, and therefore their voices were considered irrelevant. This point is the clearest explanation for understanding why progress on any justice-related matter (reparative or retributive) has lagged. Notwithstanding the absence of major changes, however, at least during the election period, the presence and voice of Indigenous victim-survivors of coercive sterilization had an impact on national politics.

CONCLUSION

The majority of victim-survivors of coercive sterilization were of Indigenous descent. As Indigenous persons, they faced an uphill battle.

For a long time the legacy of colonialism in Peruvian society hid the treatment of Indigenous women and coercive sterilizations and prevented them from being understood as human rights violations against an individual's life, dignity, and reproductive rights. The family planning policy was effectively sold using logic. However, when examining the colonialist visions of Indigenous women, one finds a case of rights violations amounting to genocide against vulnerable populations, whose identity positioned them far from any political power.

And yet there is something unique about this victimhood of Indigenous women. The victim-survivors, under threat from the government or a powerful group, did not remain weak. Instead, at the right moment and with the support of other groups, they emerged as potentially significant political actors. Initially, particularly in earlier presidential election periods, they were given some attention, as part of the broader group of those who opposed Fujimori. Later, as they continued advocating for the rights of victim-survivors, their coalition expanded (as evidenced in chapter 5 on allies and activists), their opposition to Fujimori became more consolidated, and they became more vocal about their positions. With these changes, the presence of Indigenous women during presidential election periods increased, their stories were circulated in mainstream media outlets, and these women victim-survivors of coercive sterilizations managed to generate their own power and claim their political agency.

CHAPTER TWO

Indigenous Women and the Genocide

Peru's Coercive Sterilization of Indigenous Women

"Genocide" is a word that commissioners involved with Peru's TRC (2001–2003) avoided when defining what had taken place during the two decades (1980–2000) of Peru's internal armed conflict.[1] The political violence between the state, leftist guerrilla forces (i.e., the Shining Path and the Revolutionary Movement of Tupac Amaru), and the civilians that were caught in the middle resulted in the disappearance and death of over sixty-nine thousand victims. According to the commissioners, the mass casualties were not a result of a genocide.[2] There was no plan either by the Peruvian state—the three administrations of Fernando Belaúnde Terry (1980–1985), Alan García (1985–1990), and Alberto Fujimori (1990–2000)—or the guerrilla forces to systematically destroy groups of people, making it difficult to bring up the term in connection with the conflict. This was despite the fact that the majority of the victims shared strangely similar characteristics of residing in poor rural areas and speaking Indigenous languages as their mother tongue. For this reason, genocide was not referenced in the seventy-three individual cases of violations that were investigated and then published in the TRC final report in 2003.[3]

And yet a genocide did occur. At the same time, the destruction of the collective rights of a group of people was not directly tied to the political dynamics of the internal armed conflict, in that it did not involve interactions between the state, leftist subversive groups, and civilians. Nor did it resemble the characteristics of other commonly occurring crimes from this period, such as torture, arbitrary detention, or disappearance. Instead, this was a case of genocide that involved the state acting against the reproductive rights of an ethnic minority, or an institutionalized genocide via a state policy.

Over the course of five years from 1996 to 2000, the state intentionally launched a genocidal policy, the PSRPF, which aimed to destroy, in whole or in part, a specific population within Peru.[4] The population affected by this program consisted of women (and some men) of poor, rural, and Indigenous-language-speaking backgrounds who were sterilized without their consent, misinformed about the practice, and forced to undergo surgery.[5] Chapter 3 of this book uncovers the story of a victim-survivor of Indigenous descent who recounts her experience of coercive sterilization.

In referring to the terrible practices of forced sterilization that emerged from this health program, the former deputy executive secretary of the National Coordination of Human Rights (Coordinadora Nacional de Derechos Humanos; CNDDHH), Ana María Vidal, described it as "the trashing of human rights, in this case of Indigenous women."[6] This comment reflected the stigmatized situation of the Indigenous population in Peru, as a marginalized group whose status had been fixed in this position since the adoption of the first Constitution of Peru in 1823. Under Article 17, the Constitution conditioned citizenship based on property ownership and literacy in Spanish, both of which were difficult for Indigenous populations with different linguistic traditions and notions of territory to achieve.[7] A century and a half later, the state targeted the Indigenous population with a policy of reproductive health and coercive sterilization, which undermined Indigenous women's ability to reproduce and, as a result, destroyed the future generations of Indigenous peoples.

Although from the early moments of PSRPF there were signs link-
ing this human rights violation to genocide, the case went largely unnoticed by human rights and genocide studies scholars. Consequently, the
majority of existing studies on Peru characterize forced sterilization
not as genocide, but rather as an example of sexual violence, a violation of Indigenous peoples' rights, or at most, a form of crime against
humanity.[8] Even an expanded use of the term "genocide"—exemplified,
for example, by scholars who explain that all the processes and patterns in the history of "North-American settler-Indigenous relations"
were genocidal—is missing in the coercive sterilization literature on
Peru.[9] Most recently, some scholars have mentioned genocide and
Peru's coercive sterilizations together, noting that from the perspectives of Indigenous peoples, sterilizations are genocide and that tubal
ligation "prevents lives," which is a form of silent and invisible genocide against Indigenous peoples.[10] Other scholars, however, continue to
exhibit caution, arguing that it may be difficult to make a legal case for
genocide.[11] For my own scholarship, genocide was not the first crime
that came to my mind when I began this work on coercive sterilization. It was only after an audience member (at a talk that I gave) asked
whether the Peruvian case could be considered a form of genocide that
I began thinking about the connection between forced sterilization and
the human rights norm. That interaction sparked the current study on
making the case for genocide, considering the normative and sociopolitical angles of the story.

This chapter considers the forced sterilization of Indigenous women
in Peru as a genocide. Using the normative definitions from the 1948
Convention on the Prevention and Punishment of the Crime of Genocide (or the Genocide Convention), it first categorically sets forced sterilization victim-survivors from this state-led policy as victim-survivors
of genocide. It is argued that the term genocide fits this context because
of the effects that the health malpractice had on Indigenous wom-
en's reproductive rights and future Indigenous populations. Then this
chapter grounds the discussion of genocide further and argues for the

genocidal intent of the Peruvian state, relying on victim-survivors' testimonies, interviews from human rights experts, archival data from victim-survivors' registries, government documents, and human rights ombudsman office reports. These discussions contribute to the existing body of scholarship on the link between genocide and forced sterilization of Indigenous women—namely, in the United States and Canada.[12] With the exception of Rocío Silva Santisteban's work on genocide and biopolitics, no prior scholars studying this particular situation have made the case for genocide, one of the most heinous crimes in international politics.[13] Even in the case *María Mamérita Mestanza Chávez v. Peru* there were no references to genocide, despite a petition that was lodged by domestic and international nongovernmental organizations with the IACHR against the Peruvian state for María's forced sterilization, subsequent health complications, and death on April 5, 1998.[14] The same holds true for *Celia Ramos v. Peru*, argued as a case of crimes against humanity and reproductive violence related to the death of Celia Ramos, who was forcibly sterilized and died of postoperative health complications on July 22, 1997.[15]

It is important to acknowledge the period of forced sterilization as a genocide because, first and foremost, this case was the most modern attempt by the governing apparatus of Peru—largely reflecting colonial hierarchies of power where those of European or of mixed European descent have political control—at targeting Indigenous peoples from rural and impoverished regions. Previous genocides involving the groups in power were considerably different in nature. During the historic period of the colonization of the Americas, one might argue that the Spanish Empire and its soldiers unknowingly brought about the genocide of the Indigenous peoples via the spread of diseases from Eurasia (e.g., chicken pox), which led to the death of Indigenous peoples not immunologically prepared to resist new viruses. Nor was coercive sterilization a type of genocide that resulted from the internal armed conflict, when the leftist guerrilla group Sendero Luminoso (Shining Path) killed and disappeared more than five thousand Asháninka-speaking and Nomatsiguenga-speaking Indigenous peoples from Peru's Amazon region.[16] One could perhaps argue that the state's genocidal planning with coercive sterilizations originated during the internal armed conflict from the 1989 *Plan por un Gobierno de la Reconstrucción Nacional* (Plan for a government of national reconstruction, more commonly known as *Plan Verde*), which aimed for the establishment of a massive eugenics program involving sterilization. However, *Plan Verde*'s ideas alone did not materialize in the genocidal act involving coercive sterilization of thousands of Indigenous women, as had been the case with PSRPF.[17]

The evidence that this chapter lays out confirms that the family planning program was a genocidal policy with the objective of controlling the bodies of Peru's Indigenous peoples and those of their children.[18] As such, it provides a telling example of where Indigenous peoples' rights stand in Peru today and reflects the unchanged status of Indigenous identity within Peruvian society, where Indigenous, Andean, Quechua, Aymara, and Amazonian identities are seen as having "primordial" characteristics, as identities that no one desires or wants.[19] Additionally, the weight of the word genocide can bring about positive outcomes in dealing with the needs of the victim-survivors and in ensuring they receive some form of justice and reparations related to their case. The state aimed to deliberately prevent future births in this group, and in doing so aimed to destroy at least a part of the Indigenous population. However, the search for criminal accountability with this case has faced obstacles of impunity, as evidenced in the 2016 decision by the Public Prosecutor's Office to shelve 2,074 cases of forced sterilization due to "insufficient information," and the 2023 Supreme Court's decision to annul criminal investigations into these cases.[20] Even with the opening of the criminal investigations by the Public Prosecutor's Office on November 3, 2025, as of this writing the case is still at the initial phase of evidence. Finally, with the death of Fujimori on September 11, 2024, questions have arisen about how the legal case may shift direction.

The acknowledgment of this situation as a genocide—a crime of crimes—can provide victims with even more impetus to put forth their case. Notably, by referencing genocide in cases of victim-survivors who face difficulties in their legal battles against the state, we can provide them with an additional tool to urge the state to recognize its responsibility for this heinous crime.

SEXUAL VIOLENCE, INDIGENOUS PEOPLES' RIGHTS, AND HUMAN RIGHTS

Studies on coercive sterilization in Peru examine this atrocity within the framework of sexual violations: as a case of women's reproductive rights and Indigenous peoples' rights violations. Within these rights violations, some scholars focus on the societal dynamics of discrimination that played a part in the victimhood of the Indigenous population. Alejandra Ballón Gutiérrez documents the cartography of the resistance movement in Peru against forced sterilization.[21] She describes how the resistance began when local women's and human rights groups started receiving information on abuses related to the family planning program. As the situation became worse, domestic advocacy groups communicated their concerns to international human rights organizations. The message resonated, and soon a network of international and domestic advocacy formed. This network was also strengthened by the involvement of the artistic community in Peru, who helped maintain the subject of forced sterilization in the public discourse through their artwork, performances, and exhibitions. In discussing the artistic works of resistance, Ballón explains that the resistance movement embodied a postcolonial criticism, because the family planning policy was built on abuses of political power, discrimination, classism, racism, *machismo* (patriarchal notions of society), misogyny, and a depreciation of Indigenous culture and identity.[22] Furthermore, Lucía Stavig explains that the violation of Indigenous women's rights and reproductive rights reflected ideas of neoliberal governmentality from the state, "based on economic class and specifically poverty."[23] Similar ideas were also present in other modern family planning programs, in countries such as Canada and the United States, where ideas of population control revolved around the history of colonialism, control of "aboriginal peoples' land and resources," and the "denial of indigenous sovereignty."[24]

Exploring the status of Peru's Indigenous peoples' marginalization further, Ernesto Vasquez del Aguila discusses how the Peruvian government's family planning campaign reflected deep-rooted racial discrimination and unequal treatment of this ethnic group.[25] Racial inequality and the urban-rural divide from the Spanish colonial period have set the Indigenous peoples apart from those of European heritage. In this system, the Europeans identify with the urban and superior race, while the Indigenous are associated with the rural, poor, and weaker race. Such visions were reflected in the Peruvian government's projection of the family planning policy on a predominantly Indigenous population. Vasquez del Aguila explains how Fujimori's discourse was used to manipulate Indigenous peoples in the rural areas and documents malpractice by government health practitioners coming from urban areas, who did not speak Indigenous languages and who were of mixed European heritage. These state-sponsored health practitioners subjugated Indigenous women and gave them false information so that they would accept sterilization.[26] Such societal interactions were made possible in the context of Peru's society, where Indigenous peoples in rural areas were treated as inferior to those who were from the urban centers and had a lighter skin complexion.

Ñusta Carranza Ko extends del Aguila's argument and connects it to other structural factors to argue that the crime of forced sterilization represented the intersection of gender, ethnicity, and socioeconomic class dynamics in Peruvian society, which date back to the colonial period.[27] On gender, Julissa Mantilla Falcón argues that it is important for the Peruvian state to acknowledge the case as a violation of women's reproductive rights and to recognize the international documents that protect women's rights.[28] These include the right to reproductive health, right to life without discrimination and violence on the basis of gender, right to education, and right to liberty and personal security.

Using the lens of critical interculturality, Rosario B. De La Cruz Huamán focuses on some of the same intersections, particularly on the hierarchy of order and domination (including gender) reproduced from the colonial period in different cultures that have generated multiple inequalities.[29] The identities of the victim-survivors, who are mostly women of Indigenous origin living in conditions of poverty, point to these inequalities and intersections, and the Peruvian state participated in this very process of abuse as the new oppressor. Christina Ewig further emphasizes the economic and societal aspects of this case, explaining that Fujimori launched his campaign based on Thomas Malthus's idea of overpopulation, resource depletion, and economic downturn.[30] Fujimori thus used the fight against poverty and the messaging of economic advancement as a justification for a family planning campaign that included forced sterilization. Jelke Boesten raises similar points, showing that the neo-Malthusian-motivated policies were implemented to address the "Indian problem."[31] This was a well-known practice previously used in population control policies in countries such as South Africa. As Monica Bahati Kuumba explains, Malthusian-inspired birth control programs blamed African women for "their own poverty and underdevelopment as a result of their population growth" and targeted "blacks without a concomitant emphasis on the rest of the population."[32]

Connecting the ideas of Indigenous peoples' exclusion in Peru and of their victimhood, Jocelyn E. Getgen critically evaluates the role of Peru's TRC in not documenting the forced sterilization of Indigenous women and men.[33] The TRC's voluntary omission of the state's forced sterilization of Indigenous women in its final report (2003) reveals the restrictions that the TRC faced in presenting an overarching narrative of all the human rights crimes that occurred during the internal armed conflict.[34] Unsurprisingly, the exclusion of this group of victim-survivors in the TRC's final report made it significantly more difficult for victim-survivors, who were predominantly poor Indigenous Quechua-speaking women, to seek accountability.

Other scholars have been more cautious in categorizing the Indigenous peoples in Peru as those whose identities are defined only based on victimhood. Ainhoa Molina Serra explains how victim-centric approaches to the discourse on forced sterilization evolved around the objective of identifying the victim-survivors, revealing the suffering, and urging for justice.[35] She argues that this scope of victim-based discourse contributes to stereotyping Indigenous populations as passive, vulnerable actors and that it restricts sterilizations to be examined only through a human rights lens.

While existing research on forced sterilization in Peru has extensively documented and analyzed the abuse from a victim-centric, postcolonial, and intersectional perspective, only a few studies ground coercive sterilization within the context of genocide. Studies that do discuss the violation in relation to genocide cite the aspect of "prevention of life" that results from coercive sterilizations as evidence of genocide.[36] Other scholarship on human rights argues that coercive sterilization is a crime against humanity and not genocide.[37] In fact, even the 2018/2021 formal complaint from the Instituto de Defensa Legal and DEMUS on behalf of victim-survivors of forced sterilization against the Peruvian state has been filed under "grave human rights crimes," and violation of the "right to life," but not genocide.[38] Hence, the tendency in the scholarship and among human rights nongovernmental organizations has been to not approach this case from a genocide-based angle. This chapter aims to complement the literature by introducing a scholarship of genocide (based on normative analysis) linked to the coercive sterilization of Indigenous women in the Peruvian context. In doing so, it also contributes to existing scholarship on forced sterilization of Indigenous women and genocide in North America (i.e., Canada and the United States). It is important to state the obvious connections that exist between the sterilization of Indigenous peoples and genocide in Peru and to use international instruments of human rights, namely the 1948 United Nations Genocide Convention. The categorization of the crime and rights violations defined under a genocide lens bring to light the gravity of the crime committed against the Indigenous peoples in Peru, while the continued impunity for these actions reveals the prevalence of domestic historical roots of racism, sexism, and class-related discrimination that overshadow the genocide.

THE CONTEXT AND POLICY

As anthropologist Lucía Stavig explains, since the 1970s, "Peruvian feminists had advocated for the introduction of a state-sponsored reproductive health program."[39] These demands did not materialize readily. While the state adopted a pronatalist population policy that prevented family planning and sex education during the government of Juan Velasco Alvarado in 1968, during the subsequent government of Francisco Morales Bermúdez (1975–1980), a population control policy (not pronatalist) was implemented, which as political scientist Ewig explains, "endorsed the Malthusian idea that population control was a prerequisite to sustained economic development."[40] This idea of socioeconomic development reemerged in the 1985 Law on National Population Policy during President Fernando Sergio Marcelo Marcos Belaúnde Terry's government. This law outlined the need for the state to achieve an adequate "volume, structure, dynamic, and distribution of population" for the economic development of the state.[41] Notably, this law included unique language about the government's responsibility in "providing accessible methods of contraceptives in public health services."[42] However, "abortion and sterilization" were seen as nonadvisable methods of family planning.[43]

With the 1994 International Conference on Population and Development and the 1995 United Nations Fourth World Conference on Women, women's reproductive rights and sexual rights became a central part of global women's movements. Peruvian feminists were active participants in these conferences, and as Stavig observes, they were influenced and empowered by the global movement. It is against this global backdrop that Peruvian feminists found an unlikely ally—President

Alberto Fujimori—who they originally believed supported women's rights. In a state with conservative Catholic traditions like Peru, access to contraceptive methods and education on family planning were revolutionary policies. Historically, the Church expressed opposition to state-led family planning policies, noting that while "responsible parenting" was important, the only acceptable form of contraception was "abstinence."[44] Countering such views from the Church, Fujimori publicly aligned his ideas with the feminist movement, as evidenced in his attendance as the only head of state and the speech he delivered during the 1995 Beijing Conference on Women. In the speech, he announced his plans to address the scarcity of maternity-related services and information for women to "have at their disposal with full autonomy and freedom, the tools necessary to make decisions about their lives."[45]

What the Peruvian feminists were not aware of at the time was that Fujimori's plans were intertwined with the political dynamics of the internal armed conflict, which included *Plan Verde*. This plan, developed by the armed forces in 1989, aimed to establish a "national system of control, security, and propaganda," with the goal of advancing the political, social, and economic status of the state.[46] To this end, the plan outlined that the main task of the state was to attract foreign capital to increase state power, and also to address *tendencias demográficas* (demographic tendencies) in the form of "utilización generalizada de esterilización en los grupos culturalmente atrasados y económicamente pauperizados" (general use of sterilization among culturally backwards and economically impoverished groups) and the targeting of "subversivos y a sus familiares directos . . . como excedente poblacional nocivo" (subversives and their direct family members . . . as harmful surplus populations).[47] The description of culturally backwards and impoverished peoples who were suspected to have been involved in subversive acts were code words used to refer to nonwhite, rural, and Indigenous populations. While this plan on its own did not get implemented directly, as anthropologist Alejandra Ballón Gutiérrez explains, these tenets became the outline of Fujimori's family planning plan.[48]

The PSRPF was a national health program launched in 1996 by Alberto Fujimori's administration (1990–2000). It aimed to provide services to "promote, prevent, cure, and rehabilitate reproductive health to the highest quality" for all "inhabitants in Peru," provided that they expressed "free and voluntary consent."[49] Notable program objectives included the reduction of maternal and infant mortality rates, in addition to increased national usage of contraceptive methods to reach the global average fertility rate of 2.5 children per woman.[50] And yet, and perhaps not unexpectedly due to the plan's roots in the *Plan Verde*, these progressive premises were quickly undermined during the implementation of the program. Fujimori's administration manipulated the rhetoric on advancing women's rights, connected it with the fight against poverty and controlled family planning, and justified the policy of forced sterilization.[51] According to the Defensoría del Pueblo (Human Rights Ombudsman's Office), through the PSRPF, health officials performed 272,028 sterilizations on a majority of poor, rural, Indigenous Quechua-speaking women.[52] With the PSRPF, health officials were required to meet obligatory sterilization quotas. The pressure exerted on health officials to meet their obligations even included monetary incentives when quotas were met.[53] And when quotas were not met, health officials faced threats of sanctions and the denial of promotions. On certain occasions, in efforts to fill these quotas women who worked in health clinics were also sterilized.[54] In this context of pressure and coercion, thousands of individuals were coerced into these practices without consent and at times with false information. Women were misinformed that they would be able to give birth again after surgery; were told that they were undergoing surgery to remove a tumor and not tubal ligation; or at times were simply forced on a boat, taken to a health-care location, given anesthesia, and pushed out of the recovery room immediately after surgery.[55]

At times there was no information provided. The experiences of forced sterilization were marked with difficulties of communication between the victim, who spoke an Indigenous language, and health officials, who were Spanish speaking. The majority of the victim-survivors were "illiterate and only spoke Quechua," which made accessing any legal means to pursue criminal accountability—based in the Spanish system—difficult.[56] This linguistic barrier also became the fallback used by health officials accused of forced sterilization, as they would argue that the victim ought to have asked for a translator (who spoke an Indigenous language) if they were misinformed.[57] Only in 2016, with the help of human rights organizations such as DEMUS, 2,074 cases of forced sterilization, predominantly of Indigenous women, were brought forward to the Public Prosecutor's Office.[58] Although the cases were rejected by the Public Prosecutor's Office for insufficient information and other legal efforts annulled by the Supreme Court in 2023, continued pressure from the IACHR, DEMUS, and other advocacy groups helped reopen the cases of forced sterilization victim-survivors. On November 3, 2025, the Public Prosecutor's Office announced the opening of new criminal investigations against former President Alberto Fujimori and high-level officials in his government related to the crime of coercive sterilization.

THE GENOCIDE

This is one of the many personal testimonies of the victim-survivors of coerced sterilization in Peru. Dionicia Calderón recalls the day in 1996 when she was forcibly sterilized:

> They took me to the hospital in Cangallo [in the region of Ayacucho] and forced me to undergo surgery . . . and, when we [Dionicia along with other women] went back to the health post to complain [about the pain after surgery], the nurses would say that we were hypocrites and that it didn't hurt at all, and saying those things they threw us out. So, we never went back to the health post. . . . [W]e have suffered physical pain and infections, and some of us even rupture in our marriages and families.[59]

Peru's legal system is based on a monistic system of law, in which international and internal legal systems form a unity. Under Article 55 of Peru's 1993 Constitution, international law in Peru immediately takes effect once the state becomes party to international commitments.[60] All norms enshrined in treaties ratified by the state thus form a part of national law. Peru ratified the Convention on the Prevention and Punishment of the Crime of Genocide on February 24, 1960, without any reservations or declarations. Article II of the Convention defines genocide as "acts committed with intent to destroy, in whole or in part, a national, ethnical, racial or religious group."[61] Such ideas were also found in Article 319 of Peru's Penal Code, which defines genocide as an act having the intention to "destroy, in whole or in part, a national, ethnic, and social or religious group."[62] Both emphasize the classification of victim-survivors as a collective group and the existence of the intent to harm by the contracting parties. By 1996, when the PSRPF was implemented, the norms enshrined in the Genocide Convention and Peru's domestic legal system were legally binding.

Under Sections (b) and (d) of Article II of the Genocide Convention, genocidal acts include "causing serious bodily or mental harm to members of the group" and the imposition of "measures intended to prevent births within the group," all with the intention to destroy an entire group of a population.[63] Subsection IV of Article 319 of Peru's Penal Code reiterates this point, defining genocidal acts as "methods destined to impede the births" from a group with a defined national, ethnic, and social or religious characteristic.[64] The story of Dionicia, which is but one of many similar experiences reported by Indigenous women, fits well within this framing of genocide. The surgery administered by state officials was intended to prevent births, caused bodily and mental harm, and impacted a specific ethnic group, which in her case represented the Quechua-speaking Indigenous community in Ayacucho. However, claiming genocide with her single case would be tricky. Genocidal acts may be committed against a few individuals by the state, as noted in the indictment of Goran Jelisic or the "Serb Adolf," who had instigated, ordered, and committed genocide against Bosnian Muslims.[65] Nevertheless, making the case for genocide of a collective group based on Dionicia's story alone could be difficult. Alternatively, arguing for genocide referring to a collection of cases that manifest a pattern of conduct, with documents pointing to a government's intentional targeting of women of Indigenous background, does expose the PSRPF as a policy of genocide. And grounding the genocidal intention of the state on the *mens rea* (the guilty mind) and *actus reus* (the material facts) allows the policy to be understood within the larger context of genocide. The Peruvian state had both elements: the plan to forcibly sterilize a part of a population and the implementation of conduct that resulted in the destruction of a large number of individuals of an ethnic minority.[66]

As previously noted, the state policy was intended to cause bodily harm. Dionicia testified about the pain she suffered after the surgery, which was left untreated. Luisa Pinedo Rango, an Indigenous woman of Shipibo descent from Ucayali (in the Amazonian region of Peru), told a similar story of forced sterilization. Health officials came to her native Amazonian community, urged her and other women to undergo surgery, put her on a boat, and took her and other Indigenous women to the health center. She recalls that after they gave her anesthesia without any information about what was going on, "I woke up and they told me that I could go back home . . . but I felt pain and I did not know what to do. . . . [T]hey did not even give me a pill."[67] The Quipu Project, which audio-recorded testimonies of 135 victim-survivors and victim-survivors' families, documents similar experiences of twenty-nine women from Ucayali. Many were not provided with postsurgery medication. Some continue to have "abdominal pain and stomach swelling," while others stated that they cannot "work as much as they did before," and that even daily chores such as cooking have become difficult. Often, victim-survivors asked in their testimony why the health officials insisted on the surgery, tricked them, and abandoned them.[68] Luisa and other women's stories from the Quipu Project are corroborated by TRC President Salomón Lerner, who observed numerous cases in which after coerced tubal ligation there was no postoperative follow-up, which increased the possibilities of infection and life-threatening conditions.[69]

The case of *María Mamérita Mestanza Chávez v. Peru*, mediated by the IACHR, also tells a similar story of intentional cruelty. In 1998, María and her husband Jacinto Salazar Suárez were threatened by health officials, who claimed that they had broken the law by having more than five children.[70] This false information led the couple to decide on the tubal ligation procedure on March 27, 1998. Postsurgery complications led María and her husband to seek help from medical personnel, who dismissed the symptoms as side effects of anesthesia. The denial of medical attention led to María's death on April 5, 1998. Other survivors had similar experiences, including Dionicia, Luisa, and the 135 women from the Quipu Project who make up the collective narrative from the victim-survivors. The refusal of medical personnel to respond to victim-survivors' health conditions reflected a purposeful infliction of bodily harm by the state—a sign of possible implementation of genocide.

Conforming to the categorization of genocide under Section (d), Article II, of the Convention, a group targeted by the state endured the prevention of births. Although original program objectives were to "provide surgical intervention to men and women," and vasectomies were more economical and posed a lower health risk, in the process of implementation, government documents outline the wording of genocidal intent that pushed for women to be the subjects of tubal ligation.[71] Ministerial Resolution No. 089-98-SA/DM of March 10, 1998, redacts the program's reserved plans, which included the distribution of family planning methods to no less than 50 percent of the women of fertile age and their partners.[72] The specific reference to "fertile" women as the recipients of the family planning policy coincided with the PSRPF's push for tubal ligation rather than vasectomy. Women were the state's preferred group; it aimed to sterilize this population and prevent future births. This aspect resonates with having the planned intent (*mens rea*) to get rid of a population and the categorization of genocide under the Genocide Convention.

The data from REVIESFO further supports the argument of the state's selective focus on women and the outcome (*actus reus*) backed by the number of victim-survivors. REVIESFO was established by the state via Supreme Decree No. 006-2015, to record the number of victim-survivors of forced sterilization. From REVIESFO data, women constituted the majority of the victim-survivors of forced sterilization. During the first year of its implementation in 2016, REVIESFO reported a total of 3,580 cases of forced sterilization, 97 percent of whom were women.[73] In 2017, out of 2,398 registered cases, 96.9 percent were women. In 2018, 97 percent of the 94 recorded cases were women, and in 2019, all 5 cases of forced sterilization were women.[74] Hence in total, out of 6,077 cases of forced sterilization recognized by the Ministry of Justice and Human Rights, an overwhelming majority, 5,893 (97.97%), were women, who were forced to undergo surgical procedures against their will or without their consent.

Although the policy was structured on women's reproductive health, not all women were victimized. Hence, this was not a case of femicide, the systematic killing of a population comprised of the female sex. Instead, a group of women based on an ethnic category were singled out and subjected to the state's genocidal measures. This approach conforms to the textual definition of genocide in that the perpetrator—which was the state—planned to use policies of coercive sterilization and effectively did so to an ethnic minority population with the intention to destroy that group. The national family planning program invoking women's access to medical care was a disguised colonialist policy to prevent the births of Indigenous peoples and diminish the Indigenous population. The colonial vision of society channeled in this program worked well with the justifications used by the state about population control of the poor sectors of society—namely the Indigenous population.

This intention by the state to harm the Indigenous population was apparent from the moment the state fertility program was first promoted. The launch of the PSRPF was directed toward eight specific regions, with the objective to "better the accessibility" health-care services to the local population. These were the regions of Arequipa, Cusco, Puno, San Martín, Tacna, Junín, Ancash, and Piura.[75] All eight were considered nonmetropolitan rural areas, and with the exception of Tacna, San Martín, and Piura, were majority Quechua-speaking regions. Additionally, as noted in court documents filed by victim-survivors of forced sterilization against the state, irregularities affecting the reproductive rights of women were manifested in the Amazonas, Ancash, Apurimac, Arequipa, Ayacucho, Cajamarca, Cusco, Huancavelica, Huánuco, Junín, La Libertad, Lambayeque, Lima, Piura, Tarapoto, and Tumbes. Majority Quechua-speaking populations resided in Ancash, Apurimac, Ayacucho, Cusco, Huancavelica, Huánuco, and Junín, and areas with Jíbaro-speaking populations (an Indigenous language) included the Amazonas.[76]

The emphasis on Indigenous peoples was also evident from the early moments of family planning campaign promotion. Starting in 1996, Ministry of Health officials launched Health and Fertility Festivals in rural and poor communities.[77] According to government census data, the majority of individuals who identify their mother tongue as Quechua, Aymara, or Amazonian Indigenous languages reside in rural areas. These areas include the Amazonian and Andean regions, and this group constitutes 38.8 percent of Peru's total population.[78] TRC President Salomón Lerner recalls seeing these festivals during one of his family trips to a rural Andean region.[79] The festival banners included messages such as "Festival de ligadura de trompas, vasectomía gratis" (Free tubal ligation and vasectomy festival), "Campaña gratuita de ligadura de trompas y vasectomía" (Free campaign of tubal ligation and vasectomy), "Por eso elegimos el método de ligadura de trompas y vivimos felices" (That is why we chose the method of tubal ligation and we live happy), and "Campaña de vasectomía y ligadura de trompas para vivir felices" (Vasectomy and tubal ligation campaign to live happy).[80] The messaging aimed to frame sterilization surgeries as the optimal choice, associating the practice with happiness, "correct choice," or even monetary gains. And given the festival locations primarily in rural areas with majority Indigenous populations, it was directed toward women from Indigenous, poor, and rural backgrounds.

The argument for targeting Indigenous peoples from the PSRPF was
to control those who were seen by the state as the "cause of poverty," as
the group that was "preventing Peru from modernization."[81] This was a
Malthusian-grounded assumption invoked in postcolonial state settings,
where the vulnerable population, primarily women of color or of Indigenous descent, were targeted for population "manipulation programs."[82]
As such, PSRPF was used by Fujimori's government to "combat poverty" via population reduction, which the government assumed would
result in an increase in gross domestic product per capita.[83] Economic
justifications were used to "destroy, in whole or in part" a socioeconomic
minority who were of one ethnic group, the Indigenous population of
Peru. REVIESFO's 2016 data on the reported 3,580 cases of forced sterilization pinpoints the selection of the Indigenous group apart from
others. According to the registry, the majority of the victim-survivors
of forced sterilization resided in Indigenous-language-speaking rural
areas. These included 2 cases in Pasco, 2 in Puno, 221 in Junín, 229 in
Huancavelica, 342 in Huánuco, 342 in Ayacucho, and 1,293 in Cusco.
Comparatively, regions with mixed languages (Spanish and Indigenous languages) registered 33 victim-survivors in Moquegua and 680 in
San Martín. Other areas with more Spanish-speaking populations also
reported forced sterilization cases: 73 in Lima, 101 in La Libertad, 109
in Cajamarca, and 181 in Piura. In total, out of 3,580 reported cases of
forced sterilization during the first year of the victim-survivors' registry, 67.9 percent (2,431 cases) were from Indigenous-language-speaking
areas. And 56.9 percent, or more than 2,040 individuals, identified Quechua as their mother tongue.[84] These characteristics of women of Indigenous descent were descriptive of the majority victim-survivor group
who were coerced into these practices, without consent and at times with
false information. The state knowingly focused on the sterilization campaign against these women, whose ethnic identity put them in a more
vulnerable position, particularly in the context of a state equating the
eradication of poverty with population control. Peru's story resembles
the stories of other postcolonial states, such as Canada, that depended

on "control over aboriginal peoples' land and resources" and Indigenous population growth to fuel their capitalist system built on colonial and racial structural differences.[85]

The signs of genocidal intent were present from the beginning. By 1997, a year into the PSRPF, government officials were aware of the "irregularities" manifested by the family planning program. Two key pieces of government documents attest to the prior knowledge by the state and provide the basis for the argument of genocidal intent. The Human Rights Ombudsman's Office—an autonomous organization within the Peruvian government—received complaints of tubal ligation procedures starting in 1997. In response, the Ombudsman's Office published an investigation into the cases in 1998 that determined the PSRPF's application involved coercive elements of pressure, insufficient information on family planning options, and a disproportionate push for tubal ligation compared to vasectomies.[86] Concluding the findings, the Ombudsman's Office issued a list of recommendations for the state under Resolution No. 01-98. These included the modification of the program objectives and replacement of tubal ligation and vasectomy with other family planning methods.[87] Initially, the Ministry of Health issued letter SA-DM-No. 0284-98 on March 6, 1998, noting its commitment to revise the policy and set up a commission to investigate the "irregularities" of the PSRPF.[88] And yet coerced sterilizations did not stop.

According to documents from the Congressional Investigative Commission on Crimes Related to Voluntary Tubal Ligation Procedures from 1996 to 2000, the director of the Basic Health Care Unit of Chumbivilcas in the region of Cusco admitted to performing a round of tubal ligations in 1999.[89] The surgeries in Chumbivilcas were notorious for being staffed by unqualified surgeons and for not having an anesthesiologist present during the tubal ligation procedures.[90] One of the women, Santusa Taype Chlla, who was sterilized at the Santo Tomás Health Center in Chumbivilca on July 10, 1999, died of postsurgery health complications on July 12, 1999. Yet parallel to the expression of concern issued by the Ministry of Health, the state continued pushing for coercive sterilizations. Investigations of irregularities in the family planning policies never materialized. Instead, health centers that met sterilization quotas received useful equipment from the Ministry of Health. How was this possible? Fujimori's government had a goal to accomplish: "combating poverty."[91] To do so, the central government set up a family planning policy aimed at preventing the population growth of those who were categorized as the source of poverty. The prejudices that sustained this policy reflected a colonialist mentality embedded in governing hierarchies that regarded the Indigenous peoples as a dispensable group, whose lives could be destroyed in part or whole without any repercussions of criminal accountability or justice.

Along with the Ombudsman's Office investigation, forced sterilization was brought up during the fourth meeting of the Second Regular Session of the Legislature on March 18, 1998. As redacted in congressional session notes, Congressman Roger Guerra-García informed the legislature about the government's population policy, referring to the PSRPF. He explained that a population policy need not be limited to the "control of population growth or the phenomenon of sterilization."[92] This was an indirect criticism of the restricted insights of the government policy that promulgated sterilization as the single best option. Guerra-García then noted the existence of complaints against those who "implemented" the government policy, referring to the health-care professionals, and explained the malpractice of coerced sterilizations that "put at risk the life and health" of many.[93] These were comments directed against the human rights violations caused by the state. The investigative report from the Human Rights Ombudsman's Office and the congressional speech were delivered in 1997 and 1998. Hence, the state was aware of forced sterilizations and its associated human rights violations from the early phase of PSRPF's implementation. And yet the government did not revise the policy or stop the bodily harm. Daily newspapers *El Comercio*, *El Sol*, and *La República* reported on "tricked" and "forced sterilizations" in the province of Cusco that took place in

1999.[94] The refusal to revisit the malpractice of sterilization was a consistent signal of genocidal intent by the state, one that prioritized the prevention of births in a population, the majority of whom were women of Indigenous descent.

There are questions about the intentionality of the PSRPF in destroying "in whole or in part" a particular population. Nongovernmental organizations defending the victim-survivors of forced sterilization are hesitant to admit that a genocide occurred, noting that there is not enough evidence to categorize the state's intentions as having the goal of annihilating a group of peoples who were impoverished, resided in rural areas, worked the fields, and were of Indigenous or Andean descent. The intentions had more to do with birth control in certain populations.[95] It is important to note that reference to "birth control" is not equivalent to the "prevention of births" that is explained in the Genocide Convention. The sterilization practice against women predominantly of Indigenous background was not to inform the population of birth control or family planning practices. These experiences were designed to forcibly prevent the births of more children, as had been the case with the Indigenous population in Canada.[96] The surgical acts in Peru were performed against the women's will; at times women would be locked up and in other instances forced to take anesthesia.[97] There could not be clearer evidence of a state's intention, supporting the case for genocide.

WHAT REMAINS

For over half a decade, from 1996 to 2000, the Peruvian state implemented a family planning program with supposedly progressive objectives focusing on educating the public about contraceptive methods, reducing infant and maternal mortality rates, and protecting women's reproductive rights. However, with the implementation of the program, the focus changed toward an aggressive campaign of forced sterilization that used coercion and manipulation to target a vulnerable population of society. Indigenous women from poor economic backgrounds constituted most of the victim-survivors.

Despite the evidence that points to the genocidal intentions of the state and the physical evidence of bodily harm caused by the PSRPF, this case has yet to be considered as a crime against humanity, let alone as a genocide. What remains from the family planning policy are the violations endured by the victim-survivors and their family members, many of whom are still waiting for justice and reparations. Even the family members of María Mamérita Mestanza Chávez have yet to receive the various measures of reparations. This is in spite of María Mamérita Mestanza Chávez's death and the subsequent petition from nongovernmental organizations to the IACHR that led to a friendly agreement in 2003 between the state and the victim's family. Mamérita's daughters and sons have not received financial assistance for education. Relatedly on reparations, despite the modifications to the Law on Comprehensive Reparations on February 2021, which expanded the eligibility of individuals receiving reparations from victim-survivors of internal armed conflict to now include those affected by coercive sterilizations, victim-survivors registered in the REVIESFO have not received any form of reparations as of the time of this writing.

The other factor that remains unspoken within this unacknowledged context of genocide is the identification of the majority of victim-survivors: the Indigenous populations of Peru. The targeting of these ethnic groups has gone unnoticed and has been pushed aside. In the past, the Spaniards as conquistadors and colonizers of Peru ruled with the idea of ethnic superiority. This perspective is similar to the views on ethnicity and socioeconomics that have continued in contemporary Peruvian society and have shaped society's deprecation of Indigenous peoples and cultures, as discussed in chapter 1.[98] From this perspective, the elimination in "whole or in part" of the Indigenous populations was not a problematic outcome, because it would help the state establish population control and improve national economic standards. This indeed was the goal of Fujimori's government.

In this context, the Indigenous peoples became a population that could be subject to genocide via coercive sterilization practices and the prevention of births of future generations of Indigenous children. As I have argued in this chapter, this was the intention behind the family planning policy.

CHAPTER THREE

Then, There Were the Children . . .

Indigenous leader and activist Hilaria Supa Huamán had the chance to meet Peruvian President Alberto Fujimori in Beijing at the Conference on Women in 1995. She spoke to him about the many problems Indigenous women and communities faced in Peru, including poverty and limited access to health services.[1] After speaking with Hilaria, Fujimori took the stand and gave his speech on women's rights in Peru. In the speech, he noted how women and children were the "less favored sectors of society," affirmed his position on protecting women's rights by "vigorously" enforcing the "law outlawing all forms of violence against women," and "pledged to work for the women of [his] country."[2] Contradicting his claims, however, Fujimori's government was at the same time in the process of devising plans to launch a genocidal family planning program, which would result in the coercive sterilization of thousands of women of Indigenous descent. Among these victim-survivors were children whose stories have gone unnoticed.

Through the use of storytelling of a victim-survivor's testimony, this chapter explores the story of a young woman named Sarita and her story of coercive sterilization and survival. First, I situate the violations committed against Sarita within the social and legal framework of children's rights, noting the intersections of other layers of human rights violations that resulted from the coercive sterilization campaign in Peru. Next, following the social and legal analysis, this chapter explores the concept of "justice" from both Sarita's perspective and a rights-based argument, pointing out the similarities and differences between victim-survivor-centered and rights-centered frameworks. Finally, the chapter raises questions about why the case of minors, specifically Indigenous minors, was overlooked in the discourse on coercive sterilizations and discusses how Sarita's case may change the public perception of this crime.

No one has mentioned the children, the underage girls who were victimized by the family planning program (i.e., PSRPF) during the late 1990s.[3] They were absent from *Nada Personal* (Nothing personal), the first investigative report about forced sterilization practices, published by human rights advocate and lawyer Giulia Tamayo.[4] They were also absent from subsequent reports published by the Peruvian Human Rights Ombudsman's Office and nongovernmental organizations.[5] Similarly, information about minors was absent from the court case filed in 2018 against former President Alberto Fujimori; his ministers Eduardo Yong Motta, Marino Costa Bauer, and Alejandro Aguinaga Recuenco; and other government personnel on behalf of 1,316 victim-survivors for mediated authorship of serious bodily injury resulting in death and 1,310 victim-survivors for serious bodily injury.[6] Even studies that discussed coercive sterilization in connection with the children primarily referred to them as those who were affected physically and psychologically as a result of "losing their mothers" or "drinking breast milk with anesthesia from mothers in post-operative situations."[7] Children were considered an indirectly affected group or studied using a victim-by-association framework. As Sarita's story reveals, however, there were cases in which children were indeed subject to sterilization.

It is difficult to know how many children were forcibly sterilized, as children generally have not testified on their own behalf; Most of the victim-survivors who have testified in public were above the legal age of consent.[8] Sarita is registered in REVIESFO. While REVIESFO information released to the public includes data on a victim's sex, region of residence, education level, health status (including disability status), and identifier of the mother tongue (i.e., Quechua, Asháninka, Spanish, and others), it does not list the age group of the victim-survivors who are registered.[9] Nevertheless, based on the systematic implementation of the PSPRF and its genocidal nature, as revealed by published research, it is likely that Sarita was not the only minor affected by coercive sterilization.[10] And yet there are no other cases that have come to light. For this reason, the story that Sarita told to Victoria Vigo—the non-Indigenous victim-survivor of coercive sterilization whose story is told in chapter 4—matters. Specifically, it demonstrates how the framing of the coercive sterilization case—in both public discourse in Peru and academic writing—has overlooked the victimhood of minors. While this lack of attention may have been unintentional, the unexplored nature of children as potential victim-survivors of these coercive practices ultimately neglects and denies them the right to their sufferings. Sarita's case confirms the horrors that took place during the PSPRF campaign in Peru and that further aggravated the Peruvian government's crime. Importantly, her case brings to light the government's crimes against an even more vulnerable population: minors. Sarita remains one of the forgotten children of the state campaign of coercive sterilization.

SARITA'S STORY

Victoria Vigo recalls the day she ran into Sarita. Victoria had been an active voice in the fight against impunity for those affected by coercive sterilization, having herself been a survivor of a nonconsented cesarean and involuntary sterilization in 1996. Sarita was a colleague of hers, and Victoria had gotten to know her as a participant in the movement against government practices of coercive sterilization. But that day, as Victoria remembers, Sarita did not look right.

"Is everything okay?" she asked Sarita. "You look a little bit under the weather," she remarked. Sarita responded that she had not been feeling well. Specifically, Sarita was feeling pain in her abdomen and experiencing some hemorrhaging. Victoria suggested Sarita consult a doctor, perhaps a gynecologist or an obstetrician, about her symptoms. Sarita was reticent. Then, she revealed something to Victoria that she had not told anyone until that point: "Victoria, I too was forced sterilized. They sterilized me at the age of seventeen."[11]

Sarita was born in 1980. By 1997 she was happily living with her partner in the region of Huánuco in central Peru. As she explained, "Yo tengo dos niños" (I have two kids), and she hoped to have many more children in the future. At that time she was only seventeen years old. That same year, however, life took a turn: "Señorita, me hicieron mal" (Miss, they did wrong to me).[12]

One day the nurses from the health center came to her community. "Vamos al hospital para hacerte una limpieza" (Let's take you to the hospital to give you a cleaning), said the nurses. They urged Sarita to have a "cleaning" to avoid the risk of developing cancer, diabetes, and other problems in the future. With those words, the nurses convinced a hesitant Sarita and took her to the hospital. Once at the hospital, things felt rushed. Sarita explained her initial experience: "[A]garrando me han puesto (la) bata, me pusieron anastesia" (Grabbing me, they put a hospital gown on me, then gave me anesthesia). When Sarita woke up, she was in pain: "Dolía, dolía y yo hechada al costado . . . me dolía la barriga" (Lying down on the side . . . I felt pain in my belly). Confused about what had happened, she looked around. Then one of the nurses said, "[T]u ya no vas a tener hijos" (You are not going to be able to have more children). The information the nurses presented was foreign to Sarita's ears. No more children? Before Sarita could process the statement, the nurses scoldingly told her, "[A] los diecisiete años tu ya tienes dos hijos! Tu cómo vas a mantenerlos!" (At seventeen you already have two kids! How do you think you are going to maintain them!) To Sarita, who listened incredulously to these statements, one of the nurses confidently emphasized, "Ya nunca más vas a tener hijos. ¡Mas bien, díganos a nosotros gracias!" (Now, you are never again going to be able to have more children. In fact, you should be thanking us!) That same day, Sarita was discharged from the hospital without any proper medication or a follow-up consultation about the procedure she had undergone. "Mismo día nos botan del hospital y [p]ara dolor nada nos dan. Ni pastilla." (The same day they threw us out of the hospital. For the pain, they gave us nothing. Not even pills.) The only thing she knew was that she would no longer be able to have any more children.

Sarita explained, "No me dijeron nada, nada, nada de planificación familiar, no he sabido nada yo . . . solamente me han hecho así en el hospital" (They did not tell me anything, nothing, nothing of the family planning, I did not know . . . only that this is what they had done to me at the hospital). From that point forward, Sarita described how her life became "todo un fracaso" (all a failure). As a result of the forced sterilization, Sarita had problems with her partner and is now *separada* (separated). Her partner had accused her of having "otro marido" (another husband) and insulted her. Sighing deeply and with her voice quivering, Sarita explained that she had endured numerous insults throughout her life and had become *marginalizada* (marginalized) because of her experience. In fact, she never dared speak of her experience to local authorities or anyone "por verguenza . . . porque estaba marginalizada" (out of embarrassment . . . because I was marginalized).

Fracaso (failure) is a word Sarita muttered over and over again. She said she lived in constant emotional and physical pain and was often reminded of that day in 1997 when everything changed. She explained how the experience resulted in her "no vivir la vida bien . . . no tener motivo . . . un fracaso" (not living life well . . . not having motivation . . . a failure). This is similar to what many victim-survivors of coercive sterilization have reported in terms of the effects of these procedures on their mental and physical health. This includes the loss of *ánimo*, meaning the energy to live both physically and emotionally, which causes one to experience loss of appetite, anxiety, headaches, insomnia, and shocks throughout the body.[13] Anthropologist Julieta Chaparro-Buitrago refers to these pains as symptomatic of a condition of *debilidad* (debility) and "debilitated lifeworlds," which represents the numerous harms that embody the outcomes of sterilizations in women's lives.[14] Some women refer to it as a feeling of being drunk, and others describe the *debilidad* as a condition that involves "headaches, mostly brain pain, and headache in the cranium . . . dizziness, sleep disorders, and loss of appetite." Sarita suffered similar effects.

Sarita suffered the *debilidad* alone. However, once she recognized that she was one of many who were forced to undergo the procedure of tubal ligation, Sarita gained the courage to travel to Lima to join protests demanding justice for Peru's coercive sterilization victims. This is when she met Victoria, whom she described as a *buena persona* (good person) whom she *confío* (confides in). With time, Sarita also registered her case with REVIESFO. However, telling others about her personal experience remains a difficult process. Only recently she told her story to Victoria and opened up to me about her experiences when she "solo tenía diecisiete años" (was only seventeen).

RACIALIZATION OF CHILDREN IN PERU

In thinking about children, the status of children, and children's rights, it is important to explore the racialization of children in Peru.[15] Anthropologist Krista Van Vleet explains that in postcolonial contexts such as that of Peru, "young people navigate uneven political, social, and economic terrain as they develop a sense of self."[16] This uneven terrain is saturated by hierarchies of race, gender, and class from the colonial period that condition the identity and future of the child. Particularly, Indigenous girls live in "intersected oppressions intertwined with racial, gendered, sexual, and class hegemonies." As evidenced by the decolonial feminist scholarship referenced in chapter 1, poverty, patriarchal gendered norms, and oppression associated with ethnicity all heighten the violence and resulting vulnerability that Indigenous girls face in Peruvian society.

According to the Human Rights Ombudsman's Office reports from 2024, Indigenous peoples often are victims of various types of human rights violations.[17] In 2018 alone, there were hundreds of reported cases of sexual violence against Indigenous women. Among these cases of sexual violence, 411 were against Kichwa-speaking Indigenous women, 370 were against Indigenous children under the age of eighteen, and 166 were against Indigenous children between the ages of eleven and fourteen. The Ombudsman's Office found that Indigenous children are vulnerable and are at high risk not only due to their age, but also because of where and how they suffer sexual violence. Often, sexual violence against Indigenous children occurs in educational settings.

According to Rosemary Pioc, the president of the Council of Awajún and Wampis Women, between 2010 and 2024 there were 524 reported cases of sexual violence against Awajún Indigenous children, perpetrated by teachers in the province of Condorcanqui in the Amazonian region of Peru.[18] The Condorcanqui region has one of the highest percentages of poverty, and it is where the Awajún peoples primarily reside. These peoples make up 11 percent of the Indigenous populations residing in the Amazonian areas. The aforementioned cases of sexual violence against Awajún Indigenous children (which at times resulted in unwanted pregnancies) took place in the dorm houses of students and were inflicted by the teachers. While these crimes were reported to the Ministry of Education, they have largely been dismissed. In fact, they have been labeled as normal "cultural practices" by Minister of Education Morgan Quero, and adolescent Indigenous girls have been asked by Minister of Women Ángela Hernández to hold off on their sexual behaviors.[19] The excuse and victim-blaming provided by the minister of women reflects an attitude within Peruvian society of faulting children who are of nonwhite backgrounds as "unruly subjects who need to be controlled, managed, and disciplined into appropriate behavior."[20] Sociologist Jessica K. Taft calls this an extension of "a racialized project of civilization, modernization, and national development," in which children of nonwhite backgrounds are regarded by the state as needing some form of rectification of behavior that separates them from Indigenous cultures and practices.[21]

In addition to physical and emotional harm, sexual violence against Indigenous children, which in the case of the Awajún peoples has disproportionately impacted Indigenous girls, also restricts the possibility for children to pursue their education further. As evidenced in the testimony from María, an Awajún student who was raped by her teacher on two separate occasions and received death threats from the same teacher, the entire experience impacted her health both physically and psychologically. The rapes resulted in an unwanted pregnancy and miscarriage, and they left her traumatized to the extent that pursuing education became no longer possible.[22] Legal scholar Mikaela Luttrell-Rowland explains how education has been viewed by young people in Peruvian society as "the avenue towards development and a way to become somebody."[23] Embedded in the pursuit of education are implicit ideas about progress and modernity linked with Peru's racialized colonial history, which regards Indigenous ways as being backward. Additionally, as anthropologist Jessaca Leinaweaver explains, education is seen as a way to *superar* (overcome) poverty, which is equivalent to "sloughing off the markers that might make others define you as indigenous."[24] Thus, by being subject to sexual violence and suffering the impacts of such a heinous act, Awajún girls like María were robbed of their opportunity to continue their education, which could have guaranteed them better opportunities in society. Finally, the absence of any legal processes against the abusers of these children reflects the vulnerable status of Awajún girls, Indigenous girls, and Indigenous children in Peru.

CHILDREN'S RIGHTS UNDER THE LAW

Forced sterilizations—or sterilizations performed without informed consent—against a specific group of ethnic peoples constitute a multiplicity of human rights violations, such as gender discrimination, sexual violence, torture, crimes against humanity, and genocide. More-over, when one considers the involvement of children, namely girls, as subjects of this crime, the human rights violations extend to include violations of children's rights. This section explores the case of Sarita in relation to international law, namely conventional law concerning the rights of children. The discussion of the legal norms about children's rights is intended to situate Sarita's experience from a legal perspective as a crime committed against a minor in Peru. Additionally, I hope to contrast this legal form of justice with Sarita's own vision of justice.

The earliest modern international document to recognize the specific rights of children was drafted in 1923, largely in response to the plight of children during World War I. Adopted by the League of Nations in 1924, the Geneva Declaration of the Rights of the Child asserts the right of children to be "given the means requisite for [their] normal development, both materially and spiritually."[25] Here, "normal development" refers to basic human needs, like food, health care, shelter, and protection from exploitation, all of which are noted in the declaration. Additionally, the declaration recognizes that a "child must be the first to receive relief in times of distress," and that any sick child must "be nursed."[26] Given these perspectives, forcing a child— against their will—to undergo a procedure intended to alter their body, which negatively impacts their physical and mental health, would certainly be considered a violation of these norms. Moreover, instances when children are denied postoperative care and suffer subsequent health complications or sicknesses would also be regarded as violations of children's rights under the Geneva Declaration. In other words, using the framework of these norms, Sarita's experience would constitute an egregious violation of her rights as a child.

While the Geneva Declaration is a legally nonbinding document that predated Peru's PSRPF, it is nevertheless important to outline the norms that were established in the declaration, as they set the standard for future norm developments related to children's rights. These include the Declaration of the Rights of the Child, adopted in 1959;

some of the provisions in the Universal Declaration of Human Rights; the International Covenant on Civil and Political Rights; and the International Covenant on Economic, Social and Cultural Rights. The last of these relates to the rights of the child and the safeguards established in the Convention on the Rights of the Child (CRC) to protect the child from violence.

The CRC, which became law in 1989, specifies how the Peruvian government's atrocities of coercive sterilizations can be understood within the legally binding framework of children's rights violations. Peru was one of the first states to ratify the convention, on September 4, 1990. According to Article 55 of Peru's 1993 Constitution, the state follows a monistic system of law, which allows international treaties to become domestic legal norms from the moment of treaty ratification.[27] Ratification, however, must be preceded by Congress's approval of the treaty, as specified under Article 56 of the Constitution. Once Congress approves the treaty and the president of the republic ratifies the treaty at the international level, the norms enshrined in the treaty become effective as domestic law. At this point, under Article 32 of the Constitution, international treaties and their related human rights norms cannot be subject to a referendum. Taking these standards into account, the Peruvian state, from 1990 onward, was legally bound by the children's rights norms enshrined in the CRC.

As stated in Article 1 of the CRC, a child is defined as "every human being below the age of eighteen years."[28] According to this definition, Sarita was a child when she was coercively sterilized at the age of seventeen. Furthermore, Articles 12 and 13 of the convention specify the child's right to freedom. While Article 12 states that a child has the right to express their own views "freely in all matters affecting" them, Article 13 clarifies that these rights include the "freedom to seek, receive and impart information ... either orally, in writing or in print."[29] Applying these norms to Sarita's experience as a seventeen-year-old girl who was forced to undergo tubal ligation, the state, under the standards of the CRC, had an obligation to provide her with information related to the procedure she was about to undergo. However, no information was provided orally, in writing, or in print to Sarita. It was only after the procedure was completed that she discovered what had happened to her body.

In addition to granting children their freedoms, the state is also obligated to protect children and their rights. Under Article 19 of the CRC, the state must "protect the child from all forms of physical or mental violence, injury or abuse, neglect or negligent treatment, maltreatment or exploitation."[30] It is important to note the emphasis on "all forms" of violence in Article 19 and the implied repercussions that accompany the state's negligence of this protection. In other words, the state is in violation of the CRC if it fails to protect children from any form of violence, regardless of its physical or mental nature. Along the same lines, Peru also ratified the International Covenant on Civil and Political Rights (ICCPR), on April 28, 1978. Under Article 24 of the ICCPR, the state is required to ensure the "protection" of children "required by [their] status" as minors.[31] Article 24 of ICCPR is thus consistent with the CRC. In particular, the CRC explains that children are entitled to special care and protection. Especially, children are entitled to protection against violence, since violence prevents, neglects, and denies the best interests of the child.

Additionally, Article 37 of the CRC specifies that "no child shall be subjected to torture or other cruel, inhuman or degrading treatment."[32] This point is also raised in the Convention Against Torture and Other Cruel, Inhuman or Degrading Treatment or Punishment, which was ratified by Peru on July 7, 1988.[33] The Convention Against Torture does not specify the child as the subject in question; however, it does outline a broad framework for the prevention of torture and ill treatment against all peoples.[34] Torture is understood to mean "any act by which severe pain or suffering, whether physical or mental, is intentionally inflicted on a person."[35] Regarding the act of coercive sterilization as a form of torture, it is important to consider the normative legal interpretations provided by former United Nations Special Rapporteur on Torture, and Other Cruel, Inhuman or Degrading Treatment or

Punishment Juan E. Méndez. According to Méndez, forced sterilization is an "act of violence, a form of social control," and "sterilizations carried out by State officials in accordance with coercive family planning laws or policies may amount to torture."[36] This is particularly true since the victim-survivors of coercive sterilizations, which were carried out by Peruvian state officials under PSPRF, were often forced to undergo these procedures without the use of anesthesia.[37] Consequently, these physical acts of violence are arguably a form of torture that can be categorized as ill, cruel, inhuman, or degrading treatment, meaning Peru violated both the Convention Against Torture and the CRC. Moreover, coercive sterilization also had profound, lasting effects on mental health, as in the case of Sarita. According to the Convention Against Torture, torture includes the purposeful infliction of suffering—both physical and mental forms. Given the physical and mental injuries Sarita suffered as a result of coercive sterilization, Peru was in violation of the Convention Against Torture and Article 24 of the CRC, which obligates states to ensure the "highest attainable standard of health" for children.[38]

The norms for the protection of children's health are also stated in the International Covenant on Economic, Social, and Cultural Rights (ICESCR), which the Peruvian government ratified on April 28, 1978. According to Article 10, Section (3) of the ICESCR, "special measures of protection and assistance should be taken on behalf of all children and young persons"; this includes, under Article 12, the right to the "enjoyment of the highest attainable standard of physical and mental health."[39] Hence, from these normative standards, it is clear that sterilizing children against their will and releasing them from hospitals without proper medical follow-up—as in Sarita's case—violated the ICESCR. Specifically, these actions denied children their right to access the highest standards of physical and mental health. In fact, the Peruvian government's actions put children's lives in danger. Furthermore, it should be noted that the earliest irregularities, complaints, and malpractices related to the family planning program were documented in 1996, yet the Peruvian government claimed not to be aware of these issues and did nothing to stop the atrocities.[40] By failing to stop these human rights violations, the government was knowingly violating its own international legal obligations.

Coercive sterilization against any individual is a crime against humanity, as defined under Article 7, Section (g) of the Rome Statute of the International Criminal Court.[41] The domestic court case against former President Fujimori and his government personnel, which was filed in Peru on October 31, 2018, follows this categorization and labels forced sterilization as a crime against humanity. This point is often raised in scholarship.[42] However, some scholars have argued that Peru's coercive sterilizations are both a crime against humanity as well as a form of genocide against Indigenous peoples.[43] Yet another perspective is offered by the IACHR, which has approached the crime as one that involves gender-based violence and discrimination against Indigenous women.[44] The point made by the IACHR about gender and women's rights is important and is further discussed in subsequent chapters on intersectionality and international human rights law. In sum, the discussion on international law so far suggests that coercive sterilization represented many different layers of rights violations, which—relating back to Sarita's case—now extended to children's rights.

The examination at the domestic level about children's rights also sheds more light on the legal discussion on coercive sterilizations. Peruvian law mirrors many of the norms on children's rights represented in the CRC and other international treaties. Under Article 4 of the 1993 Constitution, the state is obligated to protect children, adolescents, mothers, and the elderly in situations of "abandonment."[45] While abandonment is not the same as exposing a child to a situation that violates their physical integrity or subjects them to sexual violence, it is nonetheless one of the norms developed after the CRC to protect children, and its existence in the 1993 Constitution carries symbolic importance.

Along with the protection of children outlined in the Constitution, the state adopted more specific norms relating to the protection of children during this period. In 1992, the state approved Law No. 26102, or the Code of Children and Adolescents. The 1992 Code details the rights of children and adolescents and the role of the state in providing protection. Article VII of the 1992 Code explains the state's obligation to respect and apply the principles, rights, and norms established in the "present Code and the Convention on the Rights of the Child," adding weight to the norms set forth in the CRC. Many of the provisions of the Code of Children and Adolescents were further reinforced by Law No. 27337, or the New Code for Children and Adolescents that was instituted in 2000. Interestingly, this New Code was put in place in response to the perceived "necessity" of children and adolescents having access to legal resources in cases concerning the violation of children's rights.[46] For instance, as per Article 146 of the New Code, children and adolescents are guaranteed legal representation through the Ministry of Justice. The norms of the 1992 Code were effective during the PSPRF's implementation (i.e., from 1996 to 2000), and the New Code was put in place during the last "official" year of the PSPRF, which, despite its four-year mandate, continued its sterilization campaign until 2001.[47] Hence, the protections established in Peru's 1992 Code, New Code, and the CRC were all legally binding during the period when women and children—as Sarita's case reveals—were subject to involuntary sterilization. If Sarita's case had been brought to light, she, as a minor, would have been guaranteed legal representation by the Ministry of Justice. However, Sarita's case remained hidden for many years, and the Peruvian state was not held accountable for violating its own normative obligations toward children.

According to both the 1992 and 2000 Codes, a child is defined as being eleven years of age or younger, while adolescents are defined as being between the ages of twelve and eighteen.[48] Unlike the CRC, which defines "every human being below the age of eighteen years" as a child, both of these codes restrict the age range for children.[49] The 1992 Code more specifically asserts that its norms apply to all children and adolescents who reside in Peru, regardless of any distinctions based

on ethnicity, color, sex, language, religion, political opinion, national-
ity, and so forth. Based on the standards were laid out in both codes, and
which were used to classify the group—children and adolescents—as
needing protection, seventeen-year-old Sarita too would have needed
protection from the state.

Moreover, under Article 14 of the 1992 Code and Article 15 of the
2000 Code, the state has the responsibility to guarantee basic education for children and adolescents. Here, education includes education
on "orientation related to sex and family planning," meaning children
and adolescents have the right to learn about contraceptives and other
family-planning methods.[50] However, as Sarita's case reveals, she did
not receive any education or information on family planning. In fact,
things happened so quickly that Sarita was unable to grasp what was
happening to her. Upon arriving at the hospital, she was forcibly given
anesthesia and rushed into a surgical room, where shortly afterward
she underwent a life-altering procedure that she had not consented
to. The International Federation of Gynecology and Obstetrics notes
that, even in medical emergencies, a woman must be "given the time
and support she needs to consider her choice" for tubal ligation, and
her "informed decision must be respected."[51] Sarita was not given the
option to make an informed decision, even as a minor undergoing the
procedure. Moreover, as an underage minor, she did not have her rights
upheld because she was not protected against harm. Under Article 4 of
both the 1992 and 2000 Codes of Children and Adolescents, the state is
obligated to protect the personal integrity of the child and adolescent.
This includes the state's respect of underage persons' "moral, psychological, and physical development and well-being," such as by protecting the minor from torture and cruel and degrading treatment.[52] The
protection from torture has been previously discussed in relation to the
findings of Juan Méndez, the Convention Against Torture, and the legal
interpretation of the former United Nations Special Rapporteur, who
categorizes forced sterilization as a form of torture. In sum, despite the
1992 and 2000 Codes' requirement to protect children against physical

harm (e.g., torture), the implementation of Peru's family planning campaign involved the coercive sterilization of young underage girls, such as Sarita. These nonconsensual surgical procedures inflicted physical and mental violence—both of which had long-lasting effects—on Peru's Indigenous youth.

Sarita was forcibly sterilized at seventeen. Forced sterilizations denied children like Sarita their rights to education on family-planning methods; violated their bodily integrity by inhibiting their physical development and well-being; subjected a vulnerable population to torture; and represented a disregard for the physical and mental health of young individuals. These rights are enshrined in conventional international law (i.e., ICCPR, ICESCR, and the CRC) and in Peru's domestic legal standards safeguarding children's and adolescents' rights. Therefore, by proactively engaging in coercive sterilizations, particularly those that involved children—which resulted in Sarita's victimhood—the state in effect rejected its legal obligations and jeopardized its ability to protect children's rights norms. Justice, understood and carried out in legal terms, would entail processes of criminal accountability against specific perpetrators that had wronged Sarita. Is this the justice Sarita wanted?

THE SEARCH FOR JUSTICE

When Sarita agreed to tell her story, I asked her what she hoped to get out of the interview. Sarita responded, "Justicia. Quiero justicia para mi." (Justice. I want justice for me.)[53] What was this justice that she was referring to? As scholars note, in the past four decades there has been a movement toward the "humanization of international law" with, for instance, increased opportunities for victim-survivors to participate and become involved in national transitional justice processes.[54] This new movement was influenced by the development of international norms linked to acquiring and promoting justice for victim-survivors, such as the United Nations Declaration of Basic Principles of Justice for Victims of Crime and Abuse of Power and the Basic Principles and Guidelines on the Right to a Remedy and Reparation for Victims of Gross Violations of International Human Rights Law and Serious Violations of International Humanitarian Law. The UN Declaration was adopted by the General Assembly in 1985, and the Basic Principles were adopted later, in December 2005. The declaration specifies the need to secure national and international measures to recognize and respect the rights of victims of crime and abuse of power, in addition to noting the need to establish and "strengthen" the prosecution and sentencing of those guilty of crimes.[55] On the other hand, the Basic Principles detail the scope of the state's obligation to take "appropriate legislative and administrative" measures to "prevent violations"; investigate violations; provide victims with legal remedy or "access to justice"; and bring forth "effective remedies to victims, including reparation."[56] Both documents focus on the state's obligation to recognize victim-survivors and protect their rights tied to criminal accountability and reparations.

As a result of the emergence of new international norms that recognize victims' rights, we tend to think about matters more from a legal tradition, particularly when discussing matters that involve human rights violations, victim-survivors, and the meaning of justice. Existing research on victim-survivors and global justice also gravitates toward a legal-justice-based approach to discussing victim-survivors' rights. As Rianne Letschert and Jan van Dijk note, victims' movements have been particularly effective in putting "victims in the center" and have influenced the "improvements in procedural rights of crime victims," which are "embedded in the legal traditions and structures of domestic criminal justice systems."[57] The focus here is on the legal aspect of justice, its connections to criminal law, and the redress of the victim-survivors.

But were these the types of justice that Sarita was referring to? This is an important question to ponder and one that is more aligned with emerging perspectives that point out the differences between the claims of transitional justice policies and the view of victim-survivors. Particularly, these scholars shift the discussion on the "benefits of justice" away from the trials and toward related policies that ground justice "in the everyday lives of those affected by violence."[58] The latter perspective helps one reconsider and redefine transitional justice terms, such as "reconciliation" and "healing," by shifting the focus to victim-survivors' perspectives or victim-centered views. In essence, these conversations foreground "victims' interests—particularly the interests of those individuals most harmed by the conflict rather than bystanders or the rest of the world community—in determining the forms of justice most appropriate after mass atrocity."[59] Consequently, justice may take the form of mental health support, increased access to information, and even infrastructure building for the communities where victims reside.[60] In short, a victim-centric justice is adaptable to the needs of victims.

The growing pursuit of responses to human rights violations shifts from justice bound for retributive proceedings to justice that fulfills victim-survivors' interests.[61] Here, the victim-survivor becomes the active agent who can choose the appropriate transitional justice policy and define their own interests and preferences.[62] In this role, victim-survivors may at times reject the offer of reparations by the state. For instance, in the case of the Madres de la Plaza de Mayo in Argentina, families of victim-survivors refused to accept state reparations, as they believed accepting them would signal the end of their search for the truth about the perpetrators who killed their sons and daughters.[63] In Sarita's case, the state had yet to even recognize its crimes, let alone seek truth, legal justice, or reparations related to her experience. As a result, her demands for justice were shaped by what she believed would give her some form of peace.

In my discussion with Sarita in Spanish over the phone, when asked to elaborate on what she meant by the word *justicia* (justice), Sarita spoke in short statements. She said: "[Quiero] que me expliquen por qué me lo han hecho . . . los profesionales que me lo han hecho . . . por qué me hicieron el mal, así." (I want them to tell me why they did it . . . the professionals who have done it . . . why they did this wrongful thing, like that.") Then she explained that she wanted a *perdón* (pardon, an apology) and *justicia* from the "gobierno [que] niegan todo lo que han hecho" (government that rejects all that they have done), about "lo que me han hecho, pues . . . tanto daño que me han hecho" (all that they have done to me . . . so much harm that they had done to me), that led her to be *siempre marginada* (always marginalized). At one point, she remarked, "Justicia, no sé cuando se da justicia" (Justice, I don't know when there will be justice).

Hence, from the perspective of transitional justice initiatives, Sarita's requests for justice could be viewed as encompassing restorative (i.e., truth commission/truth telling) and reparative (i.e., reparations) initiatives. Additionally, Sarita's justice had a retributive (i.e., prosecutions and reparations policies) component, because Sarita is one of the victims included in the lawsuit that DEMUS had filed against the state in 2018. What is unique about Sarita's demands for justice is that they were not a single form of justice tied to, for instance, a legal response.[64] Instead, they were layers of justice that encompassed many dimensions. At a general level, Sarita's demands were not unrealistic expectations or "undeliverable" expectations for reparations, which is a criticism that is raised by scholars regarding the "failure to manage victim expectations" vis-à-vis transitional justice policies.[65] However, that was not the case here. Rather, Sarita wanted the state to recognize and apologize for the atrocities that it had committed against her and many others.

Her expectation was more aligned with symbolic reparations, which include the state's issuance of official apologies for human rights atrocities; creation of museums, parks, and sites of memory; enactment of days of commemoration; history rectification initiatives (i.e., changes in history textbook); and even changes to the names of public spaces.[66] The Peruvian state had previously issued state apologies for crimes committed during the internal armed conflict (1980–2000), established a place of memory (i.e., Lugar de la Memoria, Tolerancia y la Inclusión Social), and held commemorations for victim-survivors from the armed conflict period. However, no formal state apologies were issued for victim-survivors of coercive sterilization. Furthermore, victims were not provided recognition in any sites of memory, including those that are managed by nongovernmental organizations that represented victims from the internal armed conflict (e.g., El Ojo que Llora [The Eye That Cries] in Lima, Peru). Scholars have previously raised this point about the absence and rejection of coercive sterilization of victim-survivors and their victimhood in Peruvian society.[67]

Along with the apologies, Sarita mentioned the wording *reparar* when referring to reparations for the harm that the government had caused and the suffering she had to endure. There was indeed a precedent for this: the Peruvian state had developed a registry for victim-survivors; instituted a Plan Integral de Reparaciones (PIR; Comprehensive Reparations Plan); and disbursed financial, medical, and symbolic reparations for victim-survivors and their family members affected by the internal armed conflict period. In fact, the law that established the PIR had been modified in February 2021 to include victim-survivors of sexual violence in "diverse forms," giving victim-survivors of coercive sterilization access to the reparations program.[68] Up until this point, victim-survivors of coercive sterilizations were treated differently than victim-survivors of the internal armed conflict, as evidenced by a separate victim-survivor's registry (i.e., REVIESFO). Coercive sterilizations took place from 1996 to 2000, coinciding with the latter part of the internal armed conflict, which began in 1980 and ended in 2000. However, despite the changes to the PIR, the Ministry of Justice and Human Rights denied the claims for reparations from victim-survivors of coercive sterilizations a few months later.[69] They explained that only victim-survivors of the internal armed conflict would be eligible for integral reparations.

Sarita was aware of these bureaucratic obstacles. The reasoning behind her demands, however, went beyond what one may expect is attached to monetary reparations. She wanted financial reparations for the *mal* (harm) inflicted upon her. The *mal* had two components, one of physical harm and the other of an emotional correlative harm. The emotional harm referred to not only the loss of strength and feeling of *fracaso* that she often mentioned, but also the marginalization that Sarita endured within her community as a result of being coercively sterilized. The marginalization was a consequence of the violence, embodying an emotional, psychological, and relational change within her Indigenous community. In essence, Sarita was demanding reparations for being torn away from her own community. At the same time, she was seeking reparations for her community, which had to endure the hardship of her separation from the collective.

Although she did not use the term *chanintsay* directly, Sarita's approach to justice was more aligned with this conception. *Chanintsay* is a term in Kichwa (Quechua), the mother tongue of Sarita and the majority of the victim-survivors of coercive sterilizations, which means "dar un debido valor a las cosas" (to give the rightful value to things).[70] Sarita was giving value to the things she had lost as a result of being coercively sterilized at the age of seventeen. When she specified that she wanted reparations for the violence she had suffered, she was referring to feeling ostracized by her community. This suffering was more emotional than physical, but nonetheless she still suffers physically from medical malpractice after being discharged immediately after surgery.

Additionally, Sarita sought reparations for her community as well, which was also impacted by her condition. As Indigenous scholars note, in rural Indigenous communities, a person is not only an individual but an integral part of the community. This notion of community or the *ayllu* identifies a collective. It is a family established by geography, bloodline, or shared objectives. Thinking about the *ayllu* in connection to the land, the conception of "land was a sacred matter, and belonged to everyone."[71] Such ideas of the collective are commonly shared among Indigenous peoples throughout Latin America, such as Indigenous communities in Guatemala, "where communal work was the centerpiece for production and protection of the community's common interests."[72] As explained by the Indigenous activist Irma Alicia Velasquez Nimatuj, "land, natural resources" are shared collective sources and thus hold a unique significance among Indigenous communities. These elements represent the coexistence of the human being with Pachamama (Mother Nature or Mother Earth), which channels through the land, water, animals, plants, and all those who make up the habitat and ecosystem.[73] Pachamama sustains all forms of life on Earth and therefore is considered sacred.

The Indigenous woman is interconnected with the Pachamama as the producer, sustainer, and caretaker of life. Quechua scholar Francisco Carranza explains this as a connection of reciprocity, or *rantin*. Pachamama brings resources for Indigenous communities to sustain their lives. This creates the environment for Indigenous women to create life, and the new lives, in turn, are brought forth (i.e., Indigenous children and generations of Indigenous peoples) to work, take care of, and respect Pachamama.[74] The people share the *rantin*, or the process of receiving and giving, which at times is also referred to as *ayni*, with the Pachamama.[75] In this circular relationship of reciprocity, the Indigenous woman and her body, namely her womb, are both considered sacred and connected with Pachamama in the production and reproduction of her role as the bringer of new life.

This intimate connection between Pachamama and the Indigenous woman complicates our understanding of the crime that was committed against Sarita. Hers was a case that went beyond discussions of international legal norms as a violation of women's rights, children's rights, Indigenous peoples' rights, and other human rights (i.e., the rights to be protected against torture and discrimination). From the Indigenous perspective, the coercive violation of Sarita represented a violent uprooting of Pachamama. When the link between a woman's body and womb are cut off from Pachamama through forced sterilization, that abruptly disrupts the intimate connection between the Indigenous woman and Mother Earth/Mother Nature—a connection that involves fertility, life, and *rantin*. It is the ending of the sacred production of life, the final termination of the Indigenous woman, and the killing of the Indigenous community as a whole. As a result, the impact of this violence was graver than that of a common crime.

In Andean Indigenous cultures, the balance of things is considered important. Disequilibrium, as Indigenous activist and leader Hilaria Supa notes, "enferman a nuestra Sociedad" ("makes our society ill").[76] From this perspective, the violence that was inflicted upon Sarita disrupted the balance within the community, because it created an imbalance in her health, family relations, and community membership. Furthermore, the Indigenous woman is not only a single individual but also a part of the collective community, meaning anything that impacts her condition and well-being has a ripple effect on interpersonal relations within the community. Hence, Sarita's suffering took a toll on both her physical and emotional health and her relationship with the broader community. As noted by Josef Estermann, a specialist in Andean philosophy, "health and illness" in the Andean context (or within Indigenous communities) have to be understood within the broader spectrum of "collective body."[77] That is, they need to be understood in relational terms. Illness has both an exterior aspect or the physical matter, as well as the relational aspect, which is associated with life and community. For this reason, when a woman in a rural Andean Indigenous community loses her health, the community suffers the loss physically and in interpersonal relations. This dual impact of the illness makes the curing process multidimensional. Chaparro-Buitrago refers to this as a situation of "debilitated lifeworlds." Such a "gestural displacement . . . does not take infertility as the singular point of departure for understanding the multiple harms resulting from sterilization abuse." It embeds a multidimensional set of harms, which debilitate the victim-survivor's world through the loss of "fertility, loss of strength, and social and emotional turmoil."[78] Consequently, when thinking about Sarita, her physical suffering cannot be cured separately from her emotional suffering. The healing or curing of an illness involves individual, social, ritual, and communal aspects, which cannot be readily fixed with a single pill.[79]

This emotional and psychological harm was the most common suffering among victim-survivors of coercive sterilizations, which Sarita also described. The condition is referred to in Quechua as *mancharisqa* and is associated with the root word *manchay*, which denotes shock or fear, as well as the state of being frightened or terrified to the point of being shaken.[80] As anthropologist Lucía Stavig notes, "*mancharisqa* is capacious enough of an idea to hold PTSD. But PTSD is not capacious enough to hold *mancharisqa* as what Quechua people see it as the soul loss."[81] The methods that address posttraumatic stress disorder (PTSD), which often involve a series of consultative therapy sessions (i.e., trauma-focused therapies), cannot cure or solve the entirety of what constitutes soul loss or *mancharisqa*. In the Andean cosmovision, the survivor of coercive sterilization is affected in terms of their "mundo interno de la persona" (inner world of the person), which is not the inner world of an individual person but the inner world of the collective identity. As a result, curation practices involving people affected by coercive sterilization have been based on rituals that aim to "restore the personal and social equilibrium."[82] One of these sites, Casa de Sanación (House of Healing), is run by Indigenous activist Hilaria Supa. Stavig explains that Supa's Casa de Sanación is a place that heals the individual victim-survivor but also "todo el cuerpo compartido del ayllu" (all the body that is shared with the *ayllu*).[83] That is to say, the restoration of the soul by default heals and cures the individual and the collective community. Of course, this does not diminish the importance of postoperative health visits and care, which are also effective in addressing the woman's physical suffering. In sum, in transitional justice terms, the curation practices that involve an Andean Indigenous approach represent a more holistic form of reparations. Specifically, they address the individual and the community simultaneously through medical, symbolic, and financial means. This is the essence of Sarita's conception of justice.

Thinking further about the Andean Indigenous culture's conception of equilibrium, reciprocity, holistic healing, and the connection between the Indigenous woman and Pachamama or Mother Earth/Mother Nature, it is no wonder the coercive sterilization of thousands of Indigenous women had a profound impact on Indigenous communities.

Otherwise referred to as "Indigenous planning," the PSRPF destroyed Indigenous women, Indigenous communities' way of life, and future generations of Indigenous peoples.[84] Sarita's justice, namely her demand for integral reparations that include both individual and communal matters, reflects this Indigenous outlook.

BEYOND A VICTIM-SURVIVOR-CENTRIC JUSTICE

Sarita's vision of justice is different than a single legal form of justice. Her justice involves a relational process and practice between the victim-survivor, community, and nature, in the form of symbolic, medical, and material reparations. Sarita's justice is more focused on the reparative aspects, where the victim is the main actor of concern. In that, her vision of justice is victim-survivor-centric. However, it is not the victim-survivor alone as a single individual or the survivor that is important, nor their demands and expectations of deliverables related to justice. Rather, from Sarita's perspective, which embodies Andean conceptions about the world where the maintenance of balance matters and everything is defined by relational terms, the victim-survivor represents the individual and the *ayllu*, or the collective community. Therefore, when I am describing Sarita's justice as victim-survivor-centric, it is the collective victimhood of the individual and the community that I am referring to, where the individual victim-survivor's mental and physical health and the related *ayllu*'s healing are prioritized. To clarify, this form of justice is not equivalent to "collective reparations" categorized under Article 7 of Peru's PIR, which aim at "strengthening the community" through "assistance for regularizing community property ... peace education and promotion of a culture of peace ... [and] rebuilding and improvement of the infrastructure of basic services," among other things.[85] Sarita's list of reparations aligns more with organic reparative measures of healing that bring justice as a result of helping the victim-survivor with their trauma and thus reestablish their relationship with the community and the community's relationship with the victim-survivor. In doing so, these measures restore an equilibrium in the *ayllu*.

Sarita's justice does not, however, position itself in contrast to or contrary to legal visions of justice based on criminal accountability. Indeed, the engagement of the legal process is not something that is discarded or put aside completely. It is not a "neither this nor that" type of approach, in which one has to choose between retributive (involving punitive measures) or reparative justice. Rather, Sarita's conception of justice—which reflects Indigenous values, cultures, and understandings about the individual, collective, and the world—focuses on a justice process that is reparative first, prior to considering the criminal justice steps. The reparative process is one that assists in curing and healing the victim-survivor, their family, and the community in various therapeutic ways that may take a long time. The positioning of criminal accountability is therefore somewhat secondary but may be revisited after the *ayllu* and the victim-survivor have been cared for. In conceptualizing the meaning of justice for those affected by coercive sterilization and in ordering these priorities, we need to take into account the victim-survivors' perspectives.

THE FORGOTTEN INDIGENOUS CHILDREN

Children are considered a vulnerable population. According to the Committee on Economic, Social and Cultural Rights (CESCR)'s General Comment No. 14, which was issued in 2000, children are categorized as part of the "vulnerable or marginalized groups of society." In the General Comment, CESCR urges states to uphold their obligations to "protect" these groups, specifying the duty of the state to ensure there is adequate and equitable access to health care; women are not "coerced to undergo traditional practices, e.g., female genital mutilation"; women, children, and adolescents are protected from "gender-based expressions of violence"; and the state guarantees "people's access to health-related information and services," such as "reproductive, maternal (pre-natal as well as post-natal) and child health care."[86] The CESCR consists of a group of eighteen independent experts who monitor the implementation of the ICESCR by its state parties. As previously noted, Peru ratified the ICESCR in 1978 and therefore was subject to the CESCR's oversight while PSRPF was in place. Consequently, through its mass coercive sterilization campaign, the Peruvian government was violating the CESCR's General Comments; however, no one at the time acknowledged that the coercive sterilizations were being performed on individuals who were underage.

Children who are of Indigenous descent in Peru are part of an ethnic group that is even more marginalized than those of European or *mestizo* heritage for their lack of socioeconomic power. Among Indigenous children, the degree of vulnerability increases for female Indigenous children, whose identity represents the intersection of a discriminated against gender, ethnically distinct group, and lower socioeconomic class. Previous studies have examined how forced sterilizations represent the intersections of women and Indigenous peoples' rights violations. They argue that in order to fully understand the crime of coercive sterilization against Indigenous women in Peru, one ought to consider (1) the postcolonial context of Peruvian society that has historically denied Indigenous peoples' opportunities for socioeconomic achievements, and (2) how this restrictive class condition has been linked to higher levels of poverty in areas with large Indigenous populations. In other words, the legacy of colonial power, which has included the control of gender and sexuality, has undergone only minor "superficial changes in the past 500 years" and has not been dismantled.[87] Beyond class, ethnic identity, and socioeconomic class discussions, Sarita's story introduced another category of intersection: the children, whose experiences were also embedded in the forced sterilization of Indigenous women. Hence, Sarita's victimhood represented an identity that was considerably more vulnerable than that of the Indigenous women in rural or urban areas of poverty. These intersecting layers of Indigenous representation, class-related identity, and age-based category have collectively contributed to making her violation, along with the violations that were likely committed against countless other children, even more invisible and silenced in society.

With the courage to share her story, Sarita has taken the first step toward recognition of and justice for the crimes committed against children. As she says, "Hay otras … había otras en mi comunidad" (There are others … there were other [girls] in my community") who were also sterilized at a young age and have yet to come forward to share their experiences. Sarita's story may be the right catalyst for other victim-survivors to demand justice for the human rights violations committed against them when they were underage.

CHAPTER FOUR

The Other Victims

Victoria Vigo's Story

"Ya habrías escuchado mi historia" (You must have already heard my story), Victoria said at the beginning of our conversation.[1] She further explained to me, "Cuando empezó lo que me sucedió a mi, eso fue el año 1996" (When those things that happened to me began, it was in 1996). The year 1996 marked the start of the PSRPF. Although it had not been clear to Victoria at the moment, her experience became one of the first officially recorded cases of coercive sterilization linked with the PSRPF.

Victoria is from Piura, a large city in the northwestern part of Peru with over four hundred thousand residents. Her father had been a police officer, and her mother had been a teacher. Within the Peruvian social context, this meant that she grew up in comfort, which is not to say she had similar experiences to the Lima-elite families who traveled to Miami regularly and had their own social worlds in their private country clubs. But as Victoria described, she was taken care of by her family, was educated, and grew up with no worries about daily necessities or where she was going to live. After her marriage, she also lived well. Her husband was an engineer who worked at PetroPeru, a state-owned company "dedicated to the transportation, refining, distribution, and sale of fuel and other products derived from oil."[2] As a side job, he owned a construction company. Victoria's family background, upbringing, and economic condition during her marriage were clear indicators that positioned her as part of Peru's middle class.

In 1996, when she was coercively sterilized, Victoria even had health insurance from the government. In Peru, there are two types of health insurance available to the population: private plans (at times associated with a particular hospital) and public insurance from the government (either EsSalud or Seguro Integral de Salud). Victoria had public health insurance through EsSalud. According to government census documents from 2007, her status as an insured individual made her part of the privileged 57.5 percent of the total Peruvian population who reported having some form of health insurance.[3] Comparing Victoria's insured status to Indigenous populations, only 53.5 percent of Indigenous peoples had some form of medical insurance in Peru in 2007.[4] Over the past decade, the status of health insurance acquisition has improved greatly in Peru, with 69.2 percent of the population self-reporting as having public health insurance. Among this population, 69.6 percent were people who self-identified as Quechua speaking, 47.9 percent were Aymara speaking, and 78.6 percent were from other Indigenous language-speaking backgrounds.[5] Aggregating these descriptive statistics from 2007 and 2017 and reexamining Victoria's case, it is evident that she was from a privileged group of the Peruvian population who had health insurance in 1996.

Moreover, Victoria resided in the city of Piura, where health facilities were and are easily accessible.[6] This is in contrast to Indigenous communities, whose residence complicates and challenges their access to medical care, as reported by the Human Rights Ombudsman's Office in 2022.[7] In Victoria's case, in 1996 she even had a private clinic that attended to her obstetrics and gynecology (OBGYN) needs. Additionally, Victoria speaks Spanish as her mother tongue, is literate, is not from the Andes or Amazonian regions of Peru, and has no direct connections with Indigenous communities.[8] And yet, despite the privileges she has as a Spanish-speaking Piura resident (Piurana), with a police officer and teacher for parents and health insurance that gave her access to private clinics, Victoria became one of the early victims of forced sterilization.

The case of a woman of non-Indigenous descent who resided in an urban area, who spoke Spanish as her mother tongue, and whose father was in the security forces is important to examine, as she represents a different victim-survivor identity that has largely been overshadowed by the more dominant conversations about Indigenous women's victimhood under the family planning program.[9] However, her underrepresented identity as a victim-survivor among the other women affected by coercive sterilization is what gave Victoria a unique and privileged footing. Her awareness of human rights, where to go for legal help and processes, and the steps she had to take to file a formal complaint were crucial in setting her apart from other victim-survivors of coercive sterilization. This is partly why she was invited to Washington, D.C., to testify about her case during the hearing before the Subcommittee on International Operations and Human Rights of the Committee on International Relations in the House of Representatives on February 25, 1998.[10] Her persistence in seeking a legal remedy for her case also resulted in the only successful legal court case on coercive sterilization within the Peruvian domestic legal system. In 2001 the Superior Court of Justice of Piura convicted the doctor from the EsSalud Hospital in Piura for the grave injuries inflicted upon Victoria. The doctor was sentenced to four years in prison and ordered to pay 10,000 Nuevo Soles (equivalent in 2025 to US$2,968) as part of the "civil reparations" for the victim-survivor.[11]

Continuing to apply Indigenous methods of storytelling, this chapter recounts the story of Victoria Vigo. Many parts of Victoria's story are substantiated and corroborated by the litigation Victoria pursued domestically and through US congressional records (from the testimony she gave at the US House of Representatives). The chapter explores the trajectory of Victoria's story, namely how her unique victim-survivor identity helped her gain visibility, empowered her activism, and made her a target of slander and death threats. Following these discussions, this chapter raises questions about why the death of Victoria's prematurely born child was overlooked in all the efforts to establish criminal accountability regarding her case and explores a possible new legal angle in the discourse about a child's death. In doing so, it engages in heavy discussions about international human rights treaties and norms, including other ways of approaching the acts that Victoria's *hijito* (baby boy) and Victoria suffered. Finally, this chapter explores the concept of justice from Victoria's perspective, noting the similarities with Sarita, the Indigenous woman who was victimized as a minor.

VICTORIA'S STORY

"Yo he estado en 36 semanas de gestación y yo tenía mi clínica particular, mi médico particular" (I was 36 weeks pregnant, and I had my private clinic, my private doctor), noted Victoria when recalling her pregnancy.[12] The private nature of her clinic is important to consider, as not every person in Peru has had access to private doctors or clinics, let alone access to health insurance. Even with EsSalud or SIS, the public health insurance plans from the government, most patients are not able to get all the services they need on time.[13] Those who have the financial means, such as Victoria, therefore seek medical care in private clinics. On the day she was coercively sterilized, Victoria called her doctor at the private clinic and said she was feeling under the weather. According to Victoria, her doctor had wanted to bring her in for a check-up at the clinic, but she said that was not necessary; rather, she just needed a short hospital rest. The rest she had envisioned, however, was different from what took place:

> Yo le dije que solamente en el hospital, hacer un descanso, ¿no? entonces él me hace la transferencia al hospital. Yo estaba asegurada, EsSalud. Pero, cuando hacen transferencia uno entra por emergencia no por clínica. Entra por emergencia, pero ellos (del hospital) lo tomaron como emergencia y en

una hora yo ya estaba cesareada, en una hora, ni siquiera hubo una evalua-
ción, ni más. (I told him [my doctor] that just in the hospital, to have a rest,
no? Then, he files the transfer for me to the hospital. I was insured, Es-
Salud. But, when they do transfer, one enters through the emergency room
(ER) not via the clinic. I entered through the ER, but they [from the hospi-
tal] took the case as an emergency and within one hour I was already given
a cesarean, in one hour, there was not even an evaluation, not even.)[14]

Victoria mentioned that she had experienced difficulty in trying to
have a big family. She had given birth to her first child, her daughter,
when she was too young. Then she got married and was able to give
birth to her second child. She was happy in her marriage and wanted
to have more children. But by this time she had complications. Victoria
explained:

Ovulaba muy rápido. En 15 días estaba menstruando. Entonces eso me
hacía . . . no, no, no tuve un embarazo . . . y además había tenido pérdidas.
Entonces entra una frustración muy tremenda y yo pido ayuda de un
médico . . . un psiquiatra (un amigo) quien había tratado mi depresión. ([I]
ovulated too quickly. In fifteen days, I was menstruating. So that made me . . .
no, no, no I could not become pregnant . . . and besides, I had miscarriages. At
that moment, I felt tremendous frustration and I asked for help from a doctor,
a psychiatrist (a friend) who had treated me for depression.)[15]

After so many frustrating moments and miscarriages as well as dealing
with depression related to her fertility issues, she had finally become
pregnant with her third child. This pregnancy meant something special to her.

As Victoria continued to tell her story, something changed. There
were noticeable changes in her speech. She interjected a lot of "eh" (um)
moments into her sentences; there were pauses here and there, and she
repeated some of the same phrases over and over again. Then, in those
moments of pause, she would look up or away as though she was trying
to find the right words to explain the story. These hesitations manifested and were most apparent when she started describing the moment
when she had woken up after the forced cesarean and learned about the

death of her prematurely born child. Within an hour of having entered the hospital, Victoria was given a cesarean. She explained:

> "Ni siquiera hubo una evaluación, ni más. No viene ni un pediatra al costado, porque mi hijo... nace y llora, pero al ratito le entra un paro respiratorio y todo el mundo corría. No venía ni el pediatra." (There was not even an evaluation, not even. Not even a single pediatrician came by my side, well my son... is born and cries but moments later has a respiratory stop/blockage and everyone was running around. Not even the pediatrician came.)

She went on to say how, in that moment, she knew that "mi hijo estaba grave, bueno, no te dicen, pero yo sentía en mi corazón" (my son was in critical condition, well, they don't tell you, but I felt it in my heart), referring to the mother's instinct she felt about the condition of her newly born child. When she had woken up from the cesarean, her breasts were swollen, and she wanted to "dar a lactar a mi hijo" (to give milk to my son). This is when Victoria's pauses became even more pronounced, as she repeated the phrases "dar a lactar" (give milk to) and "darle a mamar" (give him to feed) in reference to her son. I could hear Victoria holding in her tears as she discussed how the doctor told her about the death of her son. Victoria told me about how hard it was, how she wanted to go home, and how, at times, she tries to block out these memories. Then, Victoria shed the tears she had been holding back when she recalled telling the doctor, "Yo me quiero ir a casa porque todos estaban con sus bebes y yo no" (I want to go home because everyone had their babies [there] except me).[16]

From that moment, Victoria's storytelling took an interesting turn. Her tears stopped, the pauses became less pronounced in her speech, and her tone became more assertive. This was the part of her story related to coercive sterilization. Victoria recalled that the doctor attending to her case had told her to stay at the hospital and stated that "sabes que, eres joven todavia, tienes 30 años y puedes volver a tener otros hijitos" (you know what, you are still young, you are thirty years old, and you can have other children [in the future]). Immediately after his comments, the intern who was accompanying the doctor inter-jected, "No, no. A la señora ya la esterilizaron." (No, no. That lady has already been sterilized.)[17] Somehow, the doctor who had been talking to Victoria had not known that she had been sterilized, but the intern had different knowledge and her medical record. When she overheard these conversations, Victoria noted that she stayed quiet. As soon as the doc-tor and the intern had left the room, however, Victoria asked the other medical personnel if she could see her medical history. Victoria knew that, if something had happened, it would be recorded there. But the record was missing. At the time she did not know this, but the absence of this medical record meant that she had become an invisible victim on whose body a grave human rights violation had been committed and yet had no document to prove it had happened.

Interestingly, though, as she noted, the medical personnel at that EsSalud hospital in Piura and what they had said in reference to her medical history were enough to substantiate the pain she had felt in her body and the suspicion that something had been done to her. This was after she had been discharged and she went back to the same hos-pital, frustrated about her situation—which was still somewhat incom-prehensible to her—and wondering if she could have children in the future. The staff at the hospital recognized her and told her "Le vamos a mandar para re-canalizarla." (We will send you to have the pipes fixed.), while the doctor repeatedly stated "Hay que tranquilizarla para que ya no diga (más)" (We have to calm her down so that she does not go around talking (more) about this).[18] Victoria had friends who were doctors. She consulted them about the things that had been said to her when she had gone back to the hospital, because she felt that the hos-pital staff were treating her like a *sonsita* (dumb one). "Victoria, es irre-versible" (Victoria, it is irreversible), noted her friends when they heard her story. And about three months from the moment she had undergone a forced cesarean, Victoria was able to confirm the status of her condi-tion at the private OBGYN clinic with her doctor. She had been ster-ilized. At this point, it became clear to her the "engaño que me hizo el hospital" (deceit that the hospital had done).[19] This was when Victoria decided that she could no longer remain silent.

After consulting her friends in the medical field, she filed an official complaint against the doctor with the Public Prosecutor's Office (i.e., the Ministerio Público Fiscalía de la Nación). Her case was immediately dropped. Then Victoria sought help from a lawyer and filed the complaint once again. Again the case was dropped. At the time, she did not know the "volumen de lo que estaba sucediendo" (magnitude of what was happening [with the family planning program]). All she knew was that she needed to hold someone accountable for what had happened, perhaps a doctor. Victoria said, "Y esto me comenzó a darme más fuerza motivarme es decir, dándome cuenta que cual difícil era con o sin abogado." (This started giving me more strength and motivation, that is to say, when I realized how difficult it was with or without a lawyer [to file a complaint].)[20] Victoria ended her statement to the Subcommittee on International Operations and Human Rights in a similar way, noting that it was "difficult for [her] to make a formal complaint" and remarked that "it is much more difficult for the women in the countryside who don't know their rights, who don't know how to do it, to lodge their complaints."[21] She further explained, "Eso me despertó la ansia de seguir luchando es decir ya pasó ser parte de mi vida cotidiana." (This awoke in me the desire to continue fighting, that is to say that it became a part of my daily life.) This is how she began her battle for justice.

FROM VICTIM-SURVIVOR TO ACTIVIST

"Todo pasó tan rápido en '98." (It happened all so quickly in '98.) Victoria recalled that two students came knocking on her door:

> "Me dijeron, Señora Vigo mire somos estudiantes . . . yo he visto su caso que está archivado, yo he trabajado en la fiscalía. Pero ella es estudiante de periodismo. Y su caso a mí me llamó la atención." (They said, Mrs. Vigo, we are students. . . . it was dismissed, I have worked at

the Public Prosecutor's Office. But she is a student of journalism. Your case has grabbed my attention.)[22]

Victoria stated that at first she was skeptical of the intentions of these students and of the things they mentioned to her. She believed that her case was distinct and not one of many that they were investigating. Then they came back a few days later with Professor Jorge Rodríguez (currently a professor in Spain), who gave her the bigger picture of the massive sterilization campaign that was happening in Peru. They highlighted that Victoria's case was the only one that had reached the Public Prosecutor's Office. This meant that there had been no other cases than hers—even though it was dismissed—that had been filed related to coercive sterilization. From that point forward, the professor and the students wrote about her experience in an article titled "Cuando los pobres molestan" (When the poor disturb), which appeared in the Piura newspaper and helped bring her case to the attention of Diakonia, a Swedish human rights organization with offices throughout Latin America. Her story began to gain momentum in the domestic and international media, with *Panorama, Telemundo,* and *Univision* reporting on her case. As a result, she became one of the key people who accompanied the US delegation that had come to Peru to investigate the irregularities being reported about the PSRPF, which was receiving funding from USAID. She remembers showing the US delegates giant walls around Piura painted with the words *planificación familiar* (family planning) and, below them, "USAID." The US delegates looked surprised and perhaps even alarmed, given the emerging news about coercive sterilization practices happening on the ground related to the family planning program funded by USAID. During her trips with the US delegation, she heard testimony from other women, some of whom noted how they were tricked into undergoing tubal ligation. Victoria explained that

en esos entonces USAID mandaba unas latas de aceite y mandaban polenta y soya y trigo y eso los cambiaban. Sí ellas recibían . . . es decir . . . haciendo filitas recibían (in those times, USAID sent cans of oil and sent polenta and soy and wheat and that was used for exchange. If they [the women] received it [tubal ligation] . . . then that is to say . . . forming lines they would receive it [cans of food]).[23]

On September 30, 1993, the Peruvian government and USAID entered into a project grant agreement for Project 2000, no. 527-0366.[24] It was a grant to fund a project on maternal, perinatal, and infant health in twelve regions and subregions in Peru for a period of seven years from 1993 to 2000. Sterilization was never directly mentioned as a goal of the USAID-funded Project 2000, which ended up sponsoring the PSRPF. In fact, education on reproductive matters (and not sterilization) was seen as a key component of the strengthening of maternal- and infant-related health services.[25] These ideas coincided with the ReproSalud project—"an innovative health and rights initiative that focuses on promoting better reproductive health through an approach based on individual and community empowerment"—which was also funded by USAID and also implemented during this period in Peru.[26] Although PSRPF and ReproSalud used drastically different strategies to achieve their goals, they were both funded by USAID.

USAID's involvement—even though indirect through financial support—in the PSRPF was evident in the recollections of victim-survivors about how they identified the organization's food aid as part of the reason they underwent sterilization surgeries. While discussing the testimony of other women, Victoria suddenly paused. Then she let out a sigh and remarked that she was unaware that her experience, which she believed had been unique and an isolated case, was happening every-where in Peru. What she noticed and what set her case apart was that she was not tricked; no one came knocking on her door for her to receive tubal ligation, as had been the case according to many women's testimo-nies. In her case, they performed the surgery on her without consent, but no vile trick had been used. That is when she "vi a realidades que nunca concocía" (saw realities that I had never known), recognized the class divisions and racial discrimination that exist in Peru, and became aware of how the family planning program channeled these ideas by targeting specific types of women (i.e., Indigenous-language-speaking, illiterate, economically marginalized, and from rural backgrounds).

Victoria was not alone in her experience of not having known what was happening in Peru. One can question how this may have been the case when there were reports about sterilization campaigns published in newspaper articles in 1996. For instance, major newspapers *La República* and *El Comercio* published seven news stories in 1996 alone about intense sterilization campaigns, and other news outlets such as *La Industria*, *Gestión*, and *El Sol* also reported on sterilizations taking place.[27] However, the reporting had been mixed. Some had discussed what was happening on the ground, while others had focused on the insistence by health authorities that there was no "sterilization being obligated" to the public.[28] Similar patterns of news reporting took place in 1997, with over twenty-two news reports emerging and some news outlets using titles such as "Government Does Not Impose Sterilization of Women."[29] The same was true in 1998, when *El Sol* ran a story with the title "There Was No Sterilization Campaign," quoting the Ministry of Promotion of Women and Human Development (which was restructured and renamed in 2002 as the Ministry of Women and Vulnerable Populations), who denied the existence of sterilization practices by the Fujimori government.[30] These diverse news reports emerging from this period obfuscated the truth and what many nongovernmental organizations had been monitoring on the ground: a massive sterilization campaign that primarily targeted women of Indigenous descent and, at times, even women like Victoria.

After the US delegation's visit to Peru, Victoria was invited to travel to Washington, D.C., to give her testimony at the House of Representatives. Victoria said, "Yo estuve en Washington y testifiqué sobre mi caso" (I was also in Washington, and testified about my case). Victoria explained that this trip was a risky one for her: "Viajamos para dar mi testimonio, yo como sobreviviente-víctima de lo que estaba sucediendo en el Perú." (We traveled to give my testimony, me as a victim-survivor of what was happening in Peru.)[31] This was true. It was a risky, if not dangerous, time to oppose any activities of the government of Alberto Fujimori (1990–2000). During this internal armed conflict period (1980–2000), there was an active confrontation between the leftist guerrilla forces, represented by Sendero Luminoso (Shining Path) and the Movimiento Revolucionario Tupac Amaru (MRTA; Revolutionary Movement of Tupac Amaru), and the state's security forces, which included paramilitary groups and death squads (e.g., Grupo Colina). Anyone speaking against the government was considered part of the leftist guerrilla forces, and as such, they faced grave human rights violations. The TRC documents the human rights violations that occurred during this period of the internal armed conflict, which included numerous death threats against opposition leaders and human rights defenders.[32] Victoria was going to Washington, D.C., to expose the sterilization campaign that had been disguised as a family planning program (i.e., PSRPF) by the Fujimori government. Surely this trip was going to make her a visible target for Fujimori supporters. But, as Victoria recalled, someone had to speak up about what was happening to the women.

The hearing before the US House of Representatives, which took place only two years after the family planning program was put into effect, noted that the sterilizations were performed "pursuant to prescribed national and regional goals rather than to patient demand."[33] In other words, it was not due to patient demand that sterilizations were being performed. Instead, the decision on sterilizations was being carried out to fulfill a government goal regarding family planning. This was carefully documented by the subcommittee's investigation on Peru, which found evidence of "goals or quotas" that had been set by the Peruvian government for the "number of people to be sterilized nationwide, in particular regions, and even in particular hospitals."[34] The same investigative committee found that "abuses" were being committed against women to meet these goals.[35]

However, the same investigative committee concluded that USAID "funding had not supported the abuses committed by the Peruvian government."[36] This is important to point out, as there were US domestic interests involved in using accounts of the victimhood emerging from the family planning program to promulgate their own political agendas. Chávez and Coe note that those who opposed the promulgation of reproductive rights seized on the coercive sterilization cases to bring charges against the USAID office in Peru to restrict funding and access to "modern contraception and abortion and promote abstinence for prevention of unintended pregnancy, HIV and other sexually transmitted infections."[37] Nevertheless, while the investigative committee may not have found any direct evidence, it is difficult to overlook the number of "irregularities" or forced sterilizations that had taken place in Peru and the testimonies from victim-survivors who discussed receiving USAID food aid in exchange for being sterilized.[38] In fact, Victoria pointed out this same issue, noting that "USAID-Perú negó todo. Pero, sabían, porque tenían que dar el balance de lo que habían gastado." (USAID-Peru rejected [responsibility in] everything. But they knew [about the coercive sterilizations] because they had to give the balance sheet of what they had spent.)

Regardless of who had knowledge about the USAID funding, it is clear that, while the victimhood of people like Victoria was real and relevant in the discussion of human rights violations, they were also being used and manipulated to serve the political agenda of conservative lawmakers in both the United States and Peru who wanted to halt the expansion of sexual and reproductive rights. These were the complexities surrounding the situation Victoria faced. As Victoria noted, she was not against family planning. What she wanted was for women to have the choice to make their own decisions about their bodies, meaning they must want to undergo tubal ligation and not be forced into any situation against their will. This was the basis of her activism and why she was willing to risk her life and status to travel to Washington, D.C., to testify about her case.

"Todos pensaban que era fácil" (Everyone thought it had been easy), said Victoria, recalling the testimony she had given to the US House of

Figure 1. Victoria Vigo (center) during protest in 2016 demanding justice for victim-survivors of forced sterilizations, accompanied by Cynthia Silva (left), former director of DEMUS, and Sayda Lucas (right), sociologist for DEMUS. Photo credit: DEMUS.

Representatives and the lawsuit she had won against the doctor at the EsSalud Hospital in Piura. She further said, "Yo fui acosada . . . me terruquean" (I was harassed . . . I was called a terrorist). Due to the publicity she received and the lawsuit she had won against the doctor, she was at times shunned by others in the human rights movement that supported victim-survivors of coercive sterilizations. Victoria explained:

> Ellos dicen, yo ya he ganado un juicio y que soy una mujer ambiciosa . . . que quería más dinero . . . aunque yo había dado testimonio para que otros puedan tener fuerza. (They say that I have already won a lawsuit and that I am an ambitious person . . . that I want more money . . . even though I had given my testimony so that others can also have the strength [to fight].)[39]

Despite these difficult moments Victoria has had to endure, she explained that she plans to continue her activism and legal fight. She is determined to continue the fight for herself, her son, and other women who suffered similar experiences. This time, her legal case is against the state as part of the collective victim-survivors' lawsuit against Fujimori and his health ministers.[40]

EL HIJITO (THE BABY BOY) AND NEW LEGAL FRAMES

Sí, mi querida Ñusta. Yo este . . . cerré, abrí el caso viendo acá la muerte de mi hijo. Pero el juez, pues no lo vio. Absolutamente, nada. Porque allí, en mí, el médico que me estaba tratando . . . fue a darle la declaración . . . donde dice que a mí no se me hubiera hecho ninguna cesárea, no era el tiempo, no era necesario, y no había nada . . . podía dar un parto normal . . . sí eso es el caso que algunos han visto pero que nunca expusieron . . . verdaderamente. (My dear Ñusta. I closed and opened the case seeing here the death of my son. But the judge did not see it. Absolutely not. In fact there, for me, the doctor who had been treating me [referring to her private OBGYN] . . .went to declare [give a declaration] . . . where he stated that they should not have done a cesarean on me, it was not the time, it was not necessary, that there was nothing [to suggest that] . . . that I could have given a normal birth. . . . [Y]es, that is the case that some had seen but never presented . . . truly.)[41]

There had been a massive sterilization campaign in Peru, disguised under the premise of a family planning program. What set Victoria's case apart from others was that her forced sterilization process was connected to the death of her prematurely born child. And yet, as evidenced by Victoria's words, despite having brought up the case about the death of her prematurely born son during her litigation against Dr. Nicolás Angulo Silva, the judge had not taken the death into consideration. Interestingly, the presence of her son is noted in the legal opinion that was issued for Victoria's case by the Superior Court of Justice of Piura. The Court specified "un recién nacido vivo prematuro" (the recently born alive premature [baby]) in describing the facts of the case.[42] However, the death of the baby is not mentioned in the Court's written sentence given against the accused doctor. The sentence, instead, focuses on the grave injuries; mutilation of a principal organ of the body; the forced nature of the sterilization, discussing nonconsent or nonprovision of informed consent; and the cesarean that accompanied the tubal ligation. The Court also referenced the testimony from Victoria's private clinic doctor, Ricardo Lip Licham, who noted the unnecessary nature of the cesarean that was performed at the EsSalud hospital.[43] Except for the single mention of the premature baby who was born alive, the death of Victoria's *hijito* (baby son) is nowhere to be found in the Court documents.

So what do we make of the death of Victoria's *hijito*? Moving away from the international legal instruments and domestic legal processes that involve coercive sterilization victims as adults, it is important to bring the conversation back to children and children's rights. In this case, we are not discussing children as girls who were subject to coercive sterilizations, as in the case of Sarita in chapter 3. Instead, we are reflecting upon the application of a human rights–based legal approach to understanding the preventable mortality of children under five years of age: specifically, the rights of preterm infants or premature babies.

What are the rights of Victoria's premature baby, who was forced to be born preterm due to medical malpractice linked with a genocidal policy of family planning that embodied multiple violations of international human rights norms (i.e., violations of women's rights, children's rights, and Indigenous people's rights)? According to Priscilla Alderson and colleagues studies on premature babies and caregivers (i.e., neonatal staff and parents), premature babies do have rights.[44] Observing premature babies' interactions with neonatal staff and their expressions of emotions, Alderson and colleagues argue that, while neonatal staff and parents may be seen as "experts" in claiming to know what is "best for children," the neonatal examples (with babies physically reacting to or emotionally pushing back against certain forms of care) suggest that "babies too can have unique insight into their best interests."[45] As such, adults and caregivers need to consider if their decisions about care, involving the baby, "are to be adequately informed and humane."[46] In short, adults and caregivers in neonatal settings have to recognize, based on babies' physical and emotional responses, what may be best for babies' health and future conditions. From this vantage point, Alderson and colleagues also argue that babies do have agency as rights holders in being able to influence the type of care that is in their best needs and interests.[47] Such findings are supported by studies on newborn infants that discuss, for instance, how "newborn infants are social beings who quickly learn to judge the safeness of a situation from the examiner's facial expression and voice, as well as from the way they are handled."[48] Similarly, Heidelise Als's study on premature infants explains that preterm babies are "socially competent and active part-ner[s]" with their caregivers, confirming, again, the agency of babies in asserting their rights.[49]

On the notion of rights, Alderson and colleagues argue that prema-ture (preterm) babies have "participation rights," which include rights such as the right to "life and survival," "inherent human dignity," and "the child's right to express views freely in all matters affecting the child."[50] The authors explain that in some cases, babies are in the pre-carious position of choosing one set of rights over that of others. For instance, the protection of the right to life may come in conflict with the right not to be subjected to torture if there is, for instance, a need for a premature baby to endure "life-sustaining treatment," which at times surmounts to "torture."[51] In other instances, the "right to survival can also potentially conflict with the quality-of-life rights," when a decision may need to be made between survival or imposition of a life-time of suffering.[52]

In all the studies that have examined babies—including preterm babies—as rights holders, the underlying assumption has been the acknowledgment of babies from birth as persons with rights. This idea stems from international normative standards, particularly the CRC, which legally recognizes the human rights of children and has been regarded as "the most authoritative standard-setting instrument in its field."[53] Paragraph 9 of the preamble of the CRC indicates that "the child, by reason of his physical and mental immaturity, needs special safeguards and care, including appropriate legal protection, before as well as after birth."[54] While numerous interpretations have been made of the notion of "before as well as after birth," particularly among those who have attempted to expand the categorization of rights of the unborn baby, this chapter is not concerned with the applicability of the rights of the unborn and thus will not address this point further.[55] However, what is clear is that there is some textual ambiguity in the CRC on the moment or timing of the applicability of the norms enshrined in it. But these ambiguities do not call into question the legality of the rights of children that are born.

Article 1 of the CRC defines a child as "every human being below the age of eighteen years unless under the law applicable to the child, majority is attained earlier."[56] Thus, from birth babies are also considered children whose rights are protected under the CRC. Article 7 of the CRC further discusses the immediacy of child status for babies, noting that "the child shall be registered immediately after birth and shall have the right from birth to a name ... and, as far as possible, the right to know and be cared for by his or her parents."[57] From the moment a baby is born, they have a right to a name and the right to adequate care by their parents. Any form of intervention that would prevent the opportunity for the baby to be given care from their parents or involving their parents would therefore constitute a form of violation of the baby's rights.

As discussed in chapter 3, Peru was one of the first states to ratify the CRC, on September 4, 1990. Furthermore, under Article 55 of Peru's 1993 Constitution, international treaty norms become a part of domestic legal norms from the moment of ratification.[58] By 1996, when Victoria was rushed into an emergency cesarean and her premature baby was delivered alive, the norms of the CRC carried legal weight in Peru. Accordingly, even for a short moment while he was alive, Victoria's prematurely born baby boy was considered a child whose rights were protected under the CRC.

Victoria described how her baby "llora, pero al ratito le entra un paro respiratorio" (cries but moments later has a respiratory stop/blockage). In this moment, Victoria said, there was "no viene ni un pediatra al costado" (no pediatrician that came by my side).[59] As research suggests, in decision-making contexts involving premature babies, there is an imbalance of "knowledge, control, and expertise in favor of medical professionals, who at times may have a different assessment of an infant's 'best interests.'"[60] The imbalance of power is often expressed through parents relying on "medical team for facts, and the physician," who may or may not exclude information in an "effort to persuade the parents to choose his or her professional recommendation."[61] In Victoria's case, there was no pediatrician or neonatologist present in the room to provide the premature infant with any medical assistance to prevent major complications of prematurity, including mechanical ventilation to resolve the baby's respiratory blockage. The absence of a pediatrician after an unconsented-to cesarean had taken place, which delivered a premature baby, was a denial of Article 24 of the CRC, which specifies the right for a child to enjoy the "highest attainable standard of health and to facilities for the treatment of illness and rehabilitation of health."[62] At the time of Victoria's surgery, there was no pediatrician or neonatologist at the EsSalud Hopsital in Piura. Additionally, there was no equipment or treatment plan to address the complications of preterm infants. Hence, there was no medical team to advise the parents on the "best interests" of the infant, as there were no medical professionals who could determine the best course of action. As Victoria noted, after her son had stopped breathing, "todo el mundo corría" (everyone was running around) instead of trying to interact with the parent to determine the best course of action.

Along with the violation of Article 24 of the CRC, the incompetence of the EsSalud Hospital in not having a pediatrician or neonatologist on call to look after any infant- or child-related health matters was a form of violence against the child that endangered their being. Article 19 of the CRC notes, "States Parties shall take appropriate legislative, administrative, social, and education measures to protect the child from all form of physical or mental violence, injury or abuses, neglect or negligent treatment, maltreatment" while under the care of a "parent (s), legal guardian (s) or any other person who has the care of the child."[63] There was no follow-up to the neglect and negligent treatment that Victoria's preterm infant received at the hospital. For instance, the doctor was not put on leave, nor were the medical licenses of any of the medical personnel involved revoked. From these facts alone, it is clear that the state was in violation of Article 19 of the CRC. In short, there were no protective measures to address what had occurred to Victoria's child.

Perhaps more importantly, Victoria's *hijito* was denied the most fundamental human right—the right to life. Article 6 of the CRC states that "every child has the inherent right to life," and "State Parties shall ensure to the maximum extent possible the survival and development of the child."[64] This was a fundamental right of Victoria's child. Because there were no appropriate health-care personnel (i.e., neonatal medical staff) present, Victoria's son was not given a chance at survival or life when he was born prematurely, which is a condition that necessitates specialized care. He was not given a choice between an adequate life or reasonable life. Simply, he was not given a right to live a life. Article 6 of the ICCPR, a legally binding document ratified by Peru on April 28, 1978, reiterates a point present in the CRC. It states that "every human being has the inherent right to life.... [N]o one shall be arbitrarily deprived of his life."[65] In General Comment No. 36, the Human Rights Committee expresses that this right to life under Article 6 of the ICCPR includes the "entitlement of individuals to be free from acts and omissions that are intended or may be expected to cause their unnatural or premature death, as well as to enjoy a life with dignity."[66] Hence, subjecting an individual to acts intended to cause premature death, such as a forced cesarean to deliver a premature infant without the presence of a neonatologist, is a violation of a child's right to life. This norm about the right to life is also present in the Universal Declaration of Human Rights (UDHR), which, although it is not

legally binding, embodies many norms that are considered part of cus-
tomary international law. Article 3 of the UDHR explains that "everyone has the right to life, liberty and security of person."[67] In the case of
Victoria's son, his right to life—protected under Article 6 of the CRC,
Article 6 of the ICCPR, and Article 3 of the UDHR—was violated.
Furthermore, by being excluded from this right, the child's right to be
"cared for by his or her parents," as noted under Article 7 of the CRC,
was simultaneously denied.[68]

Upon further reflection on this moment of Victoria's story, it is also
evident that other forms of violence and violations were taking place
that may merit a closer look. Specifically, these include obstetric violence and violations of informed consent. Obstetric violence refers to
gender-based violence that women endure in birthing and maternity
care. As the World Health Organization states, "[M]any women across
the globe experience disrespectful, abusive or neglected treatment
during childbirth in facilities."[69] Victoria was mistreated in her childbirth experience. This mistreatment was perpetrated by physicians and
nurses who were present during her forced labor and delivery. According to a 2022 ruling by the Inter-American Court of Human Rights in
Brítez Arce et. al. v. Argentina, "[W]omen have the right to live a life free
of obstetric violence and States have the obligation to prevent it, punish
it and refrain from practicing it, as well as to ensure that their agents act
accordingly."[70] The case *Brítez Arce et al. v. Argentina* dealt with Cristina
Brítez Arce, whose pregnancy presented several risk factors that "were
not adequately addressed by the health system," including her more-
than-forty-week pregnancy, a dead fetus, and induced labor to remove
the fetus, which resulted in health complications and nontraumatic car-
diorespiratory arrest.[71] The Court ruled that "women have the right to
live a life free of obstetric violence" and explained that obstetric violence "exercised by health care providers against pregnant women . . . is
expressed mostly, but not exclusively, in a dehumanizing . . . abusive or
negligent treatment of pregnant women . . . in forced or coerced medical interventions . . . in the context of health care during pregnancy,

childbirth, and postpartum."[72] Taking these decisions together, the Court recognized obstetric violence "as a form of gender-based violence" that represented a violation of the Inter-American Convention on the Prevention, Punishment, and Eradication of Violence Against Women, commonly referred to as the Convention of Belém do Pará, a legally binding international treaty that criminalized all forms of violence against women, including sexual violence.[73] Specifically, obstetric violence violated Article 7 of the Convention of Belém do Pará, which noted the duties of states to eradicate and punish such forms of gender-based violence.[74]

The Peruvian government ratified the Convention of Belém do Pará on June 4, 1996. Hence, by the time Victoria had been forced into a cesarean to deliver her premature baby—which was a form of obstetric violence—the norms of this convention carried domestic legal weight. The Peruvian state was therefore in violation of the rights enshrined in the Convention of Belém do Pará. Relatedly, as obstetric violence constitutes a form of gender-based violence that primarily impacts women, it represents a form of discrimination and challenges the norms of the legally binding Convention on the Elimination of All Forms of Discrimination Against Women (CEDAW), ratified by Peru in 1982. The Committee on the Elimination of Discrimination Against Women, which is the body of independent experts that monitors states' implementation of CEDAW, issued General Recommendation No.19, which elaborates and defines gender-based violence against women as "violence which is directed against a woman because she is a woman."[75] As such, violence against women in reproductive health services and childbirth—obstetric violence—would be a discriminatory act that results in harm or suffering to women. These ideas are also evident in the 1993 Declaration on the Elimination of Violence Against Women— the first international instrument to explicitly address violence against women. Article 1 of the declaration explains that "violence against women" includes "any act of gender-based violence that results in, or is likely to result in, physical, sexual or psychological harm or suffering to women."[76] The obstetric violence committed against Victoria during childbirth at the EsSalud Hospital—and the resulting suffering she has endured—reflects violations of various rights protected under international human rights norms.

From a more traditional standpoint, one can also view coercive sterilization as a case representing the violation of informed consent. This view is in addition to the normative arguments that have been heavily discussed in chapter 2 about the family planning policy as a form of genocide and how this case represented a violation of children's rights in reflecting upon the case of an Indigenous victim who was a "girl" at the time of coercive sterilization in chapter 3. In 2006 a historic ruling was issued by the Committee on the Elimination of Discrimination Against Women in a case that dealt with informed consent and forced sterilization. *A.S. v. Hungary* dealt with the case of a Roma woman, Andrea Szijjarto, who had a miscarriage, underwent emergency surgery, and was asked to sign a consent form that was for a cesarean and included illegible Latin wording on sterilization.[77] After failing to obtain a domestic legal remedy in Hungary for her case of coercive sterilization, Szijjarto brought a complaint before the committee, which then issued its decision on August 14, 2006. The committee determined that the Hungarian state was in violation of Article 10, Section (h) of CEDAW regarding access to information on family planning; of Article 12, on the right to "appropriate services in connection with pregnancy, confinement and the post-natal period"; and of Article 16, on the right to freely choose the number and spacing of one's children.[78] Additionally, the lack of informed consent constituted a violation of the committee's General Recommendation 24, which noted the right for women to be "fully informed, by properly trained personnel, of their options," and General Recommendation 21, which recognized that "coercive practices which have serious consequences for women, such as forced . . . sterilization" require informed decision-making being provided by the state.[79] In sum, the committee determined that the Hungarian state had failed to protect the reproductive rights of Szijjarto. This was the first time that an international human rights tribunal held a state "accountable for failing to provide necessary information to a woman to enable her to give informed consent to a reproductive health-related medical procedure."[80]

Reflecting on Victoria's case, she had not been provided even a paper to sign, as had been the case for Andrea Szijjarto. There was no Latin or Spanish wording, and there was no paper. Moreover, in Victoria's case, she was not even asked to consent to the emergency cesarean, and she had received no information about family planning, let alone tubal ligation. Hence, the doctor and the hospital that were acting in conformity with the PSRPF policy were in violation of Article 10, Section (h) of CEDAW and General Recommendations 21 and 24 of the Committee on CEDAW. Considering all these factors, the Peruvian state was accountable for having provided no informed consent to Victoria for her cesarean and her coerced sterilization. Although it had not been the principal focus of her case, the consent factor had been alluded to in the domestic legal case that Victoria had won against the doctor who performed the surgeries (i.e., the cesarean and tubal ligation). What or who was not central to Victoria's domestic court case against the individual doctor or even in the case that she is currently pursuing—along with other coercive sterilization victims, against former President Alberto Fujimori; former health ministers Eduardo Yong Motta, Marino Ricardo Costa Bauer, and Alejandro Aurelio Aguinaga Recuenco; and adviser Ulises Jorge Aguilar—was the death of her prematurely born baby.[81] Victoria's *hijito*, however, may be the central figure that changes the discourse related to this coercive sterilization case.

JUSTICIA

In listening to Victoria's story and struggles, there was a word that seemed rather absent. It was the notion of "justice." In my conversations with Sarita, the victim who had been a minor at the time of her forced sterilization, everything had been centralized in *justicia* (justice); however, the word was nearly absent in Victoria's storytelling. So when she took a moment to pause and reflect upon her thoughts, I took the opportunity to ask her directly, "¿Qué significaría justicia, para, Victoria Vigo?" (What would justice mean, for Victoria Vigo?) Victoria provided the following response:

> Mira, justicia para mi primeramente sería que reconozcan. Reconozcan lo que nos han hecho a nosotras. Y justicia será también que reconozcan aparte de que puedan pedir disculpas públicas a todas las mujeres. Para todas. La violación que han hecho terriblemente, y el tercero sería una reparación económica porque, sí, para mí, eso también es parte de la justicia. . . . Por los daños que nos han hecho. El daño psicológico y el daño económico que nos han hecho. (Look, justice for me firstly is that they recognize. Recognize what they have done to us. And justice is also that they recognize, apart [from the acknowledgment], that they apologize publicly to all the women. To all of us. The human rights violation that they have terribly done, and third, it will be an economic reparation because, yes, for me, that is also a part of justice . . . for the harms they have caused us. The psychological harm and the economic harm they have caused us.)[82]

There were remarkable similarities between the justice that Victoria defined and what Sarita had mentioned. Victoria's justice prioritized its symbolic reparative qualities, noting the recognition aspect and the public apology from the state to victim-survivors. Then she discussed the medical and economic reparations. The medical, Victoria explained, was related to the psychological damage that victims have suffered. This, too, was similar to Sarita's justice, although perhaps not as wholistic or defined in terms of justice within the Andean Indigenous world, which focused on the healing of the soul and the body. Victoria had previous experience with psychiatrist practices and depression and thus was referring to a medical reparation that was more related to Western medicine. Nonetheless, the focus was there, specifically that it was not only the physical body that needed the healing but also the mind. Last, Victoria touched upon something that had not been discussed by Sarita, economic reparations. In part, the emphasis on economic reparations may have been because Victoria had previously gone through a domestic lawsuit and understood the difficulties of navigating the legal system without financial support. Additionally, Victoria was from the city and understood that participation in every activist movement in which she wanted to engage involved economic costs, even if they were basic transportation costs. Moreover, Victoria understood that economic support would help uplift many of the women who are still suffering in pain, cannot work anymore, and are in need of restructuring their lives and livelihoods.

The justice Victoria referred to was also similar to that of Sarita in the way that the ideas were presented. Victoria always spoke from a collective perspective; it was never about her justice alone. She always referred to justice in the form of the community, emphasizing the notion of *nosotras* (us) and how the state had to recognize *todas las mujeres* (all of the women) that they had harmed. In that, while Victoria did not share an Indigenous ethnic or cultural background with Sarita, there was a shared collective or communal sentiment among the community of women who had suffered the wrongful acts together. It was a new *ayllu* that had formed among the women, an *ayllu* that was not necessarily ethnic by ties, but one shared by women with similar experiences of harm. This community was present in Victoria's notion of justice.

It was the *ayllu's* justice.

CHAPTER FIVE

Together We Fight

*Role of Activists and Allies
in the Fight Against Impunity*

The stories of Sarita and Victoria from previous chapters provide us with a glimpse into the personal experiences of Indigenous and non-Indigenous women who endured the violence caused by the PSRPF. While these women's experiences are not generalizable to the experiences of all the women affected by the violent practices of coercive sterilizations, they are useful in providing context for what was happening on the ground. Sarita's and Victoria's narratives unveil the inadequacy of government responses to their sufferings and reveal how their search for remedies and justice sharply contrasts with what the state has offered them. The women have also shown how their individual stories are connected to the structural inequality and political repression that Indigenous people and women continue to face in Peruvian society today.

These women were not alone in their suffering, engagement, and hope. Their rallying cries for justice were accompanied and supported by individuals I refer to as activists, allies, or human rights defenders.[1] In this chapter I explore and tell the stories of five of these women activists working in human rights circles, who are dedicated to fighting for victim-survivors of coercive sterilization. The stories of the allies and those who supported the victims and victim-survivors recount tireless advocacy efforts by a small group of individuals who began their work in the late 1990s. These women are Rocío Silva Santisteban, Hilaria Supa Huamán, María Ysabel Cedano, Ketty Marcelo López, and Alejandra Ballón Gutiérrez. Rocío is the head of a nongovernmental organization (DEMUS) that provides legal counsel to those impacted by coercive sterilizations, an academic, a poet, and a former congresswoman who has previously worked in various human rights organizations.[2] Hilaria Supa is an Indigenous leader, community activist, and former congresswoman who has dedicated her life to defending her community and its members' rights. Ketty is an Indigenous human rights defender and head of a nongovernmental organization (ONAMIAP) dedicated to Indigenous peoples' rights. María Ysabel is a feminist leader, human rights defender, and former head of DEMUS. Alejandra is an academic, artist, and human rights activist who has long been documenting coercive sterilizations on a digital archive platform she created.

In unweaving their stories and experiences, I first recount how each activist became involved in the human rights movement that seeks to defend those affected by coercive sterilizations. Through their stories, we see behind-the-scenes activism and the politics involved in negotiating legitimate claims. We also can begin to understand the positionalities of each ally and how these impacted their activism experiences. I then explore their reasons for continuing their work in the movement and the difficulties they encountered. Finally, I engage with their visions of justice for victim-survivors.

Before detailing their stories, it is important to discuss the debates framing victims' identities, which shape the discussion of activists and their stories. To start with the obvious, we must understand what it means to refer to affected women as "victims," "survivors," or "victim-survivors." Along with these identifier words, this chapter reviews other terminology that is used interchangeably to refer to women like Sarita and Victoria. I also discuss the origins of the allied movement against coercive sterilization. Because the five activists' stories are so closely linked to the origins of the movement, I integrate some of their stories into the discussion of these origins as well as dedicating separate sections to unpack their stories.

VICTIMS, SURVIVORS, VICTIM-SURVIVORS

The global feminist movement and activism on sexual violence "began with the necessity of making the private pain and shame of women public," and it represents "a collective refusal to keep men's secrets."[3] The movement that began in Peru and that involved women's activists and human rights defenders had similar goals: to make public what had occurred to the women and demonstrate a collective refusal to keep the state's secrets. The identification of the "victim" or "survivor" emerged in this context to recognize the harm and acknowledge the agency of those affected by coercive sterilization in their activism, actions, and strategies.

Throughout my conversations with Sarita—whose story I discuss in chapter 3—when referring to herself, she used the term "victim." In contrast, Victoria—whose story I discuss in chapter 4—did not use this term. When Victoria was telling her stories and experiences, she used the term "victim-survivor" and, at times, "activist." Many of the allies of the coercive sterilization movement interchangeably used "victims," *señoras* (ladies, ma'am), "victim-survivors," *mujeres* (women), and *hermanas* (sisters) in reference to the women who had been forcibly sterilized. How can we understand these different terms? And what meaning do they hold?

Existing research argues that it matters how we label the affected population. Feminists point to the "negative meanings attached to the word 'victim,'" which has led to the use of the term "survivor."[4] This debate about the terminology regarding populations impacted by human rights violations is centered on the notion of power and agency. Kristine Avram explains that by calling "injured persons . . . victim," a term that is "commonly equated with passivity," one is said to be "taking agency" away from this population. Alternatively, "survivor" is regarded as more appropriate or suitable when referring to an affected population.[5] Kathleen Barry's work on victims and survivors discusses these definitions in greater depth. She argues that "redefining rape," which demands recognition of "women's victimization," has led to the creation of a new identity or status: "the victim."[6] Barry explains that the process of creating the role and status of the victim involves "victimism." According to Barry, "victimism" denies the "woman the integrity of her humanity through the whole experience," as it relegates her to a person who cannot be separated from the violence she experienced rather than a "victim, someone to whom violence was done."[7] The identity of being a victim, she argues, is something that has been "assigned to her by those who are judging her experience."[8] For this reason, it is important to use the term "survivors" in reference to victims, as this term "involves will, action, initiative on the victim's part."[9] Likewise, to remove the stigma accompanying the term "victim," some affected peoples prefer to be considered "survivors."[10] Human rights nongovernmental organizations support a similar approach, arguing that the concept of "victim" is stigmatizing. The identity of being a survivor, these organizations explain, emphasizes the individual's "capacity for resistance" and "healing" while focusing less on their position as a person who has been harmed.[11]

Other approaches to the identity of affected peoples are explored in intergovernmental organizations' reports. According to the 2021 "Technical Note on the Implementation of the UN Protocol on the Provision of Assistance to Victims of Sexual Exploitation and Abuse," the United Nations deliberately uses the term "victim" instead of "survivor." According to the UN, the purpose of this word choice is to "avoid multiple terminology and to align with the UN policy framework in this area of work."[12] Despite this choice, the UN's technical note demonstrates a perspective similar to Barry's work on victimhood. This is found in a text accompanying the technical note. Specifically, the text from the UN explains that the use of "victim" is not in "any way meant to diminish the strength and courage it takes to overcome victimization of the self-determination of the individuals themselves to decide when the shift from 'victim' to 'survivor' occurs."[13] This view positions "victim" as a condition of a person who has not reconciled with the victimized self. Because being a "survivor" is seen as necessitating the processes of being a "victim" and having "courage . . . to overcome victimization," it is positioned as a step elevated to that of being a "victim."[14]

Rather than simply focus on the terminological debates, throughout the discussions about the terms "victim" and "survivor," human rights organizations—such as the Center for Justice and International Law (CEJIL)—explain that it is also important to consider the "context." Where do the victims live? What are the societal environments that condition their reactions and actions? Why is it central to consider their choice of one identity over others? For instance, identifying as a "victim" in asylum petitions or petitions about forced displacement is key in generating a response that may be favorable or unfavorable to the affected individual.[15] In other contexts, women sometimes claim the "victim" identity from a more "activist" perspective. By adopting this identity, they make visible the human rights violations they have suffered and bring attention to the responsibility of the state in "states [that] have not considered or recognized their victimhood."[16] However, being a "victim" carries a stigma in other contexts. In states that conflate "victim" with an individual who is "traumatized" and regarded as unable to contribute to society, identifying as a "victim" is not advised.[17]

Human rights scholars also use "victims" and "survivors" interchangeably in contexts in which both of these terms are acceptable. For instance, in Carmen Ileana Rogobete's work on South Africa and the life trajectories of survivors of political violence under apartheid, she explains that "victim" and "survivor" are used interchangeably. The use of both terms is context specific, as "both victim and survivor signify the experience of gross violations of human rights," which are described in the Promotion of National Unity and Reconciliation Act. Moreover, the word "victim" is the "accepted term" within the truth and reconciliation processes in South Africa.[18] At the same time, Rogobete notes that she distinguishes these terms only when the "participants themselves" have made the distinction. In other words, there is flexibility in the terminology unless specified by the affected person. Brandon Hamber's study on trauma and the South African truth-seeking process reveals similar reasoning. Hamber notes that while they favored the usage of "survivor," they later realized, after their fieldwork with community groups, that "survivor" was a term "imported into local community parlance."[19] Hence, it was not commonly used by people. Hamber explains that while "survivor" is used more widely by mental health workers now, it can "also be used to avoid talking about suffering." This point, once again, reflects the importance of considering the context in which certain terminologies are used.

The interchangeable use of terms, as evident in Rogobete's and Hamber's work, reflects the idea that while the terms "victim" and "survivor" may be seen as representing different things, they refer to an overlapping aspect of the same experience. Victimization, survival, and surviving are part of a continuum of processes, which human rights violations have conditioned. Victimization does not stop when surviving begins. Thinking about this in terms of the Andean cosmovision of the world, in which time and space exist in a circular spiral—the past connects us to the present and yet carries its legacies and continues to exist as part of the present—victimization and survival coexist together and are interconnected.[20] Therefore, victimization or being a victim as well as surviving or being a survivor are not in binary opposition. Liz Kelly and colleagues explain that "neither victim nor survivor is a useful identity over the long term in relation to sexual violence."[21] For individuals, "struggling with the confusion, guilt, sense of being unworthy and undeserving . . . claiming an identity as a 'survivor' can be a positive move forward."[22] They note that for others, "acknowledging the pain and hurt which accompanies being a 'victim' may be an important step in integrating aspects of their experiences and emotions."[23] In other words, each person has to "make decisions at the time and later which are directed towards their survival," and each decision depends on "their particular circumstances."[24] These are key factors to consider because, when we try to use either "victim" or "survivor" to refer to people, we may be making assumptions that are not respectful or reflective of each person's experiences and choices. In other words, it is necessary to incorporate the impacted individual and their voice—a victim-survivor-centered approach—to determine the appropriate terminology to use. In the legal sphere and in thinking about law reform, scholars argue that a victim-survivor-centered approach involves "listening to victim-survivors of violence . . . beyond hearing to witnessing to their experience, and to take seriously the justice interests of survivors as legal and political subjects."[25] This approach embodies the element of recognizing the individual as a victim due to their past experience and acknowledging the person as a survivor with a will and agency for justice.

There have been other efforts to contextualize experiences of human rights violations with a focus on the terminology used to refer to the women who have been impacted. For instance, multiple terms are used to refer to the "most brutal crime" that was committed by the Japanese military during the Asia-Pacific War (1931–1945), which involved the forced mobilization of "approximately 50,000–200,000 Asian women to Japanese military brothels (JMBs) to sexually serve Japanese soldiers."[26] Korean women and girls were the largest victim group of this human rights crime, and research has demonstrated that postcolonial notions of gender, class, and ethnicity factored into this overselection process. The common terminology used in reference to this affected population has been "comfort women," translated from the Japanese word *ianfu*. While this word is still the most widely used term, there have been efforts to change this label. Some scholars have expanded this term to include girls, using the hyphenated term "comfort girls-women" to inclusively underscore the young age of the victims forced into sexual enslavement.[27] Lee Young-Soo, a Korean woman who was sexually enslaved, has explained that "comfort woman" was an identity imposed upon her by the Japanese military, and thus it did not represent her identity.[28] As a result, these women have sometimes preferred to be called *halmoni*, which means "grandmother" in Korean.[29] *Halmoni*—a Korean word and not a Japanese word translated into Korean—embeds a notion of respect toward these women. Moreover, this term is regarded as more inclusive because it incorporates these women—who have been marginalized due to their experiences—into society in a more familiar and respected way.

From this vantage point, one may consider using a different term to refer to the victim-survivors of coercive sterilizations. During our conversations, Victoria Vigo—an activist and victim-survivor of forced sterilization—used the word *señoras* (ladies or ma'am) to refer to the other women who were victimized and many of whom are now part of the human rights movement. The same word was also used by human rights allies such as Rocío Silva Santisteban and Hilaria Supa, who along with *señoras* interchangeably use the terms "victims" and "victim-survivors." Similar to the use of *halmoni*, the Spanish word *señora* embeds a notion of respect and is contextually specific to Peru. On the other hand, Alejandra Ballón Gutiérrez uses the word *mujeres* (women) and Ketty López Marcelo uses the term *hermanas* (sisters) to refer to the victim-survivors. It is important to notice here that *señora(s)*, *mujeres*, and *hermanas* do not reflect—even distantly—that the referred-to individuals suffered human rights abuses; instead, they are neutral terms. If we are trying to shift the language for those wishing to adopt an identity beyond victim, survivor, or victim-survivor, then *señoras*, *hermanas*, or *mujeres* may be the solution. These terms might be preferable to a Korean *halmoni* like Lee Young-Soo, who wanted her identity to be unassociated with the crime of sexual enslavement.

Despite the heated scholarly discussions on terminology (i.e., how certain identifiers reflect agency and power and why others do not), this chapter and book do not seek to impose a term upon the affected women. Following the reasoning of Kelly and colleagues, this book and chapter hold that the affected women have the authority to determine which category of identification best suits them based on their experiences. From this vantage point, I explore the stories the activists and allies brought forward, using direct quotes to demonstrate how these individuals refer to the affected women (i.e., as victims, victim-survivors, *señoras*, *mujeres*, or *hermanas*).

THE MOVEMENT

Scholars note that violence against women persists "even after decades of research, activism, law reform and related attempts to address it" because of "how women's voices are heard and listened and responded to."[30] When considering marginalized populations, particularly women whose identity sits at the intersection of an excluded class, ethnic group, and gendered identity, their voices are likely silenced, and their experiences of gender-based violence are negated. Scholars explain that Indigenous women—whose identity represents the intersections of ethnicity, economic class, and gender dynamics—are often targets of human rights violations.[31] In the Peruvian case, sexual violence against Indigenous women is embedded with additional elements of dominion and historical power relations.[32] The PSRPF and the related consequences of coercive sterilization impacted the majority of Indigenous women. However, these abuses were excluded from the final report of the TRC of Peru.[33] Furthermore, as Hilaria Supa explains, individuals affected by these abuses were not regarded as a victim group that emerged from the internal armed conflict period and that involved the state and the leftist guerrilla forces.[34] This situation demonstrates why activists have played an important role in bringing continued attention to the case of coercive sterilizations.

As Alejandra Ballón Gutiérrez explains, the advocacy movement for women who had been coercively sterilized began when local human rights and women's rights groups received information about irregularities in the family planning program.[35] These organizations then communicated their concerns to international human rights organizations, which further disseminated the information. The Peru-based organizations involved in flagging the problems associated with the family planning program included local women's rights organizations and Indigenous rights leaders, such as Hilaria Supa Huamán; the Peru office of the Comité Latinoamericano y del Caribe para la Defensa de los Derechos de la Mujer (CLADEM; Committee for Latin America and the Caribbean for the Defense of Women's Rights); Movimiento Amplio de Mujeres Línea Fundacional (MAM Fundacional; Broad-Based Women's Movement); APRODEH; DEMUS; Flora Tristán Center of the Peruvian Woman; and the Human Rights Ombudsman's Office. Related partnering international organizations included the Center for Reproductive Law and Policy (CRLP)—now known as the Center for Reproductive Rights (CRR)—and CEJIL. Together, these groups formed a transnational advocacy network "characterized by voluntary, reciprocal, and horizontal patterns of communication and exchange" through international advocacy, intergovernmental organizations, and domestic human rights groups dedicated to promoting human rights.[36] Existing studies have documented the effectiveness and impact of transnational advocacy networks in mobilizing human rights issues and delivering messages in defense of human rights.[37] Additionally, transnational advocacy has positively influenced policymakers to continue complying with transitional justice policies in Peru's postauthoritarian transition periods.[38] Such was also the case for the movement against impunity for coercive sterilization.

Nongovernmental organizations and the Human Rights Ombudsman's Office were involved in the reports that emerged at the onset of the family planning program. Specifically, these organizations documented the sterilization practices and related human rights violations. In 1999, Peruvian human rights lawyer Giulia Tamayo from CLADEM published one of the first investigative reports about the application of the family planning program from 1996 to 1998. The report, *Nada Personal* (Nothing personal), found that there were quotas for sterilization that medical personnel had to fulfill; sanctions and threats against those who did not fill the quotas; abuses; sterilizations performed during the postpartum and postmiscarriage period, and during regular reproductive health visits; forced sterilizations of women by "exclusive authorization of their male partners"; forced sterilizations through trickery; forced sterilizations using intimidation, such as the confining of patients in waiting areas; and other practices that negated free and informed consent.[39] These reports were substantiated by the work of MAM Fundacional, which stepped in to listen, help, and investigate the cases that Indigenous rights leader Hilaria Supa had been hearing and documenting. Moreover, the Human Rights Ombudsman's Office reports in 1998, 2000, and 2001 found that sterilization occurred during "health festivals" primarily held throughout rural and majority Indigenous-language-speaking areas, where tubal ligations were framed as the ultimate health choice.[40] Together, these reports helped shine an international spotlight on Peru.

The impact of transnational advocacy networks was most prominent in the case *María Mamérita Mestanza Chávez v. Peru*. This case dealt with the coercive sterilization of an Indigenous woman named María Mamérita Mestanza Chávez, who died of health complications related to the tubal ligation procedure. Before the tubal ligation, María Mamérita lived happily with her partner Jacinto Salazar Juárez, dedicated herself to agricultural work (i.e., farming), and was a mother to seven children. Starting in 1996, María Mamérita received more than ten "intimidating visits" from health professionals who pressured her to undergo tubal ligation.[41] They threatened and intimidated María Mamérita and her partner and provided false information that having more than five children was "illegal" under the law. María Mamérita eventually underwent tubal ligation at the Health Center at La Encañada on March 27, 1998, and died on April 5, 1998, from postsurgery complications not appropriately addressed by health professionals. Her husband, Jacinto, filed a complaint against the Public Prosecutor's Office at Cajamarca. On May 18, the Provincial Prosecutor of Baños del Inca accused four health personnel (i.e., the doctor who was in charge at the Health Center at La Encañada, the obstetrician who performed the tubal ligation, the coordinator of the family planning program, and the nurse who helped administer the anesthesia) for crimes against life and health, and for the culpable homicide of María Mamérita. After numerous dismissals and appeals, the Provincial Public Prosecutor at Baños del Inca (in the city of Cajamarca) decided on December 16, 1998, that there was "no place to open the criminal case" against these individuals and ordered a definitive dismissal of the case.[42] This decision set in motion a series of strategic maneuvers involving multiple domestic and international human rights organizations, which resulted in the first transnational advocacy movement dedicated to a coercive sterilization case in Peru.

Following María Mamérita's death, Peruvian human rights organizations that had already been involved in documenting and denouncing coercive sterilization cases during the Fujimori administration—APRODEH, CLADEM, and DEMUS—mobilized their international networks and partners, namely CEJIL and CRLP/CRR.[43] Together, they took María Mamérita's case to the IACHR on June 15, 1999. Simultaneously, in May 1999, MAM Fundacional organized a press conference in Lima with Indigenous rights leader Hilaria Supa Huamán and twelve women who had been coercively sterilized, thus building the momentum on the forced sterilization issue in Peru.[44] On October 3, 2000, María Mamérita's case was accepted by the IACHR as a human rights violation of the affected individual under the norms enshrined in the American Convention on Human Rights and the Inter-American Convention on the Prevention, Punishment, and Eradication of Violence Against Women, commonly referred to as the Convention of Belém do Pará. Throughout this period from 1999 to 2000s, the transnational advocacy network (i.e., international and domestic nongovernmental organizations) remained active, supporting the family of María Mamérita. Eventually, transnational advocacy pressure resulted in a "friendly settlement" between the family of María Mamérita and the Peruvian state, with the state recognizing its culpability for the coercive sterilizations before the IACHR.[45]

Similar types of transnational advocacy efforts spearheaded by DEMUS resulted in another case of forced sterilization being accepted by the IACHR. The case *Celia Ramos v. Peru* involved the forced sterilization of Celia by health authorities working under the directive of the PSRPF campaign in 1997 and her related death due to postoperative health complications. The case concluded in 2021 with the IACHR recommending payment of reparations by the state to the victim's family. The state, however, failed to meet its obligations. In response, DEMUS was joined by CEJIL and CRR and helped to push the case forward to the IACtHR. Hearings in the case began on May 22, 2025.

The pressure the transnational advocacy network exerted in both cases of coercive sterilization led to greater social mobilization involving the women directly impacted by the family planning program. For instance, in 2004, a year after the friendly settlement in *María Mamérita Mentanza Chávez v. Peru*, the Asociación de Mujeres Afectadas por Esterilizaciones Forzadas (AMAEF; Association of Women Affected by Forced Sterilizations of Anta) was established. This group was led by the Indigenous rights leader and activist Hilaria Supa, who mobilized victim-survivors from the communities of Anta and Cusco. After the establishment of this group, other similar victim-survivor groups emerged, such as the Asociación Nacional del Mujeres Afectadas por las Esterilizaciones Forzadas (AMPAEF; Association of Peruvian Women Affected by Forced Sterilizations). These groups have organized numerous workshops on reparations and legal aid for victim-survivors, protest marches demanding justice, and collaborations with other nongovernmental organizations such as DEMUS to hold watch parties for the public hearings on *Celia Ramos v. Peru*.

Beyond these organizational developments, artistic interventions of advocacy and virtual activist efforts began. These included the photo exhibit on coercive sterilizations titled *Ikumi*, which was held at the Lugar de la Memoria, La Tolerancia y la Inclusión Social (LUM; Place of Memory, Tolerance, and Social Inclusion), the state's official place of memory for victims from the internal armed conflict period. *Ikumi* documents the testimonies of victims (in audio form), physical scars of tubal ligation (in photographs), and other historical information associated with the family planning campaign. Other efforts have included the *Alfombra Roja* (Red carpet), a "series of interventions in the public sphere to make visible—among other things women's rights related themes/subjects—forced sterilizations."[46] This artistic-feminist movement is led by Alejandra Ballón, one of the allies whose stories we visit in this chapter. The performances of *Alfombra Roja* include women dressing in red, lying on the floor, and demanding justice for women affected by coercive sterilizations. Herein, red symbolizes the color of the Peruvian flag and also blood, and the performance of lying down symbolizes the red carpet on which heads of state and other powerful individuals walk for formal ceremonies.[47] Together, these symbols represent the ways in which fundamental rights of women are trampled upon by the state and ways in which women are harmed (i.e., spilling blood). Additionally, they represent the "pressing need" or the "urgency" to address the protection of sexual and reproductive rights.

Concurrent with artistic activism, virtual activism also emerged. For example, the Quipu Project, a digital archive that aims to "shine a light on the sterilizations," provides a space for a collective memory archive.[48] The archive takes the Quechua word *quipu*—which refers to a manner of record, memory, and registry keeping during the Incan empire—and uses this as a metaphor to record voices, experiences, and stories of Indigenous women who were impacted by the PSRPF. This digital archive includes testimonies from victim-survivors who can anonymously call and record their voices, which are open and accessible to all. As scholars who lead this project have explained, their work on Quipu has facilitated the "production of participatory knowledge and has given way to new forms of involvement between those who were producing the knowledge and the general public."[49] Specifically, the Quipu Project interrupts the disputed claims about memory from this period, challenging the state's denial of this crime and preventing this memory from becoming "lost."[50] Instead, with a digital platform, the project maintains a living memory record for victim-survivors. Quipu Project's digital archive can also be referred to as a form of "digital memory activism," which involves using "digital platforms for politicized acts of commemoration."[51] Scholars explain that "memory activists" like these have used digital technologies and platforms to "amplify the memories and voices of those who are so often ignored in the memory marketplace and to disseminate these memories in accessible format."[52]

ALLIES AND ACTIVISTS

Nearly three decades have passed since the PSRPF was instituted. Advocacy efforts have spread from a few nongovernmental organizations to a transnational advocacy alliance and from an offline to an online platform. However, the primary goal has remained the same: to help victim-survivors of coercive sterilizations fight for recognition and justice. The role of activists as allies has been central to supporting this new human rights movement.

Of course, the allied movement did not just happen. There was a long, multifaceted process that involved investigations into irregularities related to the family planning program; publications emerging from human rights organizations and newspapers; activists being alerted about the situation; and finding the right time and place for a movement to develop. In many of these steps, the victim-survivors played a central role in transforming individuals from academics and human rights defenders into allies of the coercive sterilization movement by sharing space and narrating their stories. In the following pages, I discuss key activists' experiences and how they have formed this collective movement to defend victim-survivors.

THE STUDENT

When Alejandra Ballón Gutiérrez first heard about the coercive sterilization of women, she asked her colleagues and professors about it;

however, they had no information: "Nadie sabía nada, nadie sabía nada" (No one knew anything, no one knew anything).[53] This was in 1997, a year into the implementation of the PSRPF program. Alejandra was a university student at the Pontificia Universidad Católica del Perú (PUCP; Pontifical Catholic University of Lima), a world-renowned and top-ranked private university in Peru. And yet no one among her friends or colleagues knew what had been happening. Alejandra explained the situation:

> La primera vez que yo escucho sobre el tema, estaba yo en la PUCP, estudié pintura en la PUCP. Salí para comprar un cigarrillo al quiosco de la señora . . . en frente de la puerta principal y ella tenía un pequeño radio. Y justo estaba pasando una mujer que estaba hablando sobre las esterilizaciones. Yo creo que debe haber sido en el año 1997 . . . entonces claro . . . ¡Qué dolor en la voz! Y el llanto en Quechua y la traducción que estaba allí. (The first time I heard about this case, I was at PUCP, I was majoring in painting at PUCP. I had gone out to buy cigarettes at the kiosk of the lady . . . in front of the university main gate and she had a small little radio. And opportunistically a woman was just talking about the sterilizations. I believe it was in 1997, and well of course . . . what pain in her voice! And the cries in Quechua and the translation were there.)[54]

According to Alejandra, the woman at the kiosk:

> era una señora de descendiente de pueblos originarios de todas maneras, o digamos mestiza como yo también, pero seguramente ella un poco más Indígena que yo. Y las dos nos miramos y yo prendí mi cigarrillo y las dos escuchamos (was a lady who was of Indigenous ancestry, let's say mestiza like me also, but perhaps a bit more of Indigenous [ancestry] than I. And the two of us looked at one another and I lit my cigarette and both of us listened).[55]

Alejandra noted how she exchanged looks with the woman at the kiosk and said nothing. It was as if they were both trying to process the story from the radio, which no one among her colleagues and professors knew. Alejandra described that moment as "traspasadas con lo que estábamos escuchando" (pierced with what we were hearing).

The year 1997 coincided with the grave human rights violations taking place during the last years of the Fujimori dictatorship (1990–2000). Specifically, the year began with the continued hostage situation of the leftist militant group MRTA, which had infiltrated the Japanese embassy in Lima, Peru, on December 17, 1996. Despite promising a peaceful negotiation with the MRTA, the Peruvian military stormed the residence on April 22, 1997. According to the official version of the story, the military "killed all the MRTA members." It became evident that the state had extrajudicially executed some MRTA members even after they had ceased their armed aggression against the state. In other words, the MRTA had surrendered.[56] Killing individuals who had surrendered was a violation of international law and deprived some of the MRTA members of the right to life with due process. These rights violations committed by the Fujimori government dominated the discourse in Alejandra's art collective, comprised of like-minded artists and students who were human rights activists. Alejandra said she put the story of coercive sterilizations aside without knowing where to turn for more information about the case on the radio. But the voice on the radio—of a Quechua-speaking woman who was a victim-survivor—had awoken Alejandra's interest in forced sterilization cases.

Then came an opportunity for Alejandra:

> En un momento nos llamó Flora Tristán, o sea Giulia Tamayo. Giulia Tamayo con Flora Tristán querían hacer un proyecto sobre esterilizaciones y dicho ... el primero que se hizo desde el arte desde el activismo desde la cancha. (At some point [or moment], Flora Tristán [a nongovernmental organization] called, or actually Giulia Tamayo. Giulia Tamayo with Flora Tristán wanted to do a project on sterilizations and well ... it became the first one that was done from the art of activism from the ground up.)[57]

Alejandra remarked that she did not know who Giulia was, nor was she in favor of doing any artwork that a nongovernmental organization had commissioned. The art collective, from Alejandra's viewpoint, had to work on things true to their conviction and supportive of their mission while not taking any *comandas* (orders). Alejandra smiled, paused, and said that many years later, she and Giulia had a good laugh about that moment. While Alejandra did not initially agree with the art collective's work or what they created related to coercive sterilizations, she credited how the artistic rendition "en su momento cumplió su función" (in that moment served its function) by giving visibility to the case of coercive sterilizations. For Alejandra, however, this event encouraged her to reflect on the "representación de la imagen" (representation of the image), specifically how sterilizations would need to be presented, shown, and manifested without causing pain. In other words, Alejandra needed to consider the affected women and adopt a *mujeres*-based approach in thinking about artistic activism.

THE LINK: GIULIA TAMAYO

In the 1990s, Rocío Silva Santisteban's world involved work in poetry, academia, and nongovernmental organizations. Rocío said, "En esa época, salió el informe Nada Personal de Giulia Tamayo" (In that period, the report *Nada Personal* [Nothing personal] from Giulia Tamayo came out).[58] Rocío took a deep breath, looked away, and then noted how that moment changed everything for her. Since 1998, Rocío had been working in the area of communications with DEMUS, a feminist human rights nongovernmental organization based in the capital city of Lima, Peru, that was dedicated to the defense of sexual and reproductive rights of women. As small nongovernmental organizations tend to operate, Rocío also assisted with work outside the area of communications, which involved other human rights violations. DEMUS was the same organization that María Ysabel Cedano had been working at since May 1990.

When Giulia Tamayo's report came out in 1999, it confirmed some of the information published by daily newspapers. For instance, in 1998 the two largest newspapers in Peru, *El Comercio* and *La República*, published twenty-nine articles related to or on the subject of sterilizations, tubal ligations, the denial of the crime or act by Fujimori government-related health ministers (e.g., Alejandro Aguinaga), and the PSRPF.[59] In

1999 twenty articles on these topics were published in *El Comercio* and *La República*.[60] Giulia's report, however, changed the focus of those in the human rights movement. Rocío explains that, in part, it was because Giulia authored the report.

Giulia Tamayo was a respected human rights lawyer and activist and the author of the investigative report *Nada Personal*, which documented the early coercive sterilizations in Peru. She did not hesitate to gather her findings about the coercive sterilization cases and on numerous occasions spoke out against the impunity and injustice related to this situation. In interviews with news outlets, Tamayo explained that coercive sterilizations represented a case of "absolute discrimination... against groups that have less social power," especially toward Indigenous peoples who had already been impacted by the internal armed conflict.[61] Describing the gravity of the problem, Tamayo remarked that "when a crime does not have consequences towards those responsible, it sends out a message of permissiveness," meaning that such crimes can be committed without any repercussions.[62] Tamayo understood the importance of shedding more light on this case, which the state hoped to ignore and neglect. For this reason, Tamayo continued with her activism and engaged further with writings on reproductive justice for women, discussing the ways by which the control of women's sexuality and reproductive capacity is mirrored in practices of "ethnic cleansing" and "coercive sterilizations."[63]

After a short pause, Rocío continued her story about Giulia:

> Yo era amiga de Giulia, la conocía, bueno, amiga cercana, no, pero digamos la conocía, frecuentábamos movimiento juntas, ella era del movimiento feminista, entonces, igual la conocía desde muchos años antes. Entonces, en esos años es que salía a la luz este tema, fueron lo que nos impactó... porque, era como wow, que está pasando... y además todos, conociendo a Giulia, Giulia, una persona seria, seria, es entonces cuando nosotros comenzamos a entrar al tema. (I was friends with Giulia, I knew her, well, close friend, not really, but let's say that I did know her, we frequented the

[human rights] movement together, her in the feminist movement, and so, I knew her from many years back. And so, in those years when light was shed on this subject, it impacted us . . . because it was like wow, what is happening . . . and in fact all of us, knowing Giulia, Giulia, a respectful person, serious, it is when we started involving ourselves in the subject.)[64]

The human rights circles that Rocío referred to were based predominantly in and around Peru's metropolitan areas. Rocío noted how this report, the *información rotondo* (all-around information) from Giulia, and the published evidence from newspapers set in motion an expansion of DEMUS's interests, causing it to play a major role in the case of coercive sterilizations.[65] Importantly, DEMUS had already been involved in monitoring cases of sterilization. For instance, one of its cases involved a woman known by the acronym M.G.E.O. who, in 1995, consented to sterilization without a proper evaluation of her health, which would have revealed that she was a poor candidate for tubal ligation.[66] In addition, DEMUS had petitioned in 1998 for the intervention of the Human Rights Ombudsman's Office in the case of María Mamérita Mestanza Chávez. Specifically, the organization sought to ensure that the toxicology reports ordered on her would be given to the appropriate authorities in the domestic court case.[67] The publication of Giulia's report expanded the activism and work of DEMUS even further for women affected by coercive sterilization.

Giulia Tamayo's *Nada Personal* also set in motion a series of publications from the Human Rights Ombudsman's Office on coercive sterilization in 1999 and 2002.[68] The 1999 report discussed the complaints the Human Rights Ombudsman's Office had received and detailed the age, sex, education, and areas of residence of the affected population. This information proved important because (1) most people who speak Indigenous languages and are of Indigenous descent reside in nonurban rural areas, and (2) an individual's ethnicity can often be determined based on their residency in Peru.[69] The 2002 report detailed the problems associated with the family planning program. These included the restriction of access to information about family planning, problems of consent related to tubal ligation, tubal ligation performed in centers that did not comply with the norms established by the PSRPF, nonprovision of medical attention related to health complications caused by tubal ligation, denial of provision of medical exams, and a limited supply of emergency contraception pills from the Ministry of Health.[70] As Rocío had been working at DEMUS, the publication of all these reports and Giulia's report significantly influenced her interest in this case.

For Alejandra Ballón Gutiérrez, the voice of the *mujer* from the radio caught her attention and later became the link to Giulia Tamayo. For Rocío Silva Santisteban, her work at DEMUS, the publication of Giulia's work, and her respect for Giulia were the contributing factors. Relatedly, the same was true for María Ysabel Cedano, whose work at DEMUS and CLADEM—associated with Giulia's work—impacted her activism.

María Ysabel, like Alejandra Ballón Gutiérrez, was also a graduate of the PUCP in Lima. She had studied law at PUCP and heard about an internship opportunity through a colleague. To complete the *prácticas pre-profesionales* (preprofessional practices/practicum), she had applied to DEMUS and been selected. María Ysabel explained, "[T]enía noción e información básica sobre feminismo, la lucha contra la desigualdad por causa del machismo, el racismo y clasismo." (I had a basic notion and information about feminism, the struggles against inequality caused by machismo, racism, and classism.)[71] María Ysabel further explained, "No sabía qué era una ONG" (I did not know what an NGO [nongovernmental organization] was), and she was unaware of the human rights community of nongovernmental organizations. It was during her internship at DEMUS and experience as a legal assistant to the feminist lawyers at DEMUS and CLADEM that she learned and became a part of the feminist justice movement. CLADEM was the organization that published Giulia Tamayo's *Nada Personal* report in 1999 and had been involved in early efforts to support women who had been forcibly sterilized. DEMUS was also involved in women's rights matters. Working in both organizations, María Ysabel thus came to understand that the crimes she was seeing "no se trataban de delitos comunos sino de graves violaciones a los derechos humanos y crímenes de lesa humanidad" (were not dealing with common/ordinary crimes, rather, [they were grave] violations of human rights and crimes against humanity).[72] More importantly, the chilling and painful testimony from victims and their family members caused María Ysabel indignation and deeply moved her. While she did not speak the *lengua de sus ancestras* (language of her ancestors)—referring to Indigenous languages—and often missed nuances lost during the translations of testimony, María Ysabel understood the communicated messages and felt moved to join the cause to fight these grave human rights violations.

THE TURNING WHEELS OF ACTIVISM

The year 2011 was important for all activists. For Rocío Silva Santisteban, it was the year she became the executive director of the Coordinadora Nacional de Derechos Humanos (CNDDHH; National Coordination of Human Rights). Based in Lima and established in 1985, the CNDDHH served as an umbrella organization for numerous civil society organizations working on defending, promoting, and providing education on human rights. The year 2011 was also significant for heated presidential elections, with voters having to decide between two controversial candidates. The Peruvian Nobel Prize–winning novelist Mario Vargas Llosa had summarized this election as a choice between *cáncer o el sida* (cancer or AIDS).[73] Both candidates were recognized for the political baggage they carried. Presidential candidate Keiko Fujimori was the daughter of Alberto Fujimori and had held the role of First Lady of Peru from 1994 to 2000, during which time the PSRPF had been implemented. The other candidate was Ollanta Humala, a former lieutenant colonel of the armed forces responsible for the forced disappearance of civilians at the military base of Madre Mía in north Peru. In short, there was no seemingly respectable candidate. Nevertheless,

Rocío explained that, given what was at stake (i.e., the onset of another Fujimori era and what that meant for victims of human rights violations), the CNDDHH was at a critical juncture to decide whether to intervene in politics.

Rocío said:

> La Coordinadora de Derechos Humanos no había entrado tanto al tema político tan directamente, pero da las circunstancias en que Keiko Fujimori estaba a punto de convertirse Presidenta del Perú, bueno las víctimas, sobre todo las víctimas de conflicto armado solicitaron y pidieron que querían hacer algo, entonces tomamos la decisión, una decisión difícil. (The National Coordination for Human Rights had not entered in a political matter so directly, but there came the circumstance that Keiko Fujimori was about to become the President of Peru, and well, the victims, especially the victims of the internal armed conflict asked us to do something, so we made the choice, a difficult choice [to enter into politics].)[74]

The CNDDHH and other human rights organizations, such as APRODEH and the Instituto de Defensa Legal (IDL; Institute for Legal Defense), collectively launched the campaign of *Fujimori Nunca Más* (Fujimori Never Again). This was the human rights community's way of declaring their support for Ollanta Humala. As IDL Executive Director Ernesto de la Jara stated, Humala was the better choice rather than having the country return to Fujimorismo (Fujimorism) with Keiko Fujimori.[75] These ideas reflected the human rights community's staunch opposition to the legacy of human rights crimes committed under Alberto Fujimori (1990–2000), which included the years of the family planning program. After the Fujimori Never Again campaign began, Rocío, as the director of national coordination, pushed to amplify the anti-Fujimori movement to include victims of coercive sterilizations. She explained:

> Porque, no solo las víctimas del conflicto armado han sido víctimas de Alberto Fujimori. Si no que también, tendrías que pensar de las víctimas de esterilizaciones forzadas. Y es, así que conozco a Victoria Vigo. (Because the victims of the [internal] armed conflict are not the only victims of Alberto

Fujimori [administration]. In fact, you also have to think about the victims of forced sterilizations. And that is how I came to know Victoria Vigo.)[76]

Rocío explained that at the time, Victoria Vigo was one of the few women who publicly talked about her forced sterilization experience. This was largely due to Victoria's unrelenting dedication to seeking criminal accountability against the doctor who had forcibly sterilized her in Piura and her testimony before the US House of Representatives Committee on International Relations on February 25, 1998.[77] Victoria had followed a different path from most victims of the internal armed conflict. After pausing for a few seconds, Rocío explained that Victoria "es expresiva, una mujer muy inteligente" (is expressive, is an intelligent woman), comes from an urban area (the city of Piura), and endured terrible circumstances, referring to the forced cesarean, the death of Victoria's baby, and the coercive sterilization.[78] Victoria's willingness to come forward and actively participate in the Fujimori Never Again campaign—explored in greater detail in chapter 4—helped Rocío connect with the victim-survivors of coercive sterilizations. Rocío explained that Victoria became the "rostro de las esterilizaciones forzadas" (the face of forced sterilizations), a symbol of this group of affected individuals. The relationship she built with Victoria sowed the seeds for Rocío's entry into the allied movement. Put simply, Victoria had contributed to transforming Rocío's activism.

WHEN THE WORLDS CONNECT

The year 2011 represented a turning point, particularly for Rocío Silva Santisteban, as she got to know Victoria Vigo and became directly involved in launching the Fujimori Never Again campaign. Of course, this was not the only pivotal moment in Rocío's long trajectory of activism. Rather, it was the starting point of her involvement in the coercive sterilization movement. The other important event that made Rocío reflect upon her position as a human rights defender was the meeting with Hilaria Supa Huamán. This encounter eventually led to a cascade of developments for victim-survivors of coercive sterilizations. Additionally, this meeting was also important for Hilaria Supa's own activism in defense of Indigenous peoples' rights.

Hilaria Supa Huamán had been an Indigenous leader, a community activist, and the founder of Federación Campesina de la Provincia de Anta (Agricultural Farmer Federation of the Province of Anta) in the Cusco region of Peru (Southern Andes). In 1995 she even traveled to Beijing for the Conference on Women, where she met with President Alberto Fujimori and communicated her concerns about the hardships Indigenous peoples faced in the Andean areas of Peru. But in the end, none of that mattered. The violence of the internal armed conflict—which had been brewing since the 1980s—spread to communities that were majority Indigenous, who became targets of the so-called leftist movements, both from the leftist guerrilla groups and the state security forces.[79] Additionally, Indigenous women became subjects of harm as a result of the Fujimori administration's family planning policy (1996–2001).[80] Hilaria Supa explained that she could not remain silent:

> Nosotros somos pueblos originarios indígenas y, eh, y no pueden menospreciarnos. . . . [N]o tienen derecho de hacernos, imponernos nada . . . [Y]a conociendo mucho sobre derechos humanos, como porque somos ser humanos tenemos derecho vivir bien. (We are Indigenous peoples and well, they cannot disparage us. . . . [T]hey do not have the right to do things to us, to impose upon us nothing . . . [I] already [knew] a lot about human rights, like how we have the right as human beings to live well.)[81]

As an Indigenous leader, Hilaria Supa was aware of her human rights and the rights of her Indigenous community. Seeing the government commit these human rights violations, it was therefore imperative for her to engage in activism to defend her people and their rights.

Hilaria's tireless efforts in rights advocacy coincided with Rocío's work at the CNDDHH. Rocío met Hilaria Supa after Hilaria had been elected in 2011 for a five-year-term as the Peruvian representative to the Parlamento Andino (Andean Parliament). The Andean Parliament is the governing deliberative body of the Comunidad Andina (Andean Community), a trade bloc or economic group comprising Bolivia, Colombia, Ecuador, Peru, and Venezuela. Rocío recalls that Hilaria Supa had asked for the meeting, during which she was accompanied by two or three victim-survivors of coercive sterilizations. According to Rocío:

> Y yo me acuerdo de que estuve conversando con unas señoras y me impresiono una señora muy joven. Y yo le dije usted es tan joven, en qué momento la esterilizaron y me contó que la ligadura de trompas había sido cuando ella tenía 25 años y algo así. Me pareció brutal. (I remember that I was talking to one of the señoras and I was stunned that the señora was so young. I said, you are so young, when did they sterilize you and she told me that the tubal ligation had been done when she was only 25 years old or something like that. It struck me as brutal.)[82]

It was during this conversation that Rocío discovered that Hilaria Supa had traveled to Lima and requested a meeting with the CNDDHH in 1998, after being alerted about coercive sterilization cases in her community. At that time, the director of the CNDDHH told Hilaria Supa that there was nothing they could do because "el tema de esterilizaciones forzadas no forma parte del conflicto armado" (the subject of coercive sterilizations did not form a part of the [internal] armed conflict). Recalling that moment in 1998, Hilaria Supa told Rocío, "Ustedes nunca hicieron nada por nosotras" (You [all] never did anything for us [Indigenous women]). Rocío said she froze when she heard this. After all, as the executive director of the CNDDHH, she had been advocating to expand the Fujimori Nunca Más campaign to include victims of coercive sterilization. She had even formed a strong friendship with Victoria Vigo. Consequently, hearing about the failure of the CNDDHH to provide space for all victims was *terrible* (terrible) for her.

For Hilaria Supa, the unwillingness of the CNDDHH to support and help Indigenous women impacted by the coercive sterilization campaign gave her more reason to continue her advocacy. It was a dangerous time for someone like Hilaria Supa to be involved in activism, because Indigenous people were often targeted or labeled as leftists. As an Indigenous community leader, she had even experienced numerous death threats. Reflecting upon the period of the internal armed conflict during the 1990s, María Ysabel Cedano also explained that, at the time, many parts of the country were in a state of emergency, with armed forces and police personnel controlling everything and even overseeing the campaign of tubal ligations.[83] In fact, it was not easy for individuals to speak out against the government of Fujimori, which Victoria Vigo also confirmed when discussing her activism (see chapter 4). Given this sociopolitical context, as Hilaria Supa remarked, "las señoras no querían hablar, porque les daban miedo" (the ladies [who had been sterilized forcibly] did not want to speak, out of fear).[84] After all, they had been harmed by a state health policy, meaning they would need to position themselves against the state in their search for justice.

Still, something had to be done. Hilaria Supa explained, "Empezamos a defendernos, comenzar a organizarnos para poder hablar" (We started defending ourselves, started to organize ourselves to be able to speak up) about the experiences that the women had endured.[85] This included the story of one of the *señoras*. Hilaria Supa described how the nurses dragged this *señora* to the health center and locked her in a room so she could not escape. After she eventually managed to escape, she was brought back to the health center, hit, and then sterilized against her will. When the *señora* complained about feeling immense pain, the nurses insulted her, told her, "son mañosas, idiotas" ("you guys are trickster-like, idiots"), and then hit her head. Hilaria Supa described how after this mistreatment, the *señora* could no longer walk properly. Hilaria Supa said that through her continuous engagement with affected women, it became clear to her that this situation was impacting more Indigenous and Quechua-speaking peoples than others. That is when she realized that someone needed to speak up: "Sigo adelante . . . porque no hay derechos . . . no hay nadie que nos puede ayudar" (I continue marching forward . . . because there are no rights . . . no one that can help us).[86]

As a congresswoman and an Andean Parliamentarian (2006–2011), Hilaria Supa found the political footing necessary to bring attention to the case of coercive sterilizations. In her newfound role, she connected with Rocío Silva Santisteban at the CNDDHH and received the response she wanted: an alliance between Indigenous victim-survivors, an Indigenous human rights defender, and human rights activists working in Lima. This proved to be a turning point for allyship and the human rights movement because it led to the setting of a new agenda, one with a collective focus on what needed to be done for the women who had been wronged.

It was also around this time that ONAMIAP joined the movement in support of victims of coercive sterilizations. Ketty López Marcelo, the president of ONAMIAP, recalls the year when her organization became involved in the movement:

> Empezamos a acercarnos a las hermanas víctimas de esterilizaciones forzadas en el año 2016 . . . [N]os acercamos a las hermanas, como por ejemplo de Cusco y Ayacucho y comenzábamos a preocuparnos sobre hermanas de otras regiones . . . y empezamos a hacer algunos talleres con apoyo de IWGIA . . . y se hizo un pequeño documental llamado *Camino a la Justicia*. (We started becoming closer to the sisters/victims of forced sterilizations in the year 2016. . . . [W]e became closer to the sisters, like those from Cuzco and Ayacucho [in the rural highlands or the *sierra*] and we started becoming concerned about other sisters in other regions . . . and we started doing workshops with the support of IWGIA [The International Work Group for Indigenous Affairs] . . . a documentary was made named *The Road to Justice*.)[87]

Ketty described how coercive sterilizations were one of the many terrible practices that had been orchestrated by the state for decades to exterminate Indigenous peoples. But Indigenous people had held on and survived these crimes:

> Sentimos que, desde el estado, nos quieren exterminar en diferentes maneras . . . [L]as esterilizaciones forzadas también entran allí, como una muestra de que nos han querido desaparecer para que las hermanas ya no

pudieran tener decendencias como ha sucedido en comunidades nativas y campesinas. Decimos que el estado está ausente pero no está ausente, está presente, pero para exterminarnos. (We feel that from the state, they have tried to exterminate us in different ways. . . . [F]orced sterilizations also are there, as an example of how they have tried to disappear us, so that the sisters can no longer have descendants as it occurred in native and *campesino* communities. We say that the state is absent, but it is not absent, it is present for the purpose of exterminating us.)[88]

With the inclusion of ONAMIAP and its global partner IWGIA, the coercive sterilization movement gained more momentum. Ketty explained that much of the work of ONAMIAP evolved around support for the *hermanas*. ONAMIAP is unique in the sense that it is an Indigenous rights organization led by Indigenous leaders who understand Indigenous cultural practices and ways of their *ayllus*—a community or collective established by geography, bloodline, or shared objectives. The Indigenous connections of ONAMIAP were evident in the types of practices of support they offered to the women and in their approach to engaging with them, which included providing them with space and support for their healing journeys. As Ketty noted:

> Hemos estado acompañando a las hermanas, a veces lejano, a veces cercano . . . [H]emos estado sumándonos a los pronunciamientos, audiencias. . . . También hicimos talleres de cómo hacer el registro. . . . Trabajamos con círculos de sanación. Para sanar una herida [*las mujeres*] tienen que recordar. Y el momento que todas recordaban, lloraban por lo que habían pasado, y sanar todo eso era muy doloroso para uno. (We have been accompanying the sisters, at times from afar, at times from a close distance. . . . [W]e have been coming together for the declarations, hearings. . . . [A]lso we did workshops on how to register (i.e., victim's registry). . . . We worked in circles of healing. To heal a wound [the women] need to remember their past. In the moment when they remember, they cry for the things that took place, and to heal all that was painful for them.)[89]

Along with the efforts by ONAMIAP, the coercive sterilization activist movement also gained support from an unexpected entity, the Peruvian Congress. When elected to Congress in 2020, Rocío Silva

Santisteban knew this was the opportune time to channel her ally-ship into policy change. Since her meeting with Hilaria Supa (and the victims who accompanied her) and her continued engagement with Victoria Vigo, Rocío had become more interested in the coercive sterilizations. In Congress, she joined the Committee on Women but soon found that, even within this committee, no one wanted to deal with the case of forced sterilizations. According to Rocío, it was a subject that was "estigmatizado en el Fujimorismo" (stigmatized in Fujimorism).[90] Because there were too many proponents of former President Fujimori in Congress, no one wanted to work on this issue. However, despite these obstacles, Rocío wanted to modify the existing Law on Comprehensive Reparations to include victims of coercive sterilization. The Law on Comprehensive Reparations, instituted in 2005, focused on outlining an integral individual and collective reparations plan for victims of the internal armed conflict period of Peru (1980–2000). The law specified the beneficiaries of reparations, categorized victims as those who suffered "direct" abuses (e.g., victims of sexual violence; individuals who were abducted; and those gravely wounded by members of the armed forces, police, and others) and "indirect" abuses (e.g., children born out of rape), and identified the collective beneficiaries of reparations (e.g., *campesino* communities).[91] Rocío's proposed amendments to this law were to Article 3, which defined who constituted a victim, and Article 6, which described the individual beneficiaries of the reparations program. With the amendment, the words "violencia sexual en sus diversas formas" (sexual violence of diverse forms) would be added to Articles 3 and 6.[92] This change expanded the definition of victims of sexual violence and broadened the category of the beneficiaries of reparations to include individuals who were coercively sterilized.

The amendment proposal made the congressional agenda, but it kept getting tabled. Rocío, however, did not give up. She felt compelled to do something for the women who had been impacted. Fortunately, an opportunity arose to change things. When Mirtha Vásquez became the head of Congress—by request of President Francisco Sagasti

(2020–2021), whom Congress elected after the impeachment of President Martín Vizcarra (2018–2020) and the resignation of President Manuel Merino (2020–2020)—Rocío knew she finally had an ally. Rocío knew Mirtha personally, as Mirtha had also been involved in the human rights community as a lawyer for APRODEH and part of the executive council for the CNDDHH. Rocío thus asked Mirtha to put the amendments to the Law on Comprehensive Reparations on the agenda, but due to the politics of Congress and the stigmatization of coercive sterilizations as an anti-Fujimori matter, there was never a suitable time for the amendment to be debated. And then Congress went into recess. Recalling this moment, Rocío stopped talking, paused, and then smiled. She remarked that during the recess, Mirtha put forward the agenda for the amendment. With Congress in recess, there would neither be time for debate nor fierce opposition to the agenda. Since the Permanent Committee still works during the recess period, the committee simply approved the amendment without necessarily considering what they were doing. The strategy of waiting until Congress went into recess, having the allyship of Mirtha, and continuing to wait for the right moment to introduce the agenda had finally paid off. Rocío chuckled as she reflected upon that moment and said that the Permanent Committee of Congress did not know what they were doing.[93]

Unfortunately, to Rocío's dismay, nothing changed even with the modifications to the law. This was largely because the Ministry of Justice and Human Rights blocked access of victim-survivors of coercive sterilizations to any form of reparations related to the Law on Comprehensive Reparations. In response, activists and nongovernmental organizations based in Lima and other parts of the country (Asociación de Mujeres Víctimas de Esterilización Forzada de Chumbivilcas, Movimiento Amplio de Mujeres Línea Fundacional, Derechos Humanos Sin Fronteras, SISAY, Asociación SER, and DEMUS) petitioned for a writ of amparo for the ministry to recognize victims' rights to reparations. Activists called for changes and even got a judge to recognize the constitutional rights of victim-survivors of coercive sterilizations to integral reparations.[94] However, as of this writing, no reparations have been distributed. Instead, a revision to Law 27692, nicknamed Law Anti-NGO, entered into force in April 2025.[95] The law now expands government oversight of nongovernmental organization activities, and most importantly considers the use of resources to support and assist administrative or judicial actions against the government of Peru "gross misconduct" or a "serious offense." With this law, the state made clear its position of nonengagement and not recognizing its crimes against vulnerable populations, including victim-survivors of coercive sterilizations.

OF ACTIVISTS AND ALLIES

The trajectory of each of the five activists discussed in this chapter was unique and different. One was a Lima-based university student majoring in art who learned about the case of coercive sterilizations through the radio. Another was a recent law school graduate from Lima who was starting her internship in the nongovernmental organizational world. In contrast, one activist, also from Lima, had already been working in nongovernmental organizations and was involved in the human rights community. Yet another hailed from the rural areas of the Southern Andes and was a community leader. And finally, the last individual was a member of an Indigenous rights nongovernmental organization that joined forces later. Among these five activists, three were based in Lima, one resided and worked in the Southern Andean region, and one was transient and based at times in Lima and at others in diverse Andean and Amazonian regions of Peru. The three based in Lima shared Spanish as their mother tongue and did not speak Indigenous languages fluently. The other two, including the one residing in the Southern Andean region and the transient one, both spoke Quechua as their mother tongue, identified as Indigenous, and were also fluent in Spanish.

The identity of being a Spanish-speaking person and residing in the metropolitan area of Lima prevented the three activists from having direct exposure to cases of coercive sterilization. As Rocío Silva San-tisteban noted, sterilizations were not imposed in high-class neigh-borhoods of Lima.[96] Additionally, as evident in Victoria Vigo's story, forced sterilizations were relatively uncommon in metropolitan urban cities such as Piura.[97] Consequently, the PSRPF continued for so many years because people simply did not know about coercive sterilization and the extent to which the campaign was enforced in rural Indige-nous communities of Peru. Comparatively, the one activist who was an Indigenous leader and identified as an Indigenous person witnessed firsthand what was happening on the ground and immediately took notice of the human rights violations that accompanied the family planning program. This was in part because they had such direct access to the affected population. It was also likely why they attempted to shed light on this case at the onset of the implementation of the PSRPF.

What becomes evident in the trajectories of these five activists and their collective movement is how the positioning of each ally—particularly their residence in either the metropolitan or rural areas and their ethnic identity of being non-Indigenous or Indigenous—conditioned their access to resources that could help them better address the human rights violations. These conditions reflect the dis-cussion in chapter 1 about colonialism: Lima remains the center of power, where all resources are present, while the rural regions of *sierra* and *selva* remain powerless due to the continuation of postcolonial power divisions and the exclusion of Indigenous peoples. Associated with these spatial configurations are "exclusions based on rurality, lan-guage, and ethnicity," which negatively impact Indigenous peoples.[98]

Hilaria Supa Huamán understood these dynamics. For any change to occur in the region where she resided and where women were being targeted for sterilization, she knew she had to travel to Lima to appeal the case. However, Hilaria Supa did not find an ally in Lima or among those who worked on human rights matters, such as the CNDDHH. Her voice was acknowledged only after she gained political power and was elected to a government position, resulting in this case receiving greater attention. Ketty López Marcelo also spoke of similar dynamics involving Lima, although in her case, ONAMIAP is an Indigenous rights organization based in Lima.[99] Indeed, she acknowledged the privilege of having access to diverse international organizations willing to work on various Indigenous rights matters, such as IWGIA. However, she also explained how ONAMIAP as an organization was stretched thin, covering diverse issues impacting Indigenous peoples, such as *violencia extractivista* (extractive violence) that targeted Indigenous peoples' lands, among other things. Thus, the organization could not fully dedicate itself to victims of coercive sterilizations.

The three other activists had an easier time than Hilaria Supa in organizing a movement to address this situation, despite some of the challenges they too faced in government (i.e., changing an existing reparation law) or against government officials (i.e., filing a lawsuit against former government officials on behalf of victim-survivors). The three activists' positions were unique because they understood their privileges in navigating a postcolonial patriarchal society.[100] They strategically used their positions as Lima-based individuals of mixed European-Indigenous descent with a university education to navigate the system and bring attention to coercive sterilization. Moreover, they also used their connections with nongovernmental organizations to quickly mobilize and organize to defend the affected women. Specifically, they used their overseas contacts (via international nongovernmental organizations) to mobilize a transnational advocacy network. Therefore, when the time came, the three women could form an effective and well-organized allyship with the Indigenous leader, Hilaria Supa Huamán, in seeking justice. Ketty López Marcelo's organization ONAMIAP soon followed, joining forces with Hilaria and the three other activists.

Despite the varying trajectories of their lives, all five activists shared one common experience crucial to the growth of their allyship in this human rights movement: exposure to victim-survivors. For the women based in Lima, the contact with women who were affected by forced sterilizations began with hearing their stories on the radio and reading about them in published reports and developed to later working with them in the field, meeting with them to listen to their testimonies, and strategizing as well as developing human rights campaigns against impunity together. For the women based in the Southern Andes or engaged throughout Andean and Amazonian Indigenous communities' regions, the contact was more direct. At times it involved the activist accompanying the affected women to Lima to amplify their stories, defend their positions, and remind them of their rights, while in other instances, it involved the activist informing the women about resources to access reparations. Each activist played a role in shaping what is now more of a collective movement of activists and allies who have all been demanding justice for the victim-survivors.

Activism—in both individual and collective forms—effectively brought the coercive sterilization case into the political spotlight. And yet much work remains to be done. In my conversations with activists, they seem torn. They are hopeful about possible progress toward recognizing victim-survivors, yet they remain pessimistic about the future of the affected population. As Rocío Silva Santisteban stated, the main obstacle lies in the willful ignorance and rejection by the state about this case. Without any form of cooperation from the state, it is difficult to seek justice. Justice has been *lentísimo* (very slow) in coming.

LENTÍSIMO, LA JUSTICIA (VERY SLOW, THE JUSTICE)

Throughout Peru, there are numerous advocacy campaigns regarding coercive sterilization, which often involve people chanting the following: "Qué queremos? Justicia, justicia, justicia!" (What do we want? Justice, justice, justice). Similar words are also present in many testimonies of women who were affected by coercive sterilization and archived in the digital memory platform of the Quipu Project.[101] In chapters 3 and 4 I explored the conceptions of justice of two victim-survivors of forced sterilizations. What about the allies and activists working with the affected women? What justice do activists and allies envision as the ideal outcome that would serve the affected victim-survivors, *señoras*, *mujeres*, or *hermanas*?

My interviews reveal that justice is envisioned in different forms by each activist and ally. Rocío Silva Santisteban said:

> Es difícil bueno . . . la justicia es que los responsables sean procesados en manera con un proceso justo, digamos también, eh también y que haya una sanción. (It is difficult to say . . . well, justice is that those responsible are processed in a way that is just, let's say also, that, um, there is some form of sanction.)[102]

Rocío explained that this was the justice she sought for the women. As she noted, this case was complicated and challenging because there were so many victims: At present, there are over three thousand victims whose cases are being investigated by the Public Prosecutor's Office. These are the victims with serious bodily injury and include those who have died as a result of bodily injury. As Rocío remarked, this number of victims has never been dealt with, and most of their testimonies would need to be translated from Indigenous languages to Spanish. Additionally, there is the issue that the Peruvian justice system is "lento, lentísimo . . . exasperante lento" (slow, super slow . . . exasperatingly slow). The slow pace of the justice system, combined with the unwillingness of governments to listen to and believe these women, has made it nearly impossible to have a positive vision of the future. Rocío said, "Yo creo que si se pudiera desde el ámbito del gobierno la posibilidad de reparaciones, a través del Ministerio de Justicia, sería bien" (I think if it is possible from the side of the government to provide reparations, via the Ministry of Justice, that would be good), but this may be a hope far out of reach.[103]

The justice that Rocío refers to takes two forms. One is a legal form that necessitates criminal accountability and some rendering of retributive justice or punishment. The second is more reparative. This justice relies on the willingness of the Ministry of Justice and Human Rights to respect and uphold the legislative changes to the Law on

Comprehensive Reparations and to distribute reparations to the affected women. Although the legislative changes had already been made, the ministry has maintained a unified stance of not allowing victim-survivors of coercive sterilizations access to any reparations outlined in the Comprehensive Reparations Plan.[104] In that sense, Rocío's reparative justice is predicated on changes in the ministry's positioning that would bring about justice—perhaps through the influence of continued mobilization of advocacy networks domestically and internationally—by pressuring policymakers in Peru.

María Ysabel Cedano's vision of justice extends beyond reparations to include future measures of nonrepetition. She explained that she wants "una justicia que garantiza reparaciones y no repetición . . . una justicia que no discrimina y revictimize . . . una justicia de genero . . . intercultural y arcoíris" (a justice that guarantees reparations and non-repetition . . . a justice that does not discriminate and revictimize . . . a justice of gender . . . intercultural and of a rainbow [inclusive]).[105] María Ysabel was referring to a form of reparative justice that has layers. These layers include a guarantee of nonrepetition, which aligns with the UN's Basic Principles and Guidelines on the Right to a Remedy and Reparation for Victims of Gross Violations of International Human Rights Law and Serious Violations of International Humanitarian Law. This nonrepetition includes a preventative aspect against future atrocities. Naomi Roht-Arriaza explains that this preventative approach involves a transformative agenda, which would consist of making structural changes within government, tackling root causes of atrocities, and broadening institutional reform to address social and cultural concerns.[106] These would take the form of changes to the codes of conduct and ethical standards by public servants and medical personnel associated with the government.[107] In the context of coercive sterilization, the nonrepetition aspect would require reeducation and respect for a code of conduct that recognizes imposed sterilization against a specific group of people as a violation of human rights.

Other layers of justice envisioned by María Ysabel include an intercultural form of reparation, specifically respect for diverse cultures through collective reparations for communities rather than individuals, and justice focused on gender, specifically future policy changes that reflect diversity, inclusivity, and equity. Similar ideas were manifested in Hilaria Supa Huamán's conception of justice. For example, Hilaria Supa noted how justice would first include the state's recognition of its crimes *al nivel mundial* (globally). This need for recognition reflected the same vision of justice that the victim-survivor Victoria Vigo had espoused, which was a form of symbolic reparations and a public apology from the state recognizing its crimes. However, Hilaria Supa's vision for recognition went a step further, as she wanted a "global" recognition of the crimes committed against the women. Additionally, Hilaria Supa stated that she wanted justice that condemned all those responsible for the crimes in a way that serves the women who are no longer able to work or function because of forced sterilization. This vision consisted of a legal criminal accountability aspect and financial reparations to support the livelihood of the affected women. Finally, Hilaria Supa also emphasized the opportunity for education for Indigenous peoples, remarking that Indigenous peoples were not given the "oportunidad de educarse de qué significa tener más de tantos hijos etc." (opportunity to be educated as to what it means to have many children).[108] She wanted Indigenous women to have access to reproductive health education so that they could make their own decisions about their bodies. Notably, this justice also falls within the confines of symbolic reparations, which include education.

In contrast, Ketty López explained a type of justice that is more grounded, one that is *hermanas*-centric. She explained that in reality, "ningún dinero del mundo podrá reparar los daños ocasionados en los cuerpos de las hermanas y más allá de los cuerpos la autoestima, todo los impactos" (no amount of money in the world can repair the damages inflicted upon the bodies of the sisters and more than the body, even the self-esteem, all the impacts).[109] As she explained, the statement that we often hear about how we will fight until we reach justice is not achievable because the damages to the women's bodies are irreparable. What is possible according to Ketty is to decenter the discussion from money. In other words, to move beyond a discussion of assigning a monetary value to the physical and mental damage these women suffered. Instead, she proposed that we think of justice as being associated with "el acompañamiento psicológico" (a psychological treatment) that does not involve "acompañamiento psicológico de una psicóloga también con pensamiento occidental que no entiende a las hermanas" (a psychological treatment from a psychiatrist also with a Western perspective who does not understand the sisters). Instead, it has to be a form of psychological care among Indigenous women, who understand one another. Additionally, López described that the *hermanas* often want a reparation involving health and healing, which can be as simple as having the means to engage in continued conversations about the women's experiences among themselves and among those who understand them. Also, the *hermanas* want reparation for their *almas* (souls), educational support for their children, and grandchildren. In other words, reparation that is not only individual but also collective, one that seeks to better one's health and the community. Ketty noted that there is a different approach to justice from nongovernmental organizations that do not reflect Indigenous roots or ideas. Interestingly, in the justice that she described, Ketty spoke from the "us" perspective, as an Indigenous woman feeling the same amount of pain as her *hermanas*. While Hilaria Supa is also of Indigenous background, it is curious to see the slight differences between the two women's approaches to justice: While Hilaria's reflects some visions of legal justice in addition to reparations that involve education for the women directly, Ketty's is much more geared toward a reparative lens involving even future generations.

If the justice that Rocío, María Ysabel, Hilaria Supa, and Ketty López envisioned takes the form of criminal accountability and various types of reparations (i.e., symbolic, financial, medical, and one that involves a conceptualization of Indigenous ways), the justice that Alejandra envisioned is from the *cancha artística* (artistic ground). Art is central to Alejandra's conception of justice. Alejandra discussed how, in the absence of legal justice or criminal accountability, it was important to have "social justice." She said:

> Yo sí sentía que las mujeres tenían una desolación muy fuerte, cuando encima de todo lo que les paso sus propios hijos le daban la espalda.... [S]us maridos las abandonaban, sus padres les recriminaban[,] ... la sociedad las estigmatizaba y encima las negacionistas fujimoristas les decían que eran mentirosas, que era un mito y las revictimizaban, y luego encima el sistema de ... justicia.... [T]uvieron varios fiscales que las maltrataron y las revictimizaron horrible y las amenazaron. (I felt that the women were feeling a sense of strong desolation, when on top of everything that had occurred to them, their own children turned their backs on them.... [T]heir partners left them, their parents recriminated them[,] ...society stigmatized them, and on top of that the negationist Fujimori supporters called them liars, that it was all a myth and revictimized them, and later even the justice ... system.... [T]hey had many prosecutors who mistreated them and revictimized them horribly and threatened them.)[110]

Alejandra explained that social justice was a form of reparations within transitional justice, in which particularly "arte y el activismo tienen un espacio singular" (art and activism had a unique space). Alejandra Ballón Gutiérrez found a space to use art in human rights advocacy, focusing on coercive sterilization survivors and victims. This type of work is referred to as "artivism," a hybrid term that refers to work that mixes art and human rights advocacy. An "artivist" who engages in artivism uses "her artistic talents to fight and struggle against injustice and oppression."[111] From the broader literature on transitional justice, artivism would fall under the category of symbolic reparations. These types of reparations may either be tangible or involve "performative or ephemeral gestures of recognition and atonement," such as "rituals or performances."[112]

Alejandra started the work of *Alfombra Roja* because it was a way of representing "social justice" from the ground up. Faced with a society

Figure 2. *Alfombra Roja* (Red Carpet) art performance for forced sterilizations in Ayacucho involving local Indigenous women, 2015. Photo credit: Alejandra Ballón.

that chastised the affected women, legal obstacles that revictimized the women, and political pushback from Fujimori and his supporters, Alejandra found solace in artivism, and demonstrated her solidarity with the women. Alejandra chose to accompany the women, put herself in their shoes, and "visibilize their voices and amplify their voices" through her artistic performance in the *Alfombra Roja*.[113] This performance was centered on creating "solidarity" and "sorority" among the affected women, activists, and individual people from all walks of life who wanted to participate and form collective advocacy. Underlying this movement was a common understanding among the women—from the nonaffected to the affected—that "yo te creo" ("I believe you").[114] In other words, it was a movement grounded in empathy and solidarity.

For Alejandra, this movement became even more symbolic and powerful when the affected women from the rural highland areas (i.e., *sierra*) joined. These were the women with whom Alejandra had previously established contact in Ayacucho, listening to their stories and building rapport with them for a long time. At the time, the women from Ayacucho in South-Central Peru had not been well represented in the public sphere, as the conversations were dominated by women from Piura and Cuzco regions. Victoria Vigo was one such vocal activist and victim-survivor from Piura, while victim-survivors from Cuzco were supported by high-profile Indigenous leaders such as Hilaria Supa Huamán. DEMUS had invited the women from Ayacucho to travel to Lima to attend a Tribunal of Conscience for Justice for the Women Victims of Forced Sterilization and Sexual Violence During the Internal Armed Conflict on November 8, 2013. The tribunal was the result of a civil society–driven initiative. Seven domestic nongovernmental organizations (DEMUS, and others) coorganized the event, with the help of five international partners (Open Society Institute and others), who shared the goal of "making visible the human rights violations against Peruvian women, particularly involving sexual and reproductive rights."[115] It was at this tribunal that Alejandra proposed to perform *Alfombra Roja*, with open participation by anyone who wanted to be part of the performance. The ladies from Ayacucho decided to join the performance, which required wearing red-colored clothing, lying down on the ground as a way of "acting out death," and communicating using emotion-filled messages about the sterilizations or *arengas* (harangues/spiels).

The year 2013 was the first time that the affected women participated directly in the performance of *Alfombra Roja*. For Alejandra, it was a moment that showed the willingness of these affected women to connect with other women activists who formed a part of the artistic rendition of advocacy in support of victim-survivors of coercive sterilizations. It was, in essence, artivism that went beyond the performative sphere by connecting with the affected population and, as Alejandra explained, providing them with a form of "social justice." This was also a pivotal moment that marked the emergence of a national movement on coercive sterilization led by major civil society–based justice efforts.

WHICH JUSTICE IS THE RIGHT JUSTICE?

So, is there a "right" justice? Is a justice that is state driven or involving the state the right justice? Is a justice that only involves impacted communities, such as those of Indigenous descent (i.e., Indigenous communities), the justice that serves everyone? Or is justice a more complex concept that can be many things and that reflects diverse viewpoints and approaches?

This chapter, along with the previous chapters, has illustrated the various types of justice each group of actors has sought. First, the victim-survivors focused on reparative and restorative justice. In particular, the Indigenous victim-survivor Sarita emphasized collective reparations for the *ayllu* (community) that would help mend the severed ties between an individual affected by coercive sterilization—such as herself—and her community. Furthermore, Sarita and Victoria both voiced the need for justice that would repair the damage they suffered physically and mentally and restore their inner bodies. This would include medical reparations (related to Western medicinal practices) and some form of reparative and restorative approach—ideally involving Indigenous conceptions of bodily care—that would address the *soul loss*. Additionally, both victim-survivors asked for public recognition of the human rights violations by the state and society that they suffered. Second, activists and allies pushed for retributive and reparative justice. State accountability for the crimes committed was regarded as a necessary step that could not be omitted in the search for justice. Relatedly, reparative justice also appealed to the activists and allies, but at times this justice did not involve the state. Instead, it was centered on Indigenous peoples and communities and on their roles in helping to heal one another. At other times, this justice did involve the state providing financial reparations to support Indigenous medical healing practices as well as memory activities that brought conversations about coercive sterilizations to the forefront of contemporary societal and media discourse. Finally, despite the variations in types of justice sought by the actors, all sides agreed that advocacy movements had to continue domestically and internationally to pressure the state and society to deliver on the promises of justice. For instance, the state had to deliver on the promise of guaranteeing victim-survivors of coercive sterilizations access to integral reparations, which were mandated by law through the legislative amendments pursued in 2021.

This point about diverse approaches to justice and the meaning of justice does not omit a relative ordering component. As I discussed in chapters 2, 3, and 4—and as I have indicated elsewhere in this book—the justice each actor has pursued must be understood in terms of prioritization. In other words, actors are not seeking an exclusive or absolute form of a single type of justice. Rather, the main difference among actors has been in the prioritization of various forms of justice. Answers to the following questions reflect each actor's interests and objectives: Which type of justice should come first? What should the ordering of these types of justice be? In this pursuit of diverse forms of justice, however, there is no conflict among actors, as each form of justice complements the others. It is true that ordering still matters, and—above all else—the justice demanded by victim-survivors needs to be the focus of this fight against the denial of recognition and impunity for victim-survivors of coercive sterilizations. However, the larger point is that the justice sought by victim-survivors, activists, and allies has been built upon the same premise of rendering some recognition—including a retributive, reparative, and restorative component—to victim-survivors. Indeed, without this aspect of recognition or acknowledgment of the existence of the crime and the victimhood emerging from this atrocity, there is no future for *justicia*.

As the chants of "¡justicia, justicia, justicia!" over the years have shown, the movement in defense of the rights of victim-survivors of coercive sterilizations has remained steadfast in its advocacy campaigns. Within this movement, victim-survivors have emerged as active leaders, adding strength to their claims with their shared stories and experiences. They have capitalized on opportunities, such as the Peruvian presidential election periods, to make themselves more visible, promulgate their agendas, and prevent the state from silencing their exposure of human rights violations. The rights rhetoric—reproductive, women's, and Indigenous peoples' rights—plays a key role in victim-survivors' political activism. Although these groups continue to be discriminated against on the basis of ethnicity, gender, and class, they have now acquired political agency—whether as disrupters or "terrorists" (the label pushed on them by far-right Fujimori supporters)—and they can use their newfound role to resist those who attempt to silence their stories.[116]

Conclusion

Justice, Reproductive Rights, and What Remains

¡Justicia!

On January 30 and 31, 2023, non-Peruvian news media outlets published stories titled "Victims of Forced Sterilizations in Peru Continue fighting for Justice" and "Peru's Forced Sterilization Tragedy Drags on in the Courts."[1] A similar news story followed in Peruvian newspaper *La República* on April 5, 2023, titled "Thirty-One Years Since the Auto-coup of Fujimori, Victims of Forced Sterilization Continue to Push for Justice."[2] In all three stories—published in Spanish and English—in 2023, there was a common theme: the absence of justice for victim-survivors of coercive sterilizations. In that fight for justice, victim-survivors, activists, and allies have remained dedicated to ensuring that the state or society does not forget the case of coercive sterilization. That is, even with the death of Alberto Fujimori on September 11, 2024, during whose administration the PSRPF was implemented, and the questions from Fujimori sympathizers about turning the page of the past and moving on from the forced sterilization cases, victim-survivors and allies continued demanding justice.

Eventually this activism of victim-survivors, activists, and allies provided the impetus for two historic moments. One, the case of *Celia Ramos v. Peru*, was the first case to be brought before the Inter-American Court of Human Rights to address Peru's forced sterilization policy. The second was the decision issued by the United Nations Committee on the Elimination of Discrimination Against Women on October 30, 2024. The decision, reached after the committee reviewed a joint complaint filed by five victims who were forcibly sterilized as a result of the PSRPF, found that "victims were sterilized by non-specialized medical staff and in inadequate sanitary conditions." Moreover, the committee concluded that forced sterilization constituted "sex-based violence against women," and that "the sterilization program was intersectional discrimination, disproportionately targeting Indigenous, economically disadvantaged and rural women."[3] Peru has been a party to CEDAW since 1982. Pursuant to CEDAW norms, the Peruvian government had six months to inform the committee of the changes adopted to address its decision. This was a historic ruling about Peru's forced sterilization cases, the first from the CEDAW committee, which was celebrated by victim-survivors and allies.

It is against this backdrop of nearly three decades of victim-survivors and allies' activism and the counterresponse of an absent and denialist state that I have written this book. Engaging with the women over the course of five years, I have admired their struggles and *luchas* (fights) in advocating for justice. In some cases, I formed friendships that transcended space, time, and circumstances. We laughed together at joyous moments, celebrated the wins toward justice, and in other instances cried and mourned the difficult road toward justice that confronted the coercive sterilization case. Through these moments, I have built a deep level of trust, respect, and admiration for these women, and these experiences shaped my views about how to best deliver their stories in writing, which this book represents.

This book has provided a space for victim-survivors, activists, and allies to discuss their experiences confronting coercive sterilizations. The book's premise is that the actors need to speak for themselves and I, as the author, am here to communicate, channel, and transmit their voices. To do so in a context-specific and conscientious way, I have used the Indigenous methodology of storytelling to share the stories of Indigenous and non-Indigenous victim-survivors, activists, and allies. Storytelling as a method has been useful, given its nonhierarchical approach to transmitting knowledge, experiences, and stories. Additionally, my positionality as a person who understands the Indigenous landscape in Peru and the involvement of Indigenous Quechua scholars in the book have helped create an accurate presentation and portrayal of each individual's story.

Notwithstanding the important justice component of victim-survivors and ally-related advocacy movements against impunity for coercive sterilizations, this book has also emphasized the identity of the affected population. Identity matters for this victim-survivor group because their identity is what caused them to be targeted by the genocidal policy in the first place. Preexisting elements of ethnic, socioeconomic, and gender-based discrimination made Indigenous communities and Indigenous women more vulnerable to human rights violations—in this case, reproductive rights violations. These preexisting identity categories had deep connections with colonialism and its societal structures, which included gender-discriminatory practices that also led to violence against women—particularly those not directly associated with sociopolitical circles of power or places of power (i.e., Lima), which was the case for Victoria Vigo. The discriminatory and gendered family planning program thus directed its resources to women's and girls' tubal ligation—primarily in areas of economic hardship with higher levels of Indigenous populations—and produced a genocidal outcome for Indigenous communities.

SCHOLARLY AND POLICY IMPLICATIONS

For scholars, viewing this case as a genocide alone has significant analytic implications. Most basically, scholars should take a critical view of how the norms of the UN Genocide Convention can be used to analyze the Peruvian case and identify the genocidal intent (*mens rea*) and genocidal act (*actus reus*). If a similar normative argument holds for other genocides committed against Indigenous women (or other women of subaltern status in society) elsewhere, scholars should treat them as such. Adopting this approach highlights the need to differentiate the type of human rights violations targeting specific types of women, recognize the ethnic element of these atrocities, and determine how best to use the tools of genocidal framing to aid the victim-survivors in their efforts to seek justice. A genocidal frame does not neglect other rights violations. Instead, it pushes the coercive sterilization of a majority of Indigenous women to be considered one of the gravest and greatest crimes against humanity. This is a political move and part of the broader advocacy strategy that gives more weight and visibility to this case and advocacy support for victim-survivors.

Along with this analytic implication, the book's empirical chapters have sought to underline another point: the importance of understanding human rights violations and justice from actor-centric views rather than relying on politicized information reported in media outlets or from a third-person point of view. This book's chapters have sought to examine how victim-survivors from various ethnic and class backgrounds and activists and allies from diverse positions in society experienced the PSRPF and forced sterilization campaigns. This actor-centric perspective brought into focus not only the ways in which victim-survivors and allies engage with justice—both in terms of what they believe constitutes justice and what justice needs to be pursued—but also how they have struggled in achieving their objectives. The positionality of each actor, including their ethnic, class, and gendered background and their geographic location in rural or metropolitan areas—which, within Peruvian society, has direct associations with political power—influenced their trajectory.[4] The positionality and its influences on each actor's experiences deserve more attention from scholars, as it reveals the relevance of colonialism; its structural relations with gender, ethnicity, and class; and how it plays a part in dictating actors' experiences. As noted in chapters 1, 2, and 5, when colonialist visions of society interact with economic and population control, they translate into policies (e.g., the PSRPF) that oppress populations already disadvantaged in society. It is my understanding that more scholarly research is needed to explore ways to prevent the reproduction of this victimhood (primarily of Indigenous peoples) in postcolonial states. An approach that addresses past abuses and also engages in atrocity prevention is needed for cases involving Indigenous populations, particularly Indigenous women in coercive sterilization cases.

For scholars who seek to provide both sides of the story involving conflicts and human rights violations, it is important to give space to and let those on the other side speak. We need more studies of those who were involved in carrying out the PSRPF policies on the ground, the health professionals. This book did not focus on this group of people. Nevertheless, neglecting their stories of involvement, including why some resisted or agreed to carry out the tubal ligations, does a disservice to scholarship by giving a partial view of what took place. It is my hope that scholars can build on this book and explore the stories of health professionals and analyze the changes in their perspectives from the PSRPF days to the present.

In addition to these scholarly implications, this book's findings cast light on other aspects of justice that victim-survivors, allies, and activists have not overtly discussed, and thus they may also contribute to the search for justice. Despite its limited applicability, the Peruvian state has instituted a legislative change to the Law on Comprehensive Reparations. Furthermore, despite the slowness of investigations, there is an active and open case in Peru's judicial system on the coercive sterilization of victim-survivors. In situating these policies, one can argue that reparations—primarily medical and financial—along with criminal accountability are in place. What may be equally important to consider for activists, policymakers, and victim-survivors would be to engage in truth-seeking work. An official body to "investigate, document, report upon human rights abuses within a country over a specific period of time" in the form of a truth commission may be exactly what is needed to complement the work of legal justice.[5] This truth commission will not take a traditional form, as truth commissions have generally been quite widespread due to the breadth and scope of the types of crimes, years of human rights abuses, and additional role of advancing reconciliation and reforming policies to thwart future abuses.[6] Instead, this truth commission can follow South Korea's truth commission work, where individual truth commissions were established to address specific human rights atrocities. This is known as a case-specific truth commission.[7] For instance, the Jeju April 3 Commission was established to seek the truth about mass human rights violations that occurred in Jeju Province, South Korea, between 1947 and 1954.[8] The Jeju Commission produced a final report that included a set of recommendations for the state, specifically on the Jeju case and not linked to other human rights violations. The recommendations included diverse reparations policies, such as memory initiatives. In the case of the Jeju Commission, the memory initiatives—which are most often labeled and included within the broader realm of symbolic reparations—resulted in the creation of parks, spaces of memory, commemorative dates, and even history rectification initiatives for school textbooks.

A similar case-specific truth commission can work for Peru. As most truth-seeking work involves investigation, submission of a report, and a list of recommendations issued for state follow-up procedures, it may be complementary to criminal accountability efforts on coercive sterilizations. At the very least, this truth commission can provide an interpretation of the underlying causes of coercive sterilizations and give recognition to victim-survivors. This was something that the previous TRC of Peru also focused on in addition to the moral restoration of citizens on the basis of "conocimiento, reconocimiento, arrepentimiento y perdón" (understanding, recognition, repentance, and pardon).[9] Particularly for victim-survivors of coercive sterilization, the establishment of a truth commission alone may serve as the basis for further pressuring the state to comply with amendments to the reparations law. Of course there will be some difficulties in getting the state to agree to this policy initiative. Nonetheless, a truth-seeking approach that facilitates restoration, reparations, and retributive justice—forms of justice emphasized by victim-survivors and allies—may be the best policy for victim-survivors and allies to pursue. This type of approach can help ensure that the coercive sterilization case remains in the political spotlight.

THE WORK AHEAD

In some ways, this book is a guide to understanding the status of Indigenous peoples and women in Peru. It offers a crude insight into how Indigenous peoples, women, and their bodies have been "trashed" and how a modern-day genocide has taken place in Peru. Although context-specific Peruvian elements prevent this case from being generalizable to all Indigenous peoples' and women's experiences, this case unfortunately resembles similar practices in many states with colonialist experiences and Indigenous populations. If the book has succeeded, Indigenous persons, Indigenous activists, women's rights advocates, and human rights defenders (i.e., allies) will find it valuable in identifying sexual violence amounting to crimes against humanity that impacts women and genocidal state policies associated with family planning and reproductive health, developing more effective ways of preventing future genocides, and devising policies to address genocides and gender-based violence.

Some might question whether the prevention of future genocides or atrocities against Indigenous peoples and gender-based violence is even possible in a state such as Peru, where colonial logic and colonial visions of ethnicity, gender, and class remain dominant and dictate policies and societal dynamics. Changes to policy and state governance in Peru to uphold Indigenous women and women from economically underrepresented backgrounds seem—at least on the surface—not possible. Even with a registry of victims of coercive sterilizations (i.e.,

REVIESFO) and legislative changes (i.e., the Law on Comprehensive Reparations), the state has failed to deliver on its promises of reparations. In fact, it has restricted the work of victim-survivors representing nongovernmental organizations with the enactment of the Anti-NGO Law. Moreover, Peru's judicial institutions have offered no means to end any dispute related to the coercive sterilization cases. Even the coercive sterilizations cases that are being investigated by the Public Prosecutor's Office (as of this writing) have not seen much progress and have offered no resolutions. Perhaps this is not too surprising, given that gender-based violence against Indigenous women continues to be reported, with no accountability measures at hand (e.g., sexual violence against Awajún Indigenous children reported from 2010 to 2024), and the Peruvian government is more focused on victim blaming to push aside these cases. To this extent, the critics may be right that *justicia*—in every form—for victim-survivors is difficult to find, particularly in a society like Peru's.

Relatedly, victim-survivors and allies have viewed legislative changes and promises from the state with suspicion. However, they have not let this situation deter their efforts in seeking *justicia*. Refusing to accept the status quo and challenging the existing stratifications based on identity are ways to make changes. In collaboration with activists, victim-survivors have raised concerns about a continuing pattern of neglect by the government in addressing the coercive sterilizations and have challenged this state behavior on the streets and in the election booths. To strengthen their rallying cries for rights, they have also taken these rights concerns about coercive sterilization to intergovernmental organizations: the Inter-American Commission on Human Rights, the Inter-American Court of Human Rights, and the United Nations' Committee on the Elimination of Discrimination Against Women. In Peru, rights claims are resolved more swiftly after the involvement of transnational advocacy networks (networks involving domestic and international non-governmental and intergovernmental partners), as they apply pressure for resolution at the international level (e.g., the regional human rights system). This is evidenced in numerous historical human rights violations cases from the internal armed conflict period, whose lessons victim-survivors and allies have used to reach their goal (i.e., *Barrios Altos v. Peru*).[10]

Of course, not every transnational advocacy mobilization results in major advances toward justice and future rights protection. As in other aspects of transnational advocacy efforts, particularly in Peru, there are setbacks—most often involving former regime personnel (i.e., Fujimori supporters) or opponents of the rights campaign. In some cases, that may mean that justice—as envisioned by victim-survivors and allies—may not come in all forms or at the same time. Notwithstanding these caveats, there is still merit in appreciating the wins that result from rallying cries for justice and (reproductive) rights campaigns. For one thing, the expanded and visible political agency of Indigenous women is a significant matter. Political actors finally understand Indigenous women are here to stay, and they will engage in strategic moves to bolster their own side, human rights agenda, and political power. Additionally, the existence of an open investigation by the Public Prosecutor's Office, the continuing pressure from transnational advocacy networks, and the involvement of the Inter-American System of Human Rights are mechanisms that will help victim-survivors and activists reach their goals in their long fight for justice. The women, Indigenous and non-Indigenous alike, are at a critical juncture in commanding their own rights campaigns, uniting with allies in their struggles for rights, and demanding, "¡Esterilizaciones forzadas nunca más!" (Forced sterilizations never again!)

NOTES

INTRODUCTION

1. Over four million people (12% of the total population) speak Indigenous languages in Peru. According to the Ministry of Culture, in 2022 there were a total of forty-eight Indigenous languages: forty-four were from the Amazonian region and four were spoken in the Andean areas. These include languages such as Quechua, Asháninka, Aymara, Wampis, Nahua, and Jaqaru, among others. For more information see Ministerio de Cultura, "Lista de lenguas indígenas originarias," accessed April 18, 2022, https://bdpi.cultura.gob.pe/lenguas.

2. The mandate of the family planning program ended in 2000. However, the practices of coercive sterilization continued throughout 2001, as noted in Human Rights Ombudsman's Office reports.

3. Ñusta Carranza Ko, "Making the Case for Genocide, the Forced Sterilization of Indigenous Peoples of Peru," *Genocide Studies and Prevention: An International Journal* 14, no. 2 (2020): 94; Alejandra Ballón Gutiérrez, "El caso peruano de esterilizaciones forzadas: Una pieza clave del conflicto armado interno," in *Perú: Las esterilizaciones forzadas, en la década del terror*, ed. Alberto Chirif (IWGIA, 2021), 140–142.

4. Comité de América Latina y El Caribe Para la Defensa de los Derechos de la Mujer (CLADEM), *Nada Personal: Reporte de Derechos Humanos Sobre la Aplicación de la Anticoncepción Quirúrgica en el Perú 1996–1998* (CLADEM, 1999); Defensoría del Pueblo, *Anticoncepción Quirúrgica Voluntaria I: Casos Investigados por la Defensoría del Pueblo* (Defensoría del Pueblo, 1998).

5. *María Mamérita Mestanza Chávez v. Peru* was the first case about reproductive rights admitted to the Inter-American Commission on Human Rights. It involved the forced sterilization by Peruvian health officials and related death of María Mamérita Mestanza Chávez. The case was amicably settled in 2003, with the Peruvian state recognizing its crimes and agreeing to provide reparations for her family. For more information see Comisión Interamericana de Derechos Humanos, "Solución amistosa María Mamérita Mestanza Chávez v. Perú," accessed April 19, 2022, https://www.cidh.oas.org/women/peru.12191sp.htm. *Celia Ramos v. Peru* is the first case about forced sterilizations heard before the IACtHR, in 2025. The case was first brought before the IACHR in 2021. The commission declared the Peruvian state responsible for the crimes committed against Celia Ramos, who died as a result of a sterilization she was subjected to without her consent, and recommended reparations by the state. When the government of Peru did not comply with the commission's demands, the case was referred to the IACtHR. For more information see Inter-American Commission on Human Rights, "IACHR Files Case Concerning Peru with IA Court on Sterilization Without Consent," OAS, August 18, 2023, https://www.oas.org/en/iachr/jsForm/?File=/en/iachr/media_center/preleases/2023/186.asp.

6. See Archivo PSRPF, "Arte," accessed January 1, 2022, https://1996pnsrpf2000.wordpress.com/arte/.

7. The two decades of conflict involved a violent confrontation between leftist guerrilla groups (i.e., Sendero Luminoso and Movimiento Revolucionario Túpac Amaru) and state security forces, which resulted in the death and disappearance of 69,280 persons. The atrocities involving state security and armed forces included, among others, the forced disappearance and extrajudicial execution of nine students and one professor from La Cantuta University (July 18, 1992), the Barrios Altos massacre of fifteen civilians (November 3, 1991), and the kidnapping of journalist Gustavo Gorriti and businessman Samuel Dyer (April 1992). President Alberto Fujimori was found guilty of these crimes and sentenced to twenty-five years in prison on April 7, 2009. And yet, as coercive sterilizations fell "outside the political system that defined this period" of violent conflict and militarist response between leftist guerrilla groups and state security forces, the crime went undocumented by the TRC and was largely avoided by those working on the Inter-American Commission. For more information see Carranza Ko, "Making the Case for Genocide," 93; author's interview with Dr. Francisco Soberón, founder of APRODEH, May 24, 2017; Ñusta Carranza Ko, "Forcibly Sterilized: Peru's Indigenous Women and the Battle for Rights," in *Human Rights as Battlefields: Changing Practices and Contestations*, ed. Gabriel Blouin-Genest, Marie-Christine Doran, and Sylvie Paquerot (Palgrave Macmillan, 2019), 153.

8. Ministerio Público, *Resolución Fiscal No. 16* (Ministerio Público Fiscalía de la Nación, 2016).

9. Carranza Ko, "Making the Case for Genocide," 96; Rocío Silva Santisteban, "Esterilizaciones forzadas: Biopolítica, patriarcado y genocidio," in *Perú: Las esterilizaciones forzadas, en la década del terror,*" ed. Alberto Chirif (IWGIA, 2021), 57–94; Christina Ewig, "La Economía Política de Esterilización Forzada en el Perú," in *Memorias del Caso Peruano de Esterilización Forzada*, ed. Alejandra Ballón (Biblioteca Nacional del Perú, 2014).

10. US congressional records are used in discussing the story of one of the victim-survivors, Victoria Vigo, in chapter 4.

11. As addressed in chapter 4, Victoria Vigo currently resides in Ottawa, Canada. She sought asylum in Canada in 2022 due to the continuous death threats she faced for her activism in the coercive sterilization movement against the state.

12. Dan Wulff, "Unquestioned Answers: A Review of Research is Ceremony: Indigenous Research Methods," *Qualitative Report* 15, no. 5 (2010): 1290.

13. Shawn Wilson, *Research Is Ceremony: Indigenous Research Methods* (Fernwood Publishing, 2008), 32.

14. Wilson, *Research Is Ceremony*, 17.

15. Silvia Rivera Cusicanqui, "Ch'ixinakax utxiwa: A Reflection on the Practices and Discourses of Decolonization," *South Atlantic Quarterly* 111, no. 1 (2012): 99.

16. Rivera Cusicanqui, "Ch'ixinakax utxiwa," 99.

17. Congreso de la República, "Constitución para la República del Peru (12 de Julio de 1979)," 1979, https://www.leyes.congreso.gob.pe/Documentos/constituciones_ordenado/CONSTIT_1979/Cons1979_TEXTO_CORREGIDO.pdf.

18. Congreso de la República, "Constitución Política del Perú: Promulgada el 29 de Diciembre de 1993," 2019, https://www.congreso.gob.pe/Docs/files/constitucion/constitucion2019/index.html.

19. Congreso de la República, "Ley de Comunidades Nativas y de Desarrollo Agrario de la Selva y de Ceja de Selva," 1978, https://www2.congreso.gob.pe/sicr/cendocbib/con3_uibd.nsf/0D41EC1170BDE30A052578F70059D913/$FILE/(1)leyde comunidadesnativasley22175.pdf.

20. Congreso de la República, "Nueva Reforma Agraria," 1969, https://leyes.congreso.gob.pe/Documentos/Leyes/17716.pdf.

21. Adriana Arista Zerga, "La importancia de llamarse indígena: manejo y uso político del término indígena en Lircay-Perú," *Identidades, cidadanias e Estado* 7 (2010): 179.

22. Ñusta Carranza Ko, "Qishpikayqa aham," In *Indigenous Futures and Learnings Taking Place,* ed. Ligia (Licho) López López and Gioconda Coello (Routledge, 2021), 128–129.

23. Arista Zerga, "La importancia de llamarse indígena," 184.

24. Amelia Alva-Arévalo, "La identificación de los pueblos indígenas en el Perú ¿Qué está sucediendo con el criterio de autoidentificación?," *CUHSO (Temuco)* 30, no. 2 (2020): 60–77, https://dx.doi.org/10.7770/2452-610x.2020.cuhso.01.a05.

25. Alva-Arévalo, "La identificación de los pueblos indígenas en el Perú," 60–77.

26. For more information about the discourse about the capitalization of the letter "I" in writing about Indigenous peoples, see Gregory Younging, *Elements of Indigenous Style: A Guide for Writing by and About Indigenous Peoples* (Brush Education, 2018).

27. Arista Zerga, "La importancia de llamarse indígena," 179.

28. Juan M. Ossio, "Existen las poblaciones indígenas andinas en el Perú," in *Indianismo e Indigenismo*, ed. José Alcina Franch (Alianza Universidad, 1990), 164.

29. Guillermo Bonfil Batalla, "El concepto del indio en América: Una categoría de la situación colonial," *Revista semanal de la Asociación Latinoamericana de Antropología* (ALA) 3, no. 2 (2019): 15–37.

30. H. Martin Wobst, "Indigenous Archaeologies: A Worldwide Perspective on Human Materialities and Human Rights," in *Indigenous Archaeologies: A Reader on Decolonization*, ed. Margaret M. Bruchac, Siobhan M. Hart, and H. Martin Wobst (Routledge, 2016), 20–21.

31. Wobst, "Indigenous Archaeologies," 20–21.

32. Gioconda Coello and Ligia (Licho) López López, "Futures Taking Place," in *Indigenous Futures and Learnings Taking Place*, ed. Ligia (Licho) López López and Gioconda Coello (Routledge, 2021), 4.

33. Anonymous interviewee, *Quipu Project-All the Testimonies*, Interactive Quipu Project, Lima, 2017, accessed July 1, 2019, https://interactive.quipu-project.com/#/es/quipu/listen/83?currentTime=46.01&view=thread.

34. Mairi McDermott, "Mo(ve)ments of Affect: Towards an Embodied Pedagogy for Anti-Racism Education," in *Politics of Anti-Racism Education: In Search of Strategies for Transformative Learning*, ed. G. J. S. Dei and M. McDermott (Springer, 2013), 211–226.

35. Georg M. Gugelberger, *The Real Thing: Testimonial Discourse and Latin America* (Duke University Press, 1996), 112–113.

36. Linda Tuhiwai Smith, *Decolonizing Methodologies: Research and Indigenous Peoples* (Zed Books, 2021), 144–145.

37. Elizabeth Burgos, *Me llamo Rigoberta Menchú y así me nació la conciencia* (Siglo Veintiuno, 1985).

38. Wilson, *Research Is Ceremony*, 40.

39. Carranza Ko, "Qishpikayqa Aham," 117–137.

40. Carranza Ko, "Qishpikayqa Aham," 117–137.

41. Pascha Bueno-Hansen, *Feminist and Human Rights Struggles in Peru* (University of Illinois Press, 2015), 19.

42. As Cusicanqui has not affirmed that she is a "decolonial feminist," even though most of her works are referenced in discussions of decolonial feminism, I purposefully do not engage in this direct language here. Instead, I unpack these ideas further as I touch upon the points about Indigeneity and women. For more information see Silvia Rivera Cusicanqui, *Ch'ixinakax utxiwa: Una reflexión sobre prácticas y discursos descolonizadores* (Tinta Limón, 2010), 73; Asher Khan, "Reivindicar la cercanía entre los feminismos poscoloniales y decoloniales con base en Spivak y Rivera Cusicanqui," *Tabula Rasa* 30 (2019): 13–25.

43. Márgara Millán Moncayo, "Feminismos, postcolonialidad, descolonización: Del centro a los márgenes? *Andamios* 8, no. 17 (2011): 11–36.

44. Vievetha Thambinathan and Elizabeth Anne Kinsella, "Decolonizing Methodologies in Qualitative Research: Creating Space for Transformative Praxis," *International Journal of Qualitative Methods* 20 (2021): 1–9.

45. Ewig, "La Economía Política de Esterilización Forzada en el Perú," 17.

46. Priti Patel, "Forced Sterilization of Women as Discrimination," *Public Health Reviews* 38 (2017): 3–4.

47. Eduardo Galeano, *Open Veins of Latin America* (Monthly Press, 1997), 5–6.

48. Aníbal Quijano, "Colonialidad del Poder, Eurocentrismo y América Latina," in *La Colonialidad del Saber: Eurocentrismo y Ciencias Sociales*, ed. Edgardo Lander (Consejo Latinoamericano de Ciencias Sociales [CLACSO], 2000), 200–204.

49. For a complete list of international legal norms and related treaties on women's sexual and reproductive health and rights, see United Nations, "Sexual and Reproductive Health and Rights," accessed January 1, 2022, https://www.ohchr.org/en/issues/women/wrgs/pages/healthrights.aspx.

50. Carranza Ko, "Making the Case for Genocide."

51. Ministerio de Salud, *Programa de Salud Reproductiva y Planificación Familiar 1996–2000* (Ministerio de Salud, 1996), 3.

52. Ministerio de Salud, *Programa de Salud Reproductiva*, 3.

53. US Congress, House of Representatives. Committee on International Relations, *The Peruvian Population Control Program: Hearing Before the Subcommittee on International Operations and Human Rights* (US Government Printing Office, 1998).

54. It is important to note that discrimination against nondominant groups of power was also directed toward the Afro-Peruvian peoples. These ideas are documented in the works of Peruvian artists and literary figures Nicomedes and Victoria Santa Cruz, who critically noted the invisibility of Afro-Peruvian experiences

of discrimination in comparison to Indigenous populations. See Nicomedes Santa Cruz, *La décima en el Perú* [The décima in Peru] (Lima: Instituto de Estudios Peruanos, 1982); Victoria Santa Cruz, "El importante rol que cumple el obstáculo," in *El Perú en los albores del siglo XXI-4: Ciclo de conferencias 1999–2000*, ed. Fondo Editorial del Congreso del Perú (Fondo Editorial del Congreso del Perú, 1999), 231–244.

55. Quijano, "Colonialidad del Poder," 210–211.

56. Peru21, "Informe.21," January 13, 2018, https://www.inei.gob.pe/media/inei_en_los_medios/13_ene_Peru-21_14-y-15-a.pdf.

57. *El Tiempo*, "Por Programa de Planificación Familiar Enfrentamiento Fujimori-Iglesia," November 2, 1990, https://www.eltiempo.com/archivo/documento/MAM-2438; Alberto Fujimori, "Before the IV World Conference on Women, September 15, 1995, Beijing, China" (speech presented at, Beijing Conference on Women, United Nations, September 15, 1995), accessed May 1, 2019, https://www.un.org/esa/gopher-data/conf/fwcw/conf/gov/950915131946.txt.

58. Anna-Britt Coe, *Health, Rights and Realities: An Analysis of the ReprodSalud Project in Peru* (Center for Health and Gender Equity, 2001).

59. Walter D. Mignolo, *La Idea de América Latina* (Gedisa, 2005), 28.

60. Mignolo, *La Idea de América Latina*, 27–30.

61. Galeano, *Open Veins of Latin America*, 277.

62. Bartolomé de las Casas, *A Short Account of the Destruction of the Indies* (Penguin Books, 2004).

63. I do not specify the term "settler-colonial states" in this context, as settler-colonial scholarship conceptualizes "settler colonialism from experiences in former British imperial settings which often occupy dominant global positions." Hence, the terminology is often not used to describe the Latin American realities, which included drastically different relationships with settlers and Indigenous peoples than in the Anglophone settler colonies. Yet there may be much to benefit from considering what this term and its related theoretical perspectives may bring in understanding, for instance, the Indigenous struggles for justice. For more information, see Lucy Taylor and Geraldine Lublin, "Settler Colonial Studies and Latin America," *Settler Colonial Studies* 11, no. 3 (2021): 259–270.

64. I use the term "Aboriginal," following Elinghaus's work. See Katherine Elinghaus, "Biological Absorption and Genocide: A Comparison of Indigenous Assimilation Policies in the United States and Australia," *Genocide Studies and Prevention: An International Journal* 4, no. 1 (2009): 59–79.; Elinghaus, "Biological Absorption and Genocide," 59–79.

65. I use the term "native women" only in this section to reflect the work of Theobald. See Brianna Theobald, *Reproduction on the Reservation: Pregnancy, Childbirth,*

and Colonialism in the Long Twentieth Century (University of North Carolina Press, 2019). For more information on the experiences of historical trauma, cultural and economic imperialism, and their related effects on Indigenous communities, see M. Y. Brave Heart and L. M. DeBruyn, "American Indian Holocaust: Healing Historical Unresolved Grief," *American Indian and Alaska Native Mental Health Research* 8, no. 2 (1998): 56–78.

66. Robert van Krieken, "Rethinking Cultural Genocide: Aboriginal Child Removal and Settler-Colonial State," *Oceania* 75, no. 2 (2004): 126–127; Margaret D. Jacob, "The Habit of Elimination: Indigenous Child Removal in Settler Colonial Nations in the Twentieth Century," in *Colonial Genocide in Indigenous North America*, ed. Andrew Woolford, Jeff Benvenuto, and Alexander Hinton (Duke University Press, 2014), 119; Theodore Fontaine, foreword to *Colonial Genocide in Indigenous North America*, ed. Andrew Woolford, Jeff Benvenuto, and Alexander Hinton (Duke University Press, 2014), 9.

67. I want to emphasize how colonial politics shifted its discourse depending on what best benefited the economic and political interests of those in power. For instance, during the periods of colonial slavery, an enslaved woman's "reproductive labor" was seen as part of her function of work, one that would produce future generations of workers and generate capital. Once slavery was abolished, free enslaved labor's ties to capitalistic gains decreased, and social class structures were being reestablished that mirrored postcolonial policies in the twentieth century, black women became one of the most targeted populations for forced sterilization, "especially in the state of North Carolina." See Jennifer L. Morgan, "Partus Sequitur Ventrem: Law, Race, and Reproduction in Colonial Slavery," *Small Axe* 22, no. 1 (2018): 1–17; Johanna Schoen, *Choice and Coercion: Birth Control, Sterilization, and Abortion in Public Health and Welfare* (University of North Carolina Press, 2005), 106–109.

68. While not directly tied to studies about coercive sterilizations, scholarship on reproductive rights matters also discusses the disproportionate impact that women of color experienced from hostile government policies that aimed to control women's reproductive rights. Additionally, scholars have noted how even in birth control movements in the Unites States led by women activists, women of color were not included, and in fact, at times they were blatantly singled out as needing control and sterilization. For more information see Angela Y. Davis, *Women, Race and Class* (Vintage Books, 1983); Zakiya Luna, *Reproductive Rights as Human Rights* (New York University Press, 2020); SisterSong, "Mission," 2022, https://www.sistersong.net/mission.

69. The findings from the General Accounting Office conclude that 3,406 Native American women were subject to sterilization over the course of three years from 1973 to 1976. Those sterilizations had "repercussions in terms of the loss of a

generation of children and the consequences for the sterilized women and their cultures." For more information see Sally J. Torpy, "Native American Women and Coerced Sterilization: On the Trails of Tears in the 1970s," *American Indian Culture and Research Journal* 24, no. 2 (200): 1–22; Myla Vicenti Carpio, "The Lost Generation: American Indian Women and Sterilization Abuse," *Social Justice* 31, no. 4 (2004): 42.

70. Karen Stote, *An Act of Genocide: Colonialism and the Sterilization of Aboriginal Women* (Fernwood, 2015), 63–66.

71. Stote, *Act of Genocide*, 63–66.

72. Kevin Annett, *Hidden from History: The Canadian Holocaust; The Untold Story of the Genocide of Aboriginal Peoples by Church and State in Canada* (The Truth Commission into Genocide in Canada, 2001), 13.

73. Kevin Annett, *Hidden No Longer: Genocide in Canada, Past and Present* (The International Tribunal into Crimes of Church and State and The Friends and Relatives of the Disappeared, 2010), 102.

74. Mario N. Bronfman and Roberto Castro, "Discurso y practica de la planificación familiar: El caso de América Latina," *Saúde em Debate* 25 (1989): 61–68.

75. Elinghaus, "Biological Absorption and Genocide"; Fontaine, foreword, 9.

76. Jelke Boesten, *Violencia sexual en la Guerra y en la paz: Genero, poder y justicia posconflicto en el Perú*, (Biblioteca Nacional del Perú, 2016), 17–18.

77. Boesten, *Violencia sexual en la Guerra y en la paz*, 17–18.

78. Bueno-Hansen, *Feminist and Human Rights Struggles in Peru*, 19.

79. María Eugenia Ulfe, "Desaparición Feminicida en Perú," NACLA, June 25, 2024, https://nacla.org/desaparicion-feminicida-en-peru.

80. Ulfe, "Desaparición Feminicida en Perú."

81. M. Cristina Alcalde, *The Woman in the Violence: Gender, Poverty, and Resistance in Peru* (Vanderbilt University Press, 2010), 31–33.

82. Carranza Ko, "Forcibly Sterilized," 149–172; Rosario B. De La Cruz Huamán, "Análisis de las Esterilizaciones Forzadas en el Perú desde una Perspectiva de Interculturalidad Critica," *Tierra Nuestra* 12, no. 1 (2018): 105–117; Ernesto Vasquez del Aguila, "Invisible Women: Forced Sterilization, Reproductive Rights, and Structural Inequalities in Peru of Fujimori and Toledo," *Estudos e Pesquisas em Psicología UERJ RJ* 6, no. 1 (2006): 109–124.

83. Kimberly Theidon, "Guerra Reproductiva: Esterilizaciones Forzadas en Perú," in *Las esterilizaciones forzadas 25 años después: Justicia y reparación*, ed. Lucía Santos Peralta (Pontificia Universidad Católica del Perú, 2023), 58.

84. Melania Canales Poma, "La justicia es incansable para las mujeres indígenas," in *Las esterilizaciones forzadas 25 años después: Justicia y reparación*, ed. Lucía Santos Peralta (Pontificia Universidad Católica del Perú, 2023), 21–22.

85. Julissa Mantilla Falcón, "El Caso de las Esterilizaciones Forzadas en el Perú Como una Violación de los Derechos Humanos," *Ius et Veritas* 23 (2016): 10–20.

86. Ñusta Carranza Ko, "Complicating Genocide: Missing Indigenous Women's Stories," in *Oxford Research Encyclopedia of Politics*, September 29, 2021, https://doi.org/10.1093/acrefore/9780190228637.013.2008; Carranza Ko, "Making the Case for Genocide."

87. Silva Santisteban, "Esterilizaciones forzadas."

88. Ministerio de la Mujer y Poblaciones Vulnerables, "Ministra Anahí Durand Se Reúne con Mujeres Víctimas de Esterilizaciones Forzadas," Gobierno del Perú, October 19, 2021, https://www.gob.pe.

89. José Burneo Labrín, *Justicia de Genero: Esterilización Forzada En El Perú: Delito de Lesa Humanidad* (Editorial Linea Andina, 2008), 14–22.

90. Corte Superior de Justicia de Piura, "Inst. No. 2000-0785-0-2001-JR-PE-02," 2001.

91. DEMUS, "Esterilizaciones Forzadas en Perú: Luego de 18 Años de Proceso Penal se Abre Investigación Judicial Contra Alberto Fujimori y sus Exministros de Salud," December 16, 2021, https://www.demus.org.pe.

92. The Constitutional Tribunal was responding to a habeas corpus request submitted by former President Alberto Fujimori's lawyer César Nakazaki. See *Gestión*, "TC Vera Mañana Habeas Corpus Que Busca Liberar a Alberto Fujimori," February 22, 2022, https://gestion.pe.

CHAPTER 1. GENDER, CLASS, AND ETHNICITY

1. Instituto Nacional de Estadística e Informática (INEI), *Perú: Síntesis Estadística 2015* (INEI, 2015), https://www.inei.gob.pe/media/MenuRecursivo/publicaciones_digitales/Est/Lib1292/libro.pdf.

2. Instituto Nacional de Estadística e Informática (INEI), *Perú: Resultados Definitivos* (INEI, 2018), 50.

3. Ministerio de Cultura, "Lista de lenguas indígenas originarias."

4. Congreso de la República, "Constitución Política del Perú."

5. Clifford Bob, *Rights as Weapons: Instruments of Conflict, Tools of Power* (Princeton University Press, 2019), 9.

6. Silvia Cusicanqui has highlighted certain controversies regarding the positionality of Walter Mignolo and the need to refer to non–North-based scholars in discussing stories about the Global South. This book does not engage in such debates, as they do not add to the conversations on colonialism. However, by including scholars of various ethnic origins, both from Latin America and elsewhere, it

tries to present an inclusive vision of discourses on colonialism. For more information on the debate mentioned previously, see Rivera Cusicanqui, "Ch'ixinakax utxiwa."

7. Mignolo, *La Idea de América Latina Indigenismo*, 28–30.

8. Mignolo, *La Idea de América Latina Indigenismo*, 28–30.

9. Mignolo, *La Idea de América Latina Indigenismo*, 32.

10. Carranza Ko, "Forcibly Sterilized," 160.

11. Enrique Dussel, *Invention of the Americas: Eclipse of "the Other" and the Myth of Modernity* (Continuum, 1995), 12.

12. Cecilia Vicuña, "An Introduction to Mestizo Poetics," in *The Oxford Book of Latin American Poetry: A Bilingual Anthology*, ed. Cecilia Vicuna and Ernesto Livon-Grosman (Oxford University Press, 2009), xx.

13. Quijano, "Colonialidad del poder," 203.

14. Quijano, "Colonialidad del poder," 203.

15. Quijano, "Colonialidad del poder," 208

16. Quijano, "Colonialidad del poder," 205.

17. Silvia Rivera Cusicanqui, *Violencias (re) encubiertas en Bolivia* (Editorial Piedra Rota, 2010), 15.

18. Rivera Cusicanqui, *Violencias (re) encubiertas en Bolivia*, 72.

19. Vicuña, "Introduction to Mestizo Poetics," xix.

20. Cristina Iglesia and Julio Schvarztman, *Cautivas y misioneros: Mitos blancos de la Conquista* (Catálogos Editora, 1987), 39.

21. Rivera Cusicanqui, *Violencias (re) encubiertas en Bolivia*, 72.

22. Pablo González Casanova, *Sociología de la explotación* (Siglo del Hombre Editores, CLACSO, 2009), 187.

23. González Casanova, *Sociología de la explotación*, 187.

24. González Casanova, *Sociología de la explotación*, 195.

25. González Casanova, *Sociología de la explotación*, 196. Internal colonialism and colonial structures of power are distinct from "class structures" associated with Marxist ideology, in that there is not only a relation of "dominion and exploitation from workers by those who are the owners of commodities" but also a "relationship of dominion/power and exploitation of a population (with distinct classes, property status, and workers) by another population that also has distinct classes (property owners and workers)." In other words, it embeds an ethnic and people-to-people element, which distinguishes it from Marx's class structures. For more information, see González Casanova, *Sociología de la explotación*, 198.

26. Juan Carlos Callirgos, *El racismo: La cuestión del otro (y de uno)* (DESCO, 1993); Alberto Flores Galindo, *Buscando un Inca* (Editorial Horizonte, 1988), 276.

27. Flores Galindo, *Buscando un Inca*.

28. Bueno-Hansen, *Feminist and Human Rights Struggles in Peru*, 16.

29. Congreso de la República, "Diario de los Debates," 1823, https://www4 .congreso.gob.pe/dgp/constitucion/constituciones/Constitucion-1823.pdf.

30. Over the course of its political history (postindependence), the Peruvian government has had twelve different constitutions from 1823 to 1993. Constitución Política de 1826, "Constitución Política para la República del Perú" , 1826, https://www.leyes .congreso.gob.pe/Documentos/constituciones_ordenado/CONSTIT_1826/Cons1826 _TEXTO.pdf.

31. Bueno-Hansen, *Feminist and Human Rights Struggles in Peru*, 16.

32. Marisol de la Cadena, *Indigenous Mestizos: The Politics of Race and Culture in Cuzco, Peru, 1919–1991* (Duke University Press, 2000), 45.

33. Bueno-Hansen, *Feminist and Human Rights Struggles in Peru*, 16.

34. Comisión de la Verdad y Reconciliación, *Informe Final: Conclusiones*, 2003, https://www.cverdad.org.pe/ifinal/conclusiones.php.

35. El Peruano, "Ministerio de Cultura: 38.5% de la población indígena vive en situación de pobreza," June 24, 2022, https://elperuano.pe/noticia/162238-ministerio -de-cultura-385-de-la-poblacion-indigena-vive-en-situacion-de-pobreza.

36. Carranza Ko, "Forcibly Sterilized."

37. Rivera Cusicanqui, *Violencias (re) encubiertas en Bolivia*, 81.

38. Jessaca B. Leinaweaver, *The Circulation of Children: Kinship, Adoption, and Morality in Andean Peru* (Duke University Press, 2008), 109–110.

39. Leinaweaver, *Circulation of Children*, 109–110.

40. Carlos Iván Degregori, "Identidad Étnica, Movimientos Sociales y Participación Política en el Perú," in *Democracia, etnicidad y violencia política en los países andinos*, ed. Alberto Adrianzén, Jean Michel Blanquer, Ricardo Calla, and others (Instituto de Estudios Peruanos, 1993), 120.

41. Avexnim Cojti Ren, "Maya Archaeology and the Political and Cultural Identity of Contemporary Maya in Gutemala," in *Indigenous Archaeologies: A Reader on Decolonization*, ed. Margaret M. Bruchac, Siobhan M. Hart, and H. Martin Wobst (Routledge, 2016), 204.

42. Cojti Ren, "Maya Archaeology," 204.

43. Cojti Ren, "Maya Archaeology," 204.

44. Marisol de la Cadena, "Discriminación étnica," *Cuestión del Estado* 32 (2003): 1–9.

45. Carranza Ko, "Making the Case for Genocide,."

46. Judith Butler, "Performative Acts and Gender Constitution: An Essay in Phenomenology and Feminist Theory," in *Performing Feminisms: Feminist Critical Theory and Theatre*, ed. Sue-Ellen Case (Johns Hopkins University Press, 1990), 278.

47. Judith Butler, *Gender Trouble: Feminism and the Subversion of Identity* (Routledge, 1999), xv.

48. Butler, *Gender Trouble*, xv.

49. Butler, *Gender Trouble*, 6–7.

50. Butler, *Gender Trouble*, 6–7.

51. Butler, *Gender Trouble*, 6–7.

52. María Rostworowski, *Los Incas: Economía, Sociedad y Estado en la Era del Tahuantinsuyo* (Ediciones Inkamaru, 2012), 131.

53. Felipe Guaman Poma de Ayala, *Nueva corónica y buen gobierno*, ed. Franklin Pease. (Biblioteca Ayacucho, 1980).

54. Guaman Poma de Ayala, *Nueva corónica y buen gobierno*, 132.

55. Lucía Alvites Sosa, "Sistema patriarcal, articulo de importación colonial en los Andes," *Revista de Sociología* 26 (2016): 195–204.

56. María Rostworowski, *Historia del Tahuantinsuyu* (Instituto de Estudios Peruanos, 1999), 38–39.

57. To offer a comparison, in US history, only ten women have held the rank of four-star general or admiral. For more information see Norah O'Donnell and Alicia Hastey, "The 4 Highest-Ranking Women in the U.S. Military Speak About the Obstacles They Overcame," *CBS News*, March 7, 2023, https://www.cbsnews.com/news/4-highest-ranking-women-u-s-military-speak-about-obstacles-challenges/.

58. Alvites Sosa, "Sistema patriarcal," 197.

59. Alvites Sosa, "Sistema patriarcal," 197.

60. Rostworowski, *Historia del Tahuantinsuyu*, 229.

61. Rostworowski, *Historia del Tahuantinsuyu*, 38–39.

62. Rostworowski, *Historia del Tahuantinsuyu*, 41.

63. Rostworowski, *Historia del Tahuantinsuyu*, 41.

64. Men in similar classes were in charge of harvesting and transporting the crop. For more information see María Rostworowski, *La mujer en el Perú prehispánico* (Instituto de Estudios Peruanos, 1995), 18.

65. Estefanía Sanz Romero, "La mujer en el sistema sociopolítico Inca," Publicaciones Didácticas, 2016, https://core.ac.uk/download/pdf/235858099.pdf.

66. Julieta Paredes, "Entronque patriarcal. La situación de las mujeres de los pueblos originarios de Abya Yala después de la invasión colonial de 1492" (Tesis de Maestría, FLACSO, 2018), http://hdl.handle.net/10469/17739, 54–55.

67. Claudia Rivera Casanovas, "Las mujeres en Tiwanku: aproximaciones a los roles de género y aspectos de poder en una sociedad prehispánica," in *Otras miradas, presencias femeninas en una historia de larga duración*, ed. Walter Sánchez Canedo and

Claudia Rivera Casanovas (Instituto de Investigaciones Antropológicas y Museo Arqueológico de la Universidad Mayor de San Simón, 2016), 184–185.

68. Aura Estela Cumes, "Mujeres indígenas patriarcado y colonialismo: Un desafío a la segregación comprensiva de las formas de dominio," *Anuario de Hojas de Warmi* 17 (2012): 10–11, https://revistas.um.es/hojasdewarmi/article/view/180291.

69. Silvia Rivera Cusicanqui, "La noción de 'derecho' o las paradojas de la modernidad postcolonial: Indígenas y mujeres en Bolivia," *Aportes Andinos* 11 (2004): 3.

70. Rivera Cusicanqui, "La noción de 'derecho' o las paradojas de la modernidad postcolonial," 3.

71. Rivera Cusicanqui, "La noción de 'derecho' o las paradojas de la modernidad postcolonial," 2.

72. Rivera Cusicanqui, "La noción de 'derecho' o las paradojas de la modernidad postcolonial," 3.

73. María Lugones, "Colonialidad y género," *Tabula Rasa* 9 (2008): 73–101.

74. This view of the world in part challenges existing studies that describe postcolonial highland cultures as directly inheriting norms and customs from the precolonial period. For more information on *sierra* culture as being a continuation of the precolonial period, see Orin Starn, "Antropología Andina, 'andinismo' Y Sendero Luminoso," *Allpanchis* 24, no. 39 (1992): 15–71, https://doi.org/10.36901/allpanchis.v24i39.803.

75. Cumes, "Mujeres indígenas patriarcado y colonialismo," 10–11.

76. Cumes, "Mujeres indígenas patriarcado y colonialismo," 4.

77. Cumes, "Mujeres indígenas patriarcado y colonialismo," 5.

78. Cumes, "Mujeres indígenas patriarcado y colonialismo," 5.

79. Cumes, "Mujeres indígenas patriarcado y colonialismo," 5.

80. Krisa E. Van Vleet, *Hierarchies of Care* (Chicago: University of Illinois Press, 2019), 35-37.

81. Van Vleet, *Hierarchies of Care*, 38.

82. Salomón Febres Lerner, *La Rebelión de la Memoria: Selección de Discursos 2001–2003* (Centro de Estudios y Publicaciones, 2004), 208; Transfer Commission of the Truth and Reconciliation Commission of Peru, *Hatun Willakuy: Abbreviated Version of the Final Report of the Truth and Reconciliation Commission* (Transfer Commission of the Truth and Reconciliation Commission of Peru, 2014), 12.

83. Bueno-Hansen, *Feminist and Human Rights Struggles in Peru*, 3.

84. Boesten, *Violencia sexual en la Guerra y en la paz*, 115.

85. Boesten, *Violencia sexual en la Guerra y en la paz*, 115.

86. Kimberle Crenshaw, "Mapping the Margins: Intersectionality, Identity Politics, and Violence against Women of Color," *Stanford Law Review* 43, no. 6 (1991): 1243–1244.

87. Defensoría del Pueblo, *La aplicación de la anticoncepción quirúrgica y los derechos reproductivos III: Casos Investigados por la Defensoría del Pueblo* (Defensoría del Pueblo, 2002), 136.

88. Iris Lopez, *Masters of Choice: Puerto Rico Women's Struggle for Reproductive Freedom* (Rutgers University Press, 2008), xix.

89. Congreso de la República, *Informes de Comisión: Subcomisión Investigadora de la Denuncia Constitucional No. 151,* January 30, 2003, https://www2.congreso.gob.pe/Sicr /ApoyComisiones/informes.nsf/InformesPorComision/C405450DEB310E6C05256 CBE0076A35E.

90. Defensoría del Pueblo, *La aplicación de la anticoncepción quirúrgica.*

91. Defensoría del Pueblo, *La aplicación de la anticoncepción quirúrgica,* 82.

92. Silva Santisteban, "Esterilizaciones forzadas," 81.

93. Canales Poma, "La justicia es inalcanzable para las mujeres indígenas," 22.

94. Comité de América Latina y El Caribe Para la Defensa de los Derechos de la Mujer (CLADEM), *Nada Personal* (CLADEM, 1999), 41.

95. Jessica Taft, *The Kids Are in Charge* (New York University Press, 2019), 94.

96. Bianca Premo, "Pena y Protección: Delincuencia Juvenil y Minoridad Legal en Lima Virreinal, Siglo XVIII," *Histórica* 24, no. 1 (2000): 85–120. https://doi.org/10 .18800/historica.200001.004; Taft, *Kids Are in Charge.*

97. Mikaela Luttrell-Rowland, *Political Children: Violence, Labor, and Rights in Peru* (Stanford University Press, 2023), 58–59.

98. Luttrell-Rowland, *Political Children,* 59–60.

99. Taft, *Kids Are in Charge,* 96.

100. Taft, *Kids Are in Charge,* 97.

101. Van Vleet, *Hierarchies of Care,* 19.

102. Van Vleet, *Hierarchies of Care,* 18.

103. Van Vleet, *Hierarchies of Care,* 18.

104. Van Vleet, *Hierarchies of Care,* 22.

105. Leinaweaver, *Circulation of Children,* 109–110.

106. Raul Madrid, "Ethnic Proximity and Ethnic Voting in Peru," *Journal of Latin American Studies* 43, no. 2 (2011): 267–268.

107. *Inkarri* or *Inkari* is a compound word; specifically it combines the word *inka* (king in Quechua) and *rri* or *ri* (stemming from *rey* in Spanish, which means king).

108. What is unique about Peru's national ideology, however, is the idea that the purity of the Inca past is revered, while present-day Indigenous peoples—who are either still residing in rural areas or have become "assimilated" in certain ways to non-Indigenous ways—are disparaged. For more information see Shane Green,

"Incas, Indios, and Indigenism in Peru," NACLA, 2007, https://nacla.org/article/incas-indios-and-indigenism-peru#2.

109. Francisco Carranza Romero, recorded telephone interview by author, November 12, 2021.

110. For more discussion on the varying dates that suggest the origin of this myth, see Nicholas Robins, *Genocide and Millennialism in Upper Peru: The Great Rebellion of 1780–1782* (Praeger, 2002), 29.

111. Madrid, "Ethnic Proximity and Ethnic Voting in Peru," 268.

112. Madrid, "Ethnic Proximity and Ethnic Voting in Peru," 268.

113. Madrid, "Ethnic Proximity and Ethnic Voting in Peru," 268.

114. Bob, *Rights as Weapons*, 8.

115. Bob, *Rights as Weapons*, 8.

116. Marie-Christine Doran, "Indigenous Peoples in Chile: Contesting Violence, Building New Meanings for Rights and Democracy," in *Human Rights as Battlefields: Changing Practices and Contestations,* ed. Gabriel Blouin-Genest, Marie-Christine Doran, and Sylvie Paquerot (Palgrave Macmillan, 2019), 200–201.

117. Beatriz Jiménez, "Miles de peruanos marchan en Lima para pedir: Dignidad, Fujimori nunca más," *El Mundo,* May 27, 2011, https://www.elmundo.es/america/2011/05/27/noticias/1306459260.html.

118. Carmen Ilizarbe Pizarro, *La Democracia y la Calle: Protestas y contrahegemónicas en el Perú* (Instituto de Estudios Peruanos, 2022).

119. Ñusta Carranza Ko, *Truth, Justice, and Reparations in Peru, Uruguay, and South Korea: The Clash of Advocacy and Politics* (Palgrave Macmillan, 2021), 109–110.

120. Megan Haas, "Fujimori Extraditable! Chilean Supreme Court Sets International Precedent for Human Rights Violations," *University of Miami Inter-American Law Review* 39, no. 2 (2008): 396.

121. On November 15, 2022, the Ministry of Justice and Human Rights approved the expansion of the extradition request to include crimes related to coercive sterilizations. Relatedly, on June 24, 2024, the Chilean Supreme Court approved the expansion of the extradition request. And while the Peruvian Supreme Court annulled cases of coercive sterilizations in 2023, there have been some positive developments in 2025 with the opening of new criminal investigations into these cases. For more information see *DW*, "Chile amplia por tercera vez extradicion de Alberto Fujimori," June 25, 2024, https://www.dw.com/es/chile-ampl%C3%ADa-por-tercera-vez-extradici%C3%B3n-de-alberto-fujimori/a-69461905; "Alberto Fujimori declarará por esterilizaciones forzadas con miras a ampliar su extradición desde Chile," *Infobae,* May 12, 2023, https://www.infobae.com/peru/2023/05/12/alberto-fujimori

-declarara-por-esterilizaciones-forzadas-con-miras-a-ampliar-su-extradicion
-desde-chile/.

122. Carranza Ko, "Forcibly Sterilized," 149.

123. *Gestión*, "Pedro Castillo y Keiko Fujimori polemizan sobre el caso de las esterilizaciones forzadas," May 30, 2021, https://gestion.pe/peru/politica/debate -presidencial-del-jne-pedro-castillo-y-keiko-fujimori-polemizan-sobre-el-caso-de-las -esterilizaciones-forzadas-elecciones-2021-peru-libre-fuerza-popular-nndc-noticia/.

124. "Dina Boluarte: Pedro Castillo se reunirá con las victimas del caso esterilizaciones forzadas" [Dina Boluarte: Pedro Castillo Will meet with victims of the forced sterilization case], Ideele Radio, May 19, 2021, https://www.ideeleradio .pe/lo-ultimo/dina-boluarte-pedro-castillo-se-reunira-con-las-victimas-del-caso -esterilizaciones-forzadas/.

CHAPTER 2. INDIGENOUS WOMEN
AND THE GENOCIDE

1. An earlier version of this chapter has appeared as Ñusta P. Carranza Ko, "Making the Case for Genocide, the Forced Sterilization of Indigenous Peoples of Peru," *Genocide Studies and Prevention: An International Journal* 14, no. 2(2020): 90–103. The author holds the rights to the previous article publication.

2. Francisco Soberón (former Truth and Reconciliation Commission commissioner and founder of Asociación ProDerechos Humanos (APRODEH)), interview by author, Baltimore, MD, May 19, 2019.

3. Comisión de la Verdad y Reconciliación, *Final Report*, 2003, accessed August 1, 2019, http://www.cverdad.org.pe/ingles/ifinal/index.php.

4. Although the official years of the program were from 1996 to 2000, in its implementation, the PSRPF lasted until 2001.

5. Defensoría del Pueblo, *Decimonoveno Informe Anual de la Defensoría del Pueblo* (Defensoría del Pueblo, 2015), 50–53.

6. Ana María Vidal (former deputy executive secretary of the National Coordination of Human Rights), interview by author, Lima, June 1, 2017.

7. Constitución Política de la República Peruana Sancionada por el Primer Congreso Constituyente, November 12, 1823, accessed August 1, 2019, http://www .leyes.congreso.gob.pe/Documentos/constituciones_ordenado/CONSTIT_1823 / Cons1823_TEXTO. pdf.

8. Carranza Ko, "Forcibly Sterilized," 149–172; Burneo Labrín, *Justicia de Genero*, 14–22.

9. Cynthia C. Wesley-Esquimaux and Magdalena Smolewski, *Historic Trauma and Aboriginal Healing* (Aboriginal Healing Foundation, 2004), 7.

10. Hilaria Supa, "Esterilizaciones ¡Hasta dónde puede llegar un ser humano con el menosprecio y el racismo!," in *Perú: Las esterilizaciones forzadas, en la década del terror,* ed. Alberto Chirif (International Work Group for Indigenous Affairs, 2021), 17; Silva Santisteban, "Esterilizaciones forzadas," 81–85.

11. Ana María Vidal, "Por el solo hecho de ser mujeres: La impunidad y el desamparo de miles de victimas frente al crimen de lesa humanidad de las esterilizaciones forzadas," in *Perú: Las esterilizaciones forzadas, en la década del terror,* ed. Alberto Chirif (International Work Group for Indigenous Affairs, 2021), 19–56.

12. Studies on aboriginal women in Canada have determined that they were disproportionately targeted by the state to undergo tubal ligations. The coercive sterilization of Indigenous peoples is best understood within the larger relations of "colonialism, the oppression of women," and the control of Indigenous peoples' land and resources, and it constitutes a genocide. Similar studies in the United States have documented how colonizers have historically used sexual violence, such as sterilization abuse, as a primary tool of genocide against Indigenous peoples; see Karen Stote, "The Coercive Sterilization of Aboriginal Women in Canada," *American Indian Culture and Research Journal* 36, no. 3 (2012): 117; Andrea Smith, *Conquest-Sexual Violence and American Indian Genocide* (Duke University Press, 2005), 117.

13. Silva Santisteban, "Esterilizaciones forzadas," 57–94.

14. Inter-American Commission on Human Rights (IACHR), Report No. 71/03, Petition 12.191, *Friendly Settlement María Mamérita Mestanza-Chávez* (IACHR, 2003), accessed August 1, 2019, http://cidh.org/annualrep/2003eng/ Peru.12191.htm.

15. Inter-American Commission on Human Rights, "IACHR Files Case Concerning Peru"; Center for Reproductive Rights, "The Case of Celia Ramos: Seeking Justice for Women Forcibly Sterilized Under Peru's Fujimori Regime," May 19, 2025, https://reproductiverights.org/celia-ramos-forced-sterilization-peru/.

16. Julio Davila Puño, *Perú: Gobiernos Locales y Pueblos Indígenas* (Tarea Grafica Educativa, 2005), 35.

17. For scholarship that examines Plan Verde and its links with PSRPF, see Ballón Gutiérrez, "El caso peruano de esterilizaciones forzadas: Una pieza," 139–164.

18. For scholarship that examines other Indigenous peoples of the Americas and coercive sterilizations, see Carranza Ko, "Complicating Genocide."

19. Degregori, "Identidad Étnica," 116, 120.

20. "Corte Suprema anula proceso de esterilizaciones forzadas cometidas en el régimen de Alberto Fujimori," *Infobae*, December 7, 2023, https://www.infobae.com /peru/2023/12/07/alberto-fujimori-corte-suprema-anula-proceso-judicial-sobre -esterilizaciones-forzadas/.

21. Alejandra Ballón Gutiérrez, "El Caso Peruano de Esterilización Forzada: Notas Para una Cartografía de Resistencia," *Aletheia* 5, no. 9 (2014): 15.

22. Ballón Gutiérrez, "El Caso Peruano de Esterilización Forzada: Notas," 15.

23. Lucía Stavig, "Unwittingly Agreed: Fujimori, Neoliberal Governmentality, and the Inclusive Exclusion of Indigenous Women," *Latin American and Caribbean Ethnic Studies* 17, no. 1 (2021): 8.

24. Stote, "Coercive Sterilization," 117.

26. Vasquez del Aguila, "Invisible Women," 109–124.

26. Vasquez del Aguila, "Invisible Women," 115.

27. Carranza Ko, "Forcibly Sterilized."

28. Julissa Mantilla, "El Caso de las Esterilizaciones Forzadas," 19.

29. De La Cruz Huamán, "Análisis de las Esterilizaciones Forzadas," 109.

30. Ewig, "La Economía Política de Esterilización," 17.

31. Jelke Boesten, "Free Choice or Poverty Alleviation? Population Politics in Peru Under Alberto Fujimori," *European Review of Latin American and Caribbean Studies* no. 82 (2007): 3, http://www.jstor.org/stable/25676252.

32. Monica Bahati Kuumba, "Perpetuating Neo-Colonialism through Population Control: South Africa and the United States," *Africa Today* 40, no. 3 (1993): 80, http://www.jstor.org/stable/4186924 .

33. Jocelyn E. Getgen, "Untold Truths: The Exclusion of Enforced Sterilizations from the Peruvian Truth Commission's Final Report," *Boston College Third World Law Journal* 29, no. 1 (2009): 1–34, https://scholarship.law.cornell.edu/facpub /1087. The mandate of the TRC covered all forms of violations of fundamental rights, including acts perpetrated by state and armed groups from 1980 to 2000. From its work, the TRC determined that the causes of conflict were instigated by Sendero Luminoso, which had declared a popular war against the Peruvian state. The conflict and resulting human rights violations involved the state, subversive forces (such as Sendero), and civilians who were caught in the middle. From this perspective, forced sterilization practices fell outside the markers of the internal armed conflict, as they did not involve a conflict between the state, subversive forces, and civilian casualties; see Carranza Ko, "Forcibly Sterilized," 168.

34. Getgen, "Untold Truths," 4. According to human rights experts, while forced sterilization occurred during the internal armed conflict, it fell outside the political

systems that defined this period, which saw violent confrontation between leftist groups advancing their revolutionary goals and the state instituting a militarist response. Soberón, interview by author; Carmela Chávez (Superintendencia Nacional de Educación Superior Universitaria (SUNEDU)), interview by author, Lima, May 26, 2017.

35. Ainhoa Molina Serra, "Esterilizaciones (forzadas) en Perú: Poder y Configuraciones Narrativas," *Revista de Antropología Iberoamericana* 12, no. 1 (2017): 33–34, https://doi.org/10.11156/aibr.120103e.

36. Silva Santisteban, "Esterilizaciones forzadas."

37. The following pages from Labrín are dedicated to the discussion of framing the crime as a form of crimes against humanity and not as a genocide; see Burneo Labrín, *Justicia de Genero*, 14–22.

38. Ministerio Público, "Resolución Formalización Denuncia Caso EEFF Versión Comprimida," Ministerio Público Fiscalía de la Nación, October 31, 2018, accessed December 1, 2018, http://www.demus.org.pe/wpcontent/uploads/2019/01 /12-1118-Resoluci%C2%A6n-Formalizaci%C2%A6n-denuncia-caso-EEFFversi %C2%A6n-comprimida.pdf, 1.

39. Stavig, "Unwittingly Agreed," 5.

40. Christina Ewig, "Hijacking Global Feminism: Feminists, the Catholic Church, and the Family Planning Debacle in Peru," *Feminist Studies* 32, no. 3 (2006): 637.

41. "Decreto Legislativo No. 346," 1985, https://faolex.fao.org/docs/pdf/per 128573.pdf.

42. Marcos Cueto, "La vocación por volver a empezar: Las políticas de población en el Perú," *Revista Peruana de Medicina Experimental y Salud Publica* 23, no. 2 (2006): 127.

43. "Decreto Legislativo No. 346."

44. "Por Programa de Planificación Familiar Enfrentamiento Fujimori-Iglesia," *El Tiempo*, November 2, 1990, accessed November 1, 2018, https://www.eltiempo.com /archivo/documento/MAM-2438.

45. Fujimori, "Before the IV World Conference on Women," .

46. Resistencia, "El 'Plan Verde': Historia de un traición" [The Green Plan: history of treason], 2001, http://www.resistencia.org/documentos/el_plan_verde/historia _de_una_traicion.pdf, 7.

47. Resistencia, "El 'Plan Verde'," 8.

48. Ballón Gutiérrez, "El caso peruano de esterilizaciones forzadas: Una pieza," 141.

49. Ministerio de Salud, *Programa de Salud Reproductiva y Planificación Familiar,* 3.

50. Ministerio de Salud, *Programa de Salud Reproductiva y Planificación Familiar,* 26.

51. Ewig, "La Economía Política," *57.*

52. Defensoría del Pueblo, *Decimonoveno Informe,* *51.* Additionally, 22,004 men were sterilized via the PSRPF.

53. Comité de América Latina y El Caribe Para la Defensa de los Derechos de la Mujer (CLADEM), *Nada Personal,* 41.

54. Diakonia, "Las Esterilizaciones Forzadas-un Crimen Que Nadie Quiere Reconocer," accessed June 20, 2019, https://www.diakonia.se/es/donde-trabajamos /peru/demus/.

55. Anonymous interviewee, *Quipu Project—All the Testimonies,* Interactive Quipu Project, Lima, 2017, accessed July 1, 2019, https://interactive.quipu-project.com/#/es /quipu/listen/83?currentTime=46.01&view=thread.

56. Quipu Project, "The Quipu Project," 2017, https://interactive.quipu-project. com/#/en/quipu/intro.

57. Organización Nacional de Mujeres Indígenas Andinas y Amazónicas del Perú (ONAMIAP), "Testimony from Dionicia Calderón Arellano (Campesina)" (presented at ONAMIAP Public Forum and Hearing on Forced Sterilizations-Lima, 1st session, 2017).

58. La República, "Denuncia de Esterilizaciones Forzadas."

59. ONAMIAP, "Testimony from Arellano."

60. Republic of Perú, "Título II Del Estado y la Nación," 1993, http://www4 .congreso.gob.pe/comisiones/1996/constitucion/cons_t2.htm.

61. United Nations, "Convention on the Prevention and Punishment of the Crime of Genocide," December 9, 1948, https://www.un.org/en/genocideprevention /documents/atrocity-crimes/Doc.1_Convention%20on%20the%20Prevention %20and%20Punishment%20of%20the%20Crime%20of%20Genocide.pdf.

62. Ministerio de Justicia y Derechos Humanos, Decreto Legislativo No. 635 Código Penal, 2016, http://spij.minjus.gob.pe/content/publicaciones_oficiales/img /CODIGOPENAL.pdf.

63. United Nations, Convention on . . . Genocide," Art. 2.

64. Ministerio de Justicia y Derechos Humanos, Decreto Legislativo No. 635 Código Penal, 206.

65. *Prosecutor v. Goran Jelisic,* International Criminal Tribunal for the former Yugoslavia (ICTY), IT-95-10-A, para. 17, accessed February 1, 2020, https://www.icty.org/x /cases/jelisic/ind/en/jel-ii950721e.pdf.

66. William A. Schabas, *Genocide in International Law: The Crime of Crimes* (Cambridge University Press, 2009), 172–175.

67. Organización Nacional de Mujeres Indígenas Andinas y Amazónicas del Perú (ONAMIAP), "Testimony from Luisa Pinedo Rango (Campesina)" (presented at ONAMIAP Public Forum and Hearing on Forced Sterilizations-Lima, 1st session, 2017).

68. Anonymous interviewee, *Quipu Project*, Testimony 1-7.

69. Salomón Lerner Fébres (President of the Truth and Reconciliation Commission of Peru), interview by author, Lima, May 31, 2017.

70. IACHR, Report No. 71/03, Petition 12.191.

71. Vasquez del Aguila, "Invisible Women," 114; Defensoría del Pueblo, *La aplicación de la anticoncepción quirúrgica y los derechos reproductivos III*.

72. Defensoría del Pueblo, *La aplicación de la anticoncepción quirúrgica y los derechos reproductivos II: Casos investigados por la Defensoría del Pueblo* (Defensoría del Pueblo, 2000), 79.

73. Ministerio de la Mujer y Poblaciones Vulnerables, *Resumen Estadístico Victimas de Esterilizaciones Forzadas 2016* (Ministerio de la Mujer y Poblaciones Vulnerables, 2016).

74. Ministerio de la Mujer y Poblaciones Vulnerables, *Resumen Estadístico Victimas de Esterilizaciones Forzadas 2018* (Ministerio de la Mujer y Poblaciones Vulnerables, 2018); Ministerio de la Mujer y Poblaciones Vulnerables, *Resumen Estadístico Victimas de Esterilizaciones Forzadas 2019* (Ministerio de la Mujer y Poblaciones Vulnerables, 2019).

75. Ministerio Público, "Resolución Formalización," 24.

76. Instituto Nacional de Desarrollo de Pueblos Andinos, Amazónicos y Afroperuanos (INDEPA), "Mapa Etnolingüístico del Perú," *Revista Peruana de Medicina Experimental y Salud Pública* 27, no. 2 (2010): 288–291, https://www.redalyc.org/articulo.oa?id=36319368019.

77. INDEPA, "Mapa Etnolingüístico del Perú," 288–291.

78. Elin Roselia Baldárrago Estremadoyro, *Dinámicas Étnicas en el Perú: Hacia una caracterización y tipología para el diseño de políticas públicas* (Instituto Nacional de Estadística e Informática, 2017), 30.

79. Fébres, interview by author.

80. Defensoría del Pueblo, *Anticoncepción Quirúrgica Voluntaria I*, 36–38.

81. Fébres, interview by author.

82. Bahati Kuumba, "Perpetuating Neo-Colonialism," 80.

83. Ewig, "La Economía Política," 57.

84. During the first year when the victims' registry was implemented, REVIESFO gathered data on the mother tongue of victims of forced sterilization. Those who spoke Indigenous languages included 13 speaking Achuar, 7 Aymara, 6 Asháninka, 1 Cauqui, 1 Matsigenka, 1 Nomatsigenga, 1 Shipibo-Konibo, and 2,010 Quechua. In addiiton,

1,540 victims identified Spanish as their mother tongue. See Ministerio de la Mujer y Poblaciones Vulnerables, *Resumen Estadístico Victimas de Esterilizaciones Forzadas 2016*.

85. Stote, "Coercive Sterilization," 117.

86. Defensoría del Pueblo, *Anticoncepción Quirúrgica Voluntaria I*, 3.

87. Defensoría del Pueblo, *Anticoncepción Quirúrgica Voluntaria I*, 5.

88. Congreso de la República, *Informes de Comisión*.

89. Congreso de la República, "Informes de Comisión."

90. Ministerio Público, "Resolución Formalización," 24.

91. Boesten, "Free Choice or Poverty Alleviation?," 15.

92. Congreso de la República, *Diario de los debates: Segunda Legislatura Ordinaria de 1997 4ª Sesión Miércoles 18 de marzo de 1998*, March 18, 1998, http://www2.congreso.gob .pe/sicr/diariodebates/Publicad.nsf/2b66b8a68552546d05256f1000575a5c/05256d6e 0073dfe905256 5d1007dcde5?OpenDocument.

93. Congreso de la República, *Diario de los debates*.

94. Ministerio Público, "Resolución Formalización," 30.

95. Burneo Labrín, *Justicia de Genero*, 16–18.

96. Stote, "Coercive Sterilization."

97. ONAMIAP, Testimony from Arellano and Rango.

98. Degregori, "Identidad Étnica," 116–120.

CHAPTER 3. THEN, THERE WERE THE CHILDREN . . .

1. Hilaria Supa, *Hilos de Mi Vida* (Ediciones del Congreso del Perú, 2010), 76.

2. Alberto Fujimori, "Before the IV World Conference on Women."

3. For more detailed discussion on the use of specific terminology in referring to affected populations from coercive sterilizations, see chapter 5.

4. Comité de América Latina y El Caribe Para la Defensa de los Derechos de la Mujer (CLADEM), *Nada Personal*, 41.

5. Defensoría del Pueblo, *La aplicación de la anticoncepción Quirúrgica y los Derechos Reproductivos II*; Defensoría del Pueblo, *La Aplicación de la Anticoncepción Quirúrgica y los Derechos Reproductivos III* (Defensoría del Pueblo, 2002); Defensoría del Pueblo, *Decimonoveno Informe Anual* (Defensoría del Pueblo, 2015); Diakonia, "Las Esterilizaciones Forzadas." See María Ysabel Cedano, "Deuda histórica: Esterilizaciones forzadas y derecho a reparaciones integrales," March 20, 2021, https://www.demus.org.pe.

6. Mediated authorship or *autoría mediata* refers to crimes that are committed through the authorship of others. This was a term used during Alberto Fujimori's trial in 2009, when he was found guilty of "mediated authorship" and of "availing himself of the services of actors willing and able to commit the crimes at his behest."

See Juan Méndez, "Significance of the Fujimori Trial," *American University International Law Review* 25 (2010): 654. Ministerio Público, "Resolución Formalización Denuncia Caso EEFF."

7. Supa, "Esterilizaciones," 11–18.

8. See testimonies from Cuzco, Arequipa, Piura, and Lima archived under "Testimonios" [Testimonies], Archivo PSRPF, accessed October 2, 2021, https://1996pnsrpf2000.wordpress.com/testimonios-2/testimonios/.

9. Quechua and Kichwa are used interchangeably throughout this chapter. Ministerio de la Mujer y Poblaciones Vulnerables, *Resumen Estadístico Victimas de Esterilizaciones Forzadas 2016*; Ministerio de la Mujer y Poblaciones Vulnerables, *Resumen Estadístico Victimas de Esterilizaciones Forzadas 2017* (Ministerio de la Mujer y Poblaciones Vulnerables, 2017); Ministerio de la Mujer y Poblaciones Vulnerables, *Resumen Estadístico Victimas de Esterilizaciones Forzadas 2018*; Ministerio de la Mujer y Poblaciones Vulnerables, *Resumen Estadístico Victimas de Esterilizaciones Forzadas 2019*.

10. Carranza Ko, "Making the Case for Genocide," 90–103.

11. Victoria Vigo, interview by author, Zoom recording, October 19, 2021.

12. Sarita, interview by author, telephone recording, October 26, 2021.

13. Kahty Cuba Corimaita, "Huella Psicológicas de la Esterilización Forzada," *Revista Ideele* 244 (2014): 3–4.

14. Julietta Chaparro-Buitrago, "Debilitated Lifeworlds: Women's Narratives of Forced Sterilization as Delinking from Reproductive Rights," *Medical Anthropology Quarterly* 36, no. 3 (2022): 301.

15. While this section deals primarily with the racialization of children in Peru and hegemonic structures of oppression that exclude and marginalize Indigenous children, it is important to note that within Andean communities (primarily Kichwa [Quechua]-speaking), the role of the child and the position of the child is considered differently. Children are treated as more equal agents within their communities, as taking on responsibilities of communal living from an early age. For more information about Andean children's livelihoods within Andean contexts, see Patricia Ames, "Niños y niñas andinos en el Perú: crecer en un mundo de relaciones y responsabilidades," *Bulletin de l'Institut français d'études andines* 42, no. 3 (2013): 389–409.

16. Van Vleet, *Hierarchies of Care* (University of Illinois Press, 2019), 6–7.

17. Defensoría del Pueblo, *La actuación del estado frente a la violencia sexual contra la niñez y adolescencia Indígena Awajún en la provincia de Condorcanqui* (Defensoría del Pueblo, 2024).

18. Orelia Valladolid, "El infierno de las violaciones de niñas en comunidades awajún de Perú no es 'una práctica cultural,'" *El País*, August 13, 2024, https://elpais

.com/planeta-futuro/red-de-expertos/2024-08-14/el-infierno-de-las-ninas-en
-comunidades-awajun-de-peru-no-es-una-practica-cultural.html.

19. Valladolid, "El infierno de las violaciones de niñas en comunidades awajún de Perú"; Renzo Gómez Vega, "Más de 500 estudiantes de la Amazonía peruana fueron abusadas por sus profesores de manera sistemática," *El Pais*, June 24, 2024, https://elpais.com/america/2024-06-24/mas-de-500-estudiantes-de-la-amazonia -peruana-fueron-abusadas-por-sus-profesores-de-manera-sistematica.html?event _log=oklogin.

20. Taft, *Kids Are in Charge*, 97.

21. Taft, *Kids Are in Charge*, 97.

22. Gómez Vega, "Más de 500 estudiantes de la Amazonía."

23. Luttrell-Rowland, *Political Children*, 58–59.

24. Leinaweaver, *Circulation of Children*, 109–110.

25. United Nations, "Geneva Declaration of the Rights of the Child," September 26, 1924, http://www.undocuments.net/gdrc1924.htm.

26. United Nations, "Geneva Declaration of the Rights of the Child."

27. Republic of Peru, "Título II Del Estado y la Nación."

28. United Nations, "Convention on the Rights of the Child," November 20, 1989, https://www.ohchr.org/en/professionalinterest/pages/crc.aspx.

29. United Nations, "Convention on the Rights of the Child."

30. United Nations, "Convention on the Rights of the Child."

31. United Nations, "International Covenant on Civil and Political Rights," December 16, 1966, https://www.ohchr.org/en/professionalinterest/pages/ccpr.aspx.

32. United Nations, "Convention on the Rights of the Child."

33. The Convention Against Torture and Other Cruel, Inhuman or Degrading Treatment or Punishment (CAT) is a non-self-executing treaty that requires states to pass legislation for it to become applicable under domestic law, even in a monistic system of law. In 2006 Peru made legislative changes to accept the oversight of the Optional Protocol to the Convention Against Torture (OPCAT), allowing the Subcommittee on the Prevention of Torture and Other Cruel, Inhuman or Degrading Treatment or Punishment (SPT) to examine the state's prevention of torture and ill treatment.

34. United Nations, "Convention Against Torture and Other Cruel, Inhuman or Degrading Treatment or Punishment," December 10, 1984, https://www.ohchr.org /en/professionalinterest/pages/cat.aspx.

35. United Nations, "Convention Against Torture."

36. United Nations, "Report of the Special Rapporteur on Torture and Other Cruel, Inhuman or Degrading Treatment or Punishment, Juan E. Méndez," February 1, 2013,

https://www.ohchr.org/documents/hrbodies/hrcouncil/regularsession/session22/a
.hrc.22.53_english.pdf, 11.

37. Kimberly Theidon, "First Do No Harm: Enforced Sterilizations and Gender Justice in Peru," *Open Democracy*, April 29, 2015, https://www.opendemocracy
.net/en/opensecurity/first-do-no-harm-enforced-sterilizations-and-genderjustice
-in-peru/.

38. United Nations, "Convention on the Rights of the Child."

39. United Nations, "International Covenant on Economic, Social and Cultural Rights," December 16, 1966, https://www.ohchr.org/en/professionalinterest/pages
/cescr.aspx.

40. Carranza Ko, "Making the Case for Genocide."

41. International Criminal Court, "Rome Statute of the International Criminal Court," 2002, https://www.icccpi.int/nr/rdonlyres/ea9aeff7-5752-4f84-be94-0a655eb
30e16/0/rome_statute_english.pdf.

42. Burneo Labrín, *Justicia de Genero*, 14-22.

43. Carranza Ko, "Making the Case for Genocide"; Ministerio Público, "Resolución Formalización."

44. Inter-American Commission on Human Rights, "IACHR Expresses Its Deep Concern over the Claim of Sterilizations Against Indigenous Women in Canada," OAS, January 18, 2019, http://www.oas.org/en/iachr/media_center/PReleases
/2019/010.asp.

45. Republic of Peru, "Título II Del Estado y la Nación."

46. Ministerio de la Mujer y Poblaciones Vulnerables, "Conociendo el Servicio de la Defensoría del Niño y del Adolescente," accessed October 2, 2021, https://www
.mimp.gob.pe/files/direcciones/dgnna/conociendo_servicio_dna.pdf, 3.

47. As noted by the Human Rights Ombudsman's Office, actually, sterilization practices continued until 2001. Hence, it is important to take into consideration the program's impacts from 1996 to 2001. See Defensoría del Pueblo, *Decimonoveno Informe Anual.*

48. Ministerio de la Mujer y Poblaciones Vulnerables, "Ley No. 27337—Aprueba el nuevo código de los niños y adolescentes," 2000, accessed October 1, 2021, https://
www.mimp.gob.pe/files/direcciones/dga/nuevo-codigoninos-adolescentes.pdf;
Republica del Perú, "D.L. No. 26102—Aprueba código de los niños y adolescentes,"
1992, accessed October 2, 2021, https://docs.peru.justia.com/federales/decretos-leyes
/26102-dec-28-1992.pdf.

49. United Nations, "Convention on the Rights of the Child."

50. Ministerio de la Mujer y Poblaciones Vulnerables, "Ley No. 27337"; República del Perú, "D.L. No. 26102."

51. International Federation of Gynecology and Obstetrics, "Executive Board Meeting: Female Contraceptive Sterilization," June 2011, https://www.women enabled.org.

52. Ministerio de la Mujer y Poblaciones Vulnerables, "Ley No. 27337."

53. Sarita, interview by author, telephone recording, October 26, 2021.

54. Thorsten Bonacker, "Global Victimhood: On the Charisma of the Victim in Transitional Justice Processes," *World Political Science Review* 9, no. 1 (2013): 98.

55. United Nations, "Declaration of Basic Principles of Justice for Victims of Crime and Abuse of Power," 1985, https://www.un.org/en/ga/search/view_doc.asp ?symbol=A/RES/40/34.

56. United Nations, "Basic Principles and Guidelines on the Right to a Remedy and Reparation for Victims of Gross Violations of International Human Rights Law and Serious Violations of International Humanitarian Law," December 2005, https://www.ohchr.org/en/professionalinterest/pages/remedyandreparation .aspx.

57. Rianne Letschert and Jan van Dijk, "New Faces of Victimhood: Reflections on the Unjust Sides of Globalization," in *The New Faces of Victimhood: Globalization, Transnational Crimes and Victim Rights*, ed. Rianne Letschert and Jan van Dijk (Springer, 2011), 4.

58. Eric Stover, *The Witness: War Crimes and the Promise in The Hague* (University of Pennsylvania Press, 2011), 11.

59. Susan F. Hirsch, "The Victim Deserving of Global Justice: Power, Caution, and Recovering Individuals," in *Mirrors of Justice. Law and Power in the Post-Cold War Era*, ed. Kamari Maxine Clarke and Mark Goodale (Cambridge University Press, 2010), 149–170.

60. Grupo de Trabajo sobre Justicia Transicional y el ODS16+, "Hacia un cambio centrado en las victimas [Towards a change centered on victims]," ICTJ, June 2024, https://www.ictj.org/sites/default/files/2024-06/jac_report_wg-tj-sdg16_2023 _sp.pdf.

61. This approach is not synonymous with the approach to justice that is solely local, "non-Western," and "representative of the context of the violence," as specified by Susan F. Hirsch, "Victim Deserving of Global Justice."

62. Diane F. Orentlicher, "Settling Accounts Revisited: Reconciling Global Norms with Local Agency," *International Journal of Transitional Justice* 1, no. 1 (2007): 20.

63. Claire Moon, "'Who'll Pay Reparations on My Soul?' Compensation, Social Control and Social Suffering," *Social & Legal Studies* 21, no. 2 (2012): 187–199.

64. Sarita, interview by author, telephone recording, October 26, 2021.

65. Kieran McEnvoy and Kirsten McConnachie, "Victimology in Transitional Justice: Victimhood, Innocence, and Hierarchy," *European Journal of Criminology* 9, no. 5 (2012): 528.

66. Pablo De Greiff, "Justice and Reparations," in *The Handbook of Reparations*, ed. Pablo de Greiff (Oxford University Press, 2006), 453.

67. Ñusta Carranza Ko, "Repairing and Reconciling with the Past: 'El Ojo que Llora' and Peru's Public Monuments," in *Monument Culture: International Perspectives on the Future of Monument in a Changing World*, ed. Laura A. Macaluso (Rowman & Littlefield, 2019), 71–84.

68. *El Peruano*, "Ley No. 31119," accessed October 9, 2021, https://busquedas.el peruano.pe.

69. Cedano, "Deuda histórica."

70. Francisco Carranza Romero, interview by author, telephone recording, November 12, 2021.

71. Carranza Romero interview; Carranza Ko, "Qishpikayqa Aham," 117–134.

72. Gladys Tzul Tzul, "Forma Comunal de la Resistencia" (Revista de la Universidad de México, 2019), 107.

73. Irma Alicia Velásquez Nimatuj, "Acceso de las mujeres indígenas a la tierra, el territorio y los recursos naturales en América Latina y el Caribe," ONU Mujeres, October 2018, https://genderandsecurity.org/sites/default/files/Velasquez_Nimatuj _-_Acceso_de_m_indigenas_a_la_tierra.pdf.

74. Carranza Romero, interview by author, telephone recording, November 12, 2021.

75. *Ayni* is a term that has often been used interchangeably to refer to the process of giving and receiving. However, *rantin* is the term most directly associated with the notion of reciprocity. See Francisco Carranza Romero, *Diccionario Quechua-Ancashino* (Iberoamericana Vervuert, 2003).

76. Supa, *Hilos de Mi Vida*.

77. Josef Estermann, *Filosofía Andina* (Instituto Superior Ecuménico Andino de Teología, 2006), 236–237.

78. Chaparro-Buitrago, "Debilitated Lifeworlds," 298.

79. Estermann, *Filosofía Andina*, 237; Supa, *Hilos de Mi Vida*.

80. Carranza Romero, interview by author, telephone recording, November 12, 2021. See Carranza Romero, *Diccionario Quechua-Ancashino*.

81. Lucía Stavig, interview by author, Zoom recording, October 14, 2021.

82. Cuba Corimaita, "Huella Psicológicas de la Esterilización Forzada."

83. Lucía Stavig, interview by author, Zoom recording, October 14, 2021.

84. Supa, *Hilos de Mi Vida*, 126.

85. International Center for Transitional Justice, *Reparations in Peru: From Recommendations to Implementations* (ICTJ, 2013), 13.

86. United Nations, "Twenty-Second Session, Geneva, 25 April–12 May 2000, Agenda Item 3," August 11, 2000, https://docs.un.org/en/E/C.12/2000/4#:~:text=In%20conformity%20with%20articles%2022,of%20the%20right%20to%20health.

87. Mignolo, *La Idea de América Latina*, 36.

CHAPTER 4. THE OTHER VICTIMS

1. Victoria Vigo, author interview, Zoom/WhatsApp recording, October 19, 2021, and October 12, 2022.

2. "Acerca de PetroPeru," PetroPeru, February 1, 2023, https://www.petroperu.com.pe/acerca-de-petroperu/-que-hacemos-/.

3. The 1993 census documents did not include information on health insurance. For more information see https://cdn.www.gob.pe/uploads/document/file/4157945/C%C3%A9dula%20Censal%201993%3A%20%20IX%20de%20Poblaci%C3%B3n%20y%20IV%20de%20Vivienda..pdf?v=1677015392.

4. "Censos Nacionales 2007: XI de Población y VI de Vivienda: Resumen Ejecutivo," INEI, 2007, https://www.inei.gob.pe/media/MenuRecursivo/publicaciones_digitales/Est/Lib0789/Libro.pdf.

5. Baldárrago Estremadoyro, *Dinámicas Étnicas en el Perú*, 18.

6. I specify that Victoria "resided" in Piura, as she no longer is living in either Piura or Peru. Victoria has given me permission to disclose her journey to Canada, where she currently resides as an asylum seeker. Her asylum case was built upon the continuous death threats she received while in Peru that posed a threat to her life, livelihood, and health.

7. Defensoría del Pueblo, *Informe de la Defensoría del Pueblo del Peru para el cuarto ciclo del examen periódico universal* (Defensoría del Pueblo, 2022), 6.

8. I note this aspect of her ethnic background, as this is not something she disclosed and, by assumption of her residence and livelihood in Piura, it becomes clear that she had no direct links with Indigenous ethnicities. However, I am cautious about making a deterministic statement about ethnicity, as the identification with being a mestizo or mestiza by default implies a background of violent ethnic intersection between Indigenous and European ethnic groups.

9. Carranza Ko, "Making the Case for Genocide," 90–103.

10. US Congress, House of Representatives, Committee on International Relations, *The Peruvian Population Control Program: Hearing before the Subcommittee on International Operations and Human Rights*, 105th Cong., 2nd sess. (1998), 1–190.

11. Supreme Court of Justice of Piura, "Sentencia," July 5, 2001, https://1996pnsrpf 2000.files.wordpress.com/2014/09/victoriavigo_sentenciaef_autor-inmediato.pdf.

12. Vigo interview.

13. *El Comercio*, "Estado le debe mas de S/100 millones a clínicas privadas por atender asegurados del SIS y EsSalud, según ACP," June 16, 2022, https:// elcomercio.pe/economia/peru/estado-le-debe-mas-de-s-100-millones-a-clinicas -privadas-por-atender-asegurados-del-sis-y-essalud-segun-acp-rmmn-noticia/ ?ref=ecr.

14. Vigo interview.

15. Vigo interview.

16. Vigo interview.

17. Vigo interview.

18. The term "re-canalizar" literally translated refers to fixing the pipes. In medical terms, it refers to tubal ligation reversal surgery, which cannot always be done. It depends on the extent of the fallopian tubes left or the damage to the fallopian tubes. For more information see Mount Sinai, "Tubal Ligation," https://www.mountsinai .org/health-library/surgery/tubal-ligation-reversal#:~:text=Description,or%20if %20it%20is%20damaged.

19. Vigo interview.

20. Vigo interview.

21. US Congress, *Peruvian Population Control Program*, 26.

22. Vigo interview.

23. Vigo interview.

24. Ministerio de Salud (MINSA) and USAID, *Los primeros años del Proyecto 2000* (Ministerio de Salud, 1997).

25. Ministerio de Salud (MINSA) and USAID, *Los primeros años del Proyecto 2000*, 6.

26. Coe, *Health, Rights, and Realities*, 7.

27. Alejandra Ballón Gutiérrez, "PRENSA," *Archivo PNSRPF* (blog), 2023, https:// 1996pnsrpf2000.wordpress.com/prensa/.

28. "Autoridades de salud aseguran que no obligan a esterilizarse," *La Industria*, September 26, 1996, https://1996pnsrpf2000.files.wordpress.com/2012/10/la-industria -chimbote-24-de-setiembre-de-1996.pdf.

29. Ballón Gutiérrez, "PRENSA"; "Schenone: Gobierno no impone esteriliza-ción de mujeres," *Expreso*, December 9, 1997, https://1996pnsrpf2000.files.wordpress .com/2012/10/expreso-9-de-diciembre-de-1997.pdf.

30. "No hay campaña de esterilización," *El Sol*, January 6, 1998, https://1996 pnsrpf2000.files.wordpress.com/2012/10/el-sol-6-de-enero-de-1998.pdf.

31. Vigo interview.

32. Carranza Ko, *Truth, Justice, and Reparations.*

33. US Congress, *Peruvian Population Control Program*, 2.

34. US Congress, *Peruvian Population Control Program*, 2.

35. US Congress, *Peruvian Population Control Program*, 2.

36. Susana Chávez and Anna-Britt Coe, "Emergency Contraception in Peru: Shifting Government and Donor Policies and Influences," *Reproductive Health Matters* 15, no. 29 (2007): 141, https://doi.org/10.1016/S0968-8080(07)29296-1.

37. Chávez and Coe, "Emergency Contraception in Peru," 141.

38. Comité de América Latina y El Caribe Para la Defensa de los Derechos de la Mujer (CLADEM), *Nada Personal*; Defensoría del Pueblo, *Anticoncepción Quirúrgica Voluntaria I.*

39. Vigo interview.

40. DEMUS, "Cédula de notificación: Resolución formalización de denuncia esterilizaciones forzadas," 2018, http://www.demus.org.pe/wp-content/uploads /2019/01/12-11-18-Resoluci%C2%A6n-Formalizaci%C2%A6n-denuncia-caso-EEFF -versi%C2%A6n-comprimida.pdf.

41. Vigo interview.

42. Supreme Court of Justice of Piura, "Sentencia."

43. Supreme Court of Justice of Piura, "Sentencia."

44. Priscilla Alderson, Joanna Hawthorne, and Margaret Killen, "Are Premature Babies Citizens with Rights? Provision Rights and the Edges of Citizenship," *Journal of Social Sciences* 9 (2005): 71–81; Priscilla Alderson, Margaret Killen, and Joanna Hawthorne, "The Participation Rights of Premature Babies," *The International Journal of Children's Rights* 13, nos. 1–2 (2005): 31–50, https://doi.org/10.1163/1571818054545231.

45. Alderson et al., "Are Premature Babies Citizens with Rights?," 79.

46. Alderson et al., "Are Premature Babies Citizens with Rights?," 79.

47. Alderson et al., "Are Premature Babies Citizens with Rights?," 79.

48. T. Berry Brazelton and J. Kevin Nugent, *Neonatal Behavioral Assessment Scale*, 3rd ed., Clinics in Developmental Medicine no. 137 (MacKeith Press/Cambridge University Press, 1995), 2, 7.

49. Heidelise Als, "Reading the Premature Infant," in *Development Interventions in the Neonatal Intensive Care Nursery*, ed. Edward Goldson (Oxford University Press, 1999), 31.

50. Alderson et al., "Participation Rights of Premature Babies," 31.

51. Alderson et al., "Participation Rights of Premature Babies," 31.

52. Alderson et al., "Participation Rights of Premature Babies," 31.

53. Lawrence J. LeBlanc, *The Convention the Rights of the Child: United Nations Law-making on Human Rights* (University of Nebraska Press, 1995), xii.

54. United Nations, "Convention on the Rights of the Child."

55. Abby F. Janoff, "Rights of the Pregnant Child vs. Rights of the Unborn under the Convention on the Rights of the Child," *Boston University International Law Journal* 22 (2004): 165.

56. United Nations, "Convention on the Rights of the Child."

57. United Nations, "Convention on the Rights of the Child."

58. The only exception are treaties that are non-self-executing, such as the Convention against Torture, which would necessitate an additional step of domestic legislative reform for the norms to be internalized as domestic law. See chapter 3 for more a thorough discussion of these matters.

59. Vigo interview.

60. G. R. Baer and R. M. Nelson, "A Review of Ethical Issues Involved in Premature Birth," in *Institute of Medicine (US) Committee on Understanding Premature Birth and Assuring Healthy Outcomes: Preterm Birth; Causes, Consequences, and Prevention,* ed. Richard E. Behrman and Adrienne Stith Butler (National Academies Press, 2007), 648.

61. Baer and Nelson, "Review of Ethical Issues Involved in Premature Birth," 648.

62. United Nations, "Convention on the Rights of the Child."

63. United Nations, "Convention on the Rights of the Child."

64. United Nations, "Convention on the Rights of the Child."

65. United Nations, "International Covenant on Civil and Political Rights."

66. Human Rights Committee, "General Comment No. 36," September 3, 2019, https://documents-dds-ny.un.org/doc/UNDOC/GEN/G19/261/15/PDF/G1926115 .pdf?OpenElement.

67. United Nations, "Universal Declaration of Human Rights," 1949, https:// www.un.org/en/udhrbook/pdf/udhr_booklet_en_web.pdf.

68. United Nations, "Convention on the Rights of the Child."

69. World Health Organization, "The Prevention and Elimination of Disrespect and Abuse During Facility-Based Childbirth," 2015, http://www.who.int /reproductivehealth/topics/maternal_perinatal/ statement-childbirth/en/.

70. Corte Interamericana de Derechos Humanos, "Caso Brítez Arce y Otros v. Argentina" [Case Brítez Arce and others vs. Argentina], November 16, 2022, https:// www.corteidh.or.cr/docs/casos/articulos/resumen_474_esp.pdf.

71. Corte Interamericana de Derechos Humanos, "Caso Brítez Arce y Otros v. Argentina," November 16, 2022. https://www.corteidh.or.cr/docs/casos/articulos /resumen_474_esp.pdf.

72. Corte Interamericana de Derechos Humanos, "Caso Brítez Arce."

73. Corte Interamericana de Derechos Humanos, "Caso Brítez Arce."

74. Organization of American States, "Inter-American Convention on the Prevention, Punishment, and Eradication of Violence Against Women (Convention of Belém do Pará)," 2023, https://www.oas.org/en/mesecvi/docs/BelemDoPara-ENGLISH.pdf.

75. CEDAW, "General Recommendation Adopted by the Committee on the Elimination of Discrimination Against Women," 1992, https://www.oursplatform.org/wp-content/uploads/CEDAW-Committee-General-Recommendation-19-Violence-against-Women.pdf.

76. United Nations, "Declaration on the Elimination of Violence against Women," December 20, 1993, https://www.ohchr.org/en/instruments-mechanisms/instruments/declaration-elimination-violence-against-women.

77. CEDAW, "Views Communication No. 4/2004," August 29, 2006, https://www.escr-net.org/sites/default/files/CEDAW_Committee_Decision_0.pdf.

78. CEDAW, "Views Communication No. 4/2004."

79. United Nations Committee on the Elimination of Discrimination Against Women, "CEDAW General Recommendation No. 24: Article 12 of the Convention (Women and Health)," 1999, https://www.refworld.org/docid/453882a73.html; CEDAW, "Views Communication No. 4/2004."

80. Center for Reproductive Rights, "A.S. v. Hungary: Informed Consent; A Signature Is Not Enough," December 2008, https://reproductiverights.org/wp-content/uploads/2020/12/AS_v_Hungary_Informed_Consent.pdf.

81. DEMUS, "Cédula de notificación."

82. Vigo interview.

CHAPTER 5. TOGETHER WE FIGHT

1. This chapter uses the terms "activists," "human rights defenders," and "advocates" interchangeably.

2. Rocío Silva Santisteban assumed the leadership position at DEMUS on February 1, 2025.

3. Liz Kelly, Sheila Burton, and Linda Regan, "Beyond Victim or Survivor: Sexual Violence, Identity and Feminist Theory and Practice," in *Sexualizing the Social*, ed. Lisa Adkins and Vicki Merchant (Palgrave Macmillan, 1996), 81.

4. Kelly et al., "Beyond Victim or Survivor," 81.

5. Kristine Avram, "Courts as a Site to Tell the 'Truth': The Case of Former Prisoner Commander Alexandru Visinescu," in *The Impact of Human Rights Prosecutions*, ed. Ulrike Capdepon and Rosario Figari Layus (Leuven University Press, 2020), 52.

6. Kathleen Barry, *Female Sexual Slavery* (New York University Press, 1979), 44–45.

7. Barry, *Female Sexual Slavery*, 44–45.

8. Barry, *Female Sexual Slavery*, 46.

9. Barry, *Female Sexual Slavery*, 47.

10. Carlos Martín Beristain, *Manual sobre perspectiva psicosocial en la investigación de derechos humanos* (Center for Justice and International Law [CEJIL], 2015), 37.

11. Martín Beristain, *Manual sobre perspectiva psicosocial.*

12. United Nations, "Technical Note on the Implementation of the United Nations Protocol on the Provision of Assistance to Victims of Sexual Exploitation and Abuse," 2021, https://www.un.org/preventing-sexual-exploitation-and-abuse /sites/www.un.org.preventing-sexual-exploitation-and-abuse/files/technical_note _on_the_implementation_of_the_un_protocol_on_the_provision_of_assistance _to_victims_of_sea_eng.pdf.

13. United Nations, "Technical Note on the Implementation of the United Nations Protocol."

14. United Nations, "Technical Note on the Implementation of the United Nations Protocol."

15. Martín Beristain, *Manual sobre perspectiva psicosocial*, 38

16. Martín Beristain, *Manual sobre perspectiva psicosocial*, 39.

17. Martín Beristain, *Manual sobre perspectiva psicosocial*, 39.

18. Ileana Carmen Rogobete, *Reconstructing Trauma and Meaning: Life Narratives of Survivors of Political Violence During Apartheid in South Africa* (Cambridge Scholars Publishing, 2015), 6.

19. Brandon Hamber, *Transforming Societies after Political Violence: Truth, Reconciliation, and Mental Health* (Springer, 2009), 40.

20. Ñusta Carranza Ko, "Qishpikayqa Aham," 125–126.

21. Kelly et al., "Beyond Victim or Survivor," 96.

22. Kelly et al., "Beyond Victim or Survivor," 96.

23. Kelly et al., "Beyond Victim or Survivor," 96.

24. Kelly et al., "Beyond Victim or Survivor," 96.

25. Sarah Ailwood, Rachel Loney-Howes, Nan Seuffert, and Cassandra Sharp, "Beyond Women's Voices: Towards a Victim-Survivor-Centered Theory of Listening in Law Reform on Violence Against Women," *Feminist Legal Studies* 31 (2023): 217–241, https://doi.org/10.1007/s10691-022-09499-1.

26. Pyong Gap Min, *Korean "Comfort Women": Military Brothels, Brutality, and the Redress Movement* (Rutgers University Press, 2021).

27. Margaret D. Stetz, "Making Girl Victims Visible: A Survey of Representations That Have Circulated in the West," in *Japanese Military Sexual Slavery: The*

Transnational Redress Movement for the Victims, ed. Pyong Gap Min, Thomas Chung, and Sejung Sage Yim (De Gruyter, 2020), 215–227.

28. Jae-wook Jung, "위안부 피해자 할머니 "내 소원은 한국과 일본이 원수지지 않는 것," *Future Korea Weekly*, June 24, 2015, http://www.futurekorea.co.kr/news/articleView.html?idxno=28466.

29. Angella Son, "Translator's Preface," in *Stories That Make History: The Experience and Memories of the Japanese Military Comfort Girls-Women*, ed. The Research Team of the War & Women's Human Rights Center and The Korean Council for the Women Drafted for Military Sexual Slavery by Japan (De Gruyter, 2020), vii.

30. Ailwood et al., "Beyond Women's Voices."

31. Boesten, *Violencia sexual en la guerra y en la paz* (Biblioteca Nacional del Perú, 2016), 18.

32. Pascha Bueno-Hansen, *Feminist and Human Rights Struggles in Peru*, 109–110.

33. Getgen, "Untold Truths," 1–34.

34. Hilaria Supa Huamán, interview by author, WhatsApp recording, April 1, 2022.

35. Ballón Gutiérrez, "El caso peruano de esterilización forzada. Notas."

36. Margaret E. Keck and Kathryn Sikkink, *Activists Beyond Borders: Advocacy Networks in International Politics* (Cornell University Press, 1998), 3.

37. Alison Brysk, "From Above and Below Social Movements, the International System, and Human Rights in Argentina," *Comparative Political Studies* 26, no. 3 (1993): 259–285; Charli R. Carpenter, "Setting the Advocacy Agenda: Theorizing Issue Emergence and Nonemergence in Transitional Advocacy Networks," *International Studies Quarterly* 51, no. 1 (2007): 99–120; Charli R. Carpenter, "Studying Issue (Non)-Adoption in Transnational Advocacy Networks," *International Organizations* 61, no. 3 (2007): 643–667; Ann Marie Clark, *Diplomacy of Conscience* (Princeton University Press, 2001).

38. Carranza Ko, *Truth, Justice, and Reparations in Peru, Uruguay, and South Korea* (Palgrave Macmillan, 2021).

39. Tamayo, *Nada Personal*, 43–44.

40. Defensoría del Pueblo, *Anticoncepción Quirúrgica Voluntaria I* (Defensoría del Pueblo, 1998), 36–38; Defensoría del Pueblo, *La Aplicación de la Anticoncepción Quirúrgica y los Derechos Reproductivos II* (Defensoría del Pueblo, 2000); Defensoría del Pueblo, *La Aplicación de la Anticoncepción Quirúrgica y los Derechos Reproductivos III* (Defensoría del Pueblo, 2002).

41. CEJIL, "Caso Mamérita Mestanza Chávez," 2023, https://cejil.org/caso/caso-mamerita-mestanza-chavez/.

42. Comisión Interamericana de Derechos Humanos, "Informe No. 66/00," 2000, https://www.cidh.oas.org/annualrep/2000sp/CapituloIII/Admisible/Peru12.191.htm.

43. Since 1997, CLADEM had been involved in presenting its first official complaint against the Hospital Rural de Tocache, where María Mamerita Mestanza Chávez had died as a result of complications related to tubal ligation. CLADEM was also involved in transmitting video testimony of María Mamerita's husband to the Human Rights Ombudsman's Office during the same year. For more information see, Alejandra Ballón Gutiérrez, "Fechas" [Dates], *Archivo PNSRPF* (blog), 2023, https://1996pnsrpf2000.wordpress.com/fechas/.

44. Congreso de la República del Perú, "Hilaria Supa Huamán," 2006, https://www4.congreso.gob.pe/congresista/2006/hsupa/_hoja-vida.htm.

45. Inter-American Commission on Human Rights (IACHR), Report No. 71/03, Petition 12.191.

46. Alejandra Ballón Gutiérrez, "ARTE" [Art], *Archivo PNSRPF* (blog), 2023, https://1996pnsrpf2000.wordpress.com/arte/.

47. Alejandra Ballón Gutiérrez, "Una forma posible de política afectiva," *Revista Arte y Diseño A&D* 2 (2013): 41.

48. Quipu Project, "The Quipu Project."

49. Matthew Brown and Karen Tucker, "Esterilizaciones forzadas, narrativa participativa y contramemoria digital en el Perú," *Conexión* 7, no. 9 (2018): 59.

50. Brown and Tucker, "Esterilizaciones forzadas," 63.

51. Emilie Pine, "Digital Campaigns, Forums, and Archives," in *Routledge Handbook of Memory Activism*, ed. Yifat Gutman and Jenny Wustenberg (Routledge, 2023), 405.

52. Pine, "Digital Campaigns, Forums, and Archives," 405.

53. Alejandra Ballón, interview by author, Zoom recording, December 3, 2021.

54. Ballón, interview.

55. Ballón, interview.

56. Inter-American Court of Human Rights, "Caso Eduardo Nicolás Cruz Sánchez y otros (Chavín de Huántar) v. Perú," 2012, https://www.corteidh.or.cr/docs/casos/cruz-sanchez/esap.pdf.

57. Ballón interview.

58. Rocío Silva Santisteban, interview by author, Zoom recording, October 4, 2021.

59. Ballón Gutiérrez, "PRENSA."

60. Ballón Gutiérrez, "PRENSA."

61. Giulia Tamayo, Entrevista, https://www.verdadyreconciliacionperu.com/admin/files/articulos/760_digitalizacion.pdf.

62. Tamayo, Entrevista.

63. Giulia Tamayo, *Derechos sexuales: Bajo la piel* (Centro de la Mujer Peruana Flora Tristán, 2001).

64. Rocío Silva Santisteban, interview by author, Zoom recording, October 4, 2021.

65. Silva Santisteban interview.

66. Defensoría del Pueblo, *La aplicación de la anticoncepción quirúrgica y los derechos reproductivos II*, 59–60.

67. Defensoría del Pueblo, *La aplicación de la anticoncepción quirúrgica y los derechos reproductivos II*, 50.

68. Defensoría del Pueblo, *La aplicación de la anticoncepción quirúrgica y los derechos reproductivos* II; Defensoría del Pueblo, *La aplicación de la anticoncepción quirúrgica y los derechos reproductivos III*.

69. Guiliana Campos and Ronny Condor, "La etnicidad en el Perú y su naturaleza multidimensional: una propuesta de medición" [Ethnicity in Peru and its multidimensional nature: a proposal for mediation], *Desde el Sur* 14, no. 1 (2002), 15–16, https://doi.org/10.21142/DES-1401-2022-0012.

70. Defensoría del Pueblo, *La aplicación de la anticoncepción quirúrgica y los derechos reproductivos III*, 5.

71. María Ysabel Cedano, interview by author, WhatsApp recording, November 3, 2021.

72. Cedano interview.

73. *Gestión*, "Elegir entre Keiko Fujimori y Humala, es como optar por el cáncer o el sida," 2011, https://archivo.gestion.pe/noticia/290532/elegir-entre-keiko-fujimori-humala-como-optar-cancer-sida.

74. Rocío Silva Santisteban, interview by author, Zoom recording, October 4, 2021.

75. WOLA (Washington Office on Latin America), "Why I Will Vote for Humala," May 31, 2011, https://www.wola.org/analysis/why-i-will-vote-for-humala/.

76. Silva Santisteban interview.

77. Supreme Court of Justice of Piura, "Sentencia"; US Congress, House of Representatives, Committee on International Relations, *Peruvian Population Control Program*, 1–190.

78. Silva Santisteban interview.

79. Comisión de la Verdad y Reconciliación, *Final Report*.

80. Carranza Ko, *Truth, Justice, and Reparations in Peru, Uruguay, and South Korea*, 72.

81. Hilaria Supa Huamán, interview by author, WhatsApp recording, April 1, 2022.

82. Silva Santisteban interview.

83. According to the Inter-American Commission on Human Rights, the state of emergency continued throughout 1997 in certain parts of the Peruvian state. This is

something about which the Commission and the Committee against Torture (i.e., the body that monitors the implementation of the Convention against Torture by member states) had expressed significant concerns, as they had received evidence of torture and abuse of power by the anti-terrorist police forces (i.e., DINCOTE) and the armed forces. For more information, see Comisión Interamericana de Derechos Hermanos, Organización de los Estados Americanos, "Peru," https://www.cidh.oas.org/annualrep/97span/cap.5d.htm. María Ysabel Cedano, interview by author, WhatsApp recording, November 3, 2021.

84. Hilaria Supa Huamán, interview by author, WhatsApp recording, April 1, 2022.

85. Huamán interview.

86. Huamán interview.

87. Ketty Marcelo López, interview by author, Zoom recording, October 24, 2024.

88. López interview.

89. López interview.

90. Silva Santisteban interview.

91. *El Peruano*, "Normas Legales," July 29, 2005, https://www.mimp.gob.pe/homemimp/direcciones/ddcp/normas/4_5_Ley_28592_Crea_el_PIR.pdf.

92. *El Peruano*, "Normas Legales," February 6, 2021, https://busquedas.elperuano.pe/download/url/ley-que-modifica-los-articulos-3-y-6-de-la-ley-28592-ley-qu-ley-n-31119-1926075-2.

93. Silva Santisteban interview.

94. Asociación de Mujeres Peruanas Afectadas por las Esterilizaciones Forzadas, Facebook page, 2022, https://www.facebook.com/photo.php?fbid=553588463472961&set=pb.100064654363391.-2207520000.&type=3&locale=nl_NL; DEMUS, "Poder judicial ordena al ejecutivo cumplir con reparaciones integrales a las víctimas de esterilizaciones forzadas," December 2, 2022, https://www.demus.org.pe/noticias/poder-judicial-ordena-al-ejecutivo-cumplir-con-reparaciones-integrales-a-las-victimas-de-esterilizaciones-forzadas/

95. Amnistía International, "Perú: Rechazo de Amnistía Internacional a una ley anti ONG," April 15, 2025, https://amnistia.org.ar/noticias/peru-rechazo-de-amnistia-internacional-a-una-ley-anti-ong; Juan Carlos Ruiz Molleda, "Análisis de la Constitucionalidad de la Nueva Ley Anti-ONG aprobada por el Congreso," March 14, 2025, https://www.idl.org.pe/analisis-de-la-constitucionalidad-de-la-nueva-ley-anti-ong-aprobada-por-el-congreso/.

96. Silva Santisteban interview.

97. Victoria Vigo, interview by author, Zoom/WhatsApp recording, October 19, 2021 and October 12, 2022.

98. Bueno-Hansen, *Feminist and Human Rights Struggles in Peru*, 16.

99. Marcelo López interview.

100. Cedano interview.

101. Quipu Project, "Quipu Project."

102. Silva Santisteban interview.

103. Silva Santisteban interview.

104. Asociación de Mujeres Peruanas Afectadas por las Esterilizaciones Forzadas, Facebook page; DEMUS, "Poder judicial ordena al ejecutivo cumplir."

105. Cedano interview.

106. Naomi Roht-Arriaza, "Measures of Non-Repetition in Transitional Justice: The Missing Link?," in *From Transitional to Transformative Justice*, ed. Paul Gready and Simon Robins (Cambridge University Press, 2019), 105–130.

107. United Nations Office of the High Commissioner, "Basic Principles and Guidelines on the Right to a Remedy and Reparation for Victims of Gross Violations of International Human Rights Law and Serious Violations of International Humanitarian Law," 2005, https://www.ohchr.org/en/instruments-mechanisms/instruments/basic-principles-and-guidelines-right-remedy-and-reparation.

108. Huamán interview.

109. Marcelo López interview.

110. Ballón interview.

111. M. K. Asante, *It's Bigger Than Hip Hop: The Rise of the Post-Hip-Hop Generation* (St. Martin's Press, 2008), 6.

112. Robin Adéle Greeley, Michael R. Orwicz, José Luis Falconi, Ana María Reyes, Fernando J. Roseberg, and Lisa J. Laplante, "Repairing Symbolic Reparations: Assessing the Effectiveness of Memorialization in the Inter-American System of Human Rights," *International Journal of Transitional Justice* 14 (2020): 166.

113. Ballón interview.

114. Ballón interview.

115. Municipalidad de Lima, "Realizan Tribunal de Conciencia por Justicia Para las Mujeres Víctimas del Conflicto Armado Interno," November 8, 2013, https://www.youtube.com/watch?v=54gYcGyFo3I.

116. Vigo interview.

CONCLUSION

1. "Víctimas de esterilizaciones forzadas en Perú siguen luchando por la justicia," *France24*, January 30, 2023, https://www.france24.com/es/programas/boleto-de-vuelta/20230130-v%C3%ADctimas-de-esterilizaciones-forzadas-en-per%C3%BA

-siguen-luchando-por-justicia; Michael Cook, "Peru's Forced Sterilization Tragedy Drags on in the Courts," *BioEdge*, January 31, 2023, https://bioedge.org/public_health/population/perus-forced-sterilization-tragedy-drags-on-in-the-courts/.

2. Lisandro Libertad and Eduardo Brenis Pita, "Entrevista: A 31 años de auto-golpe de Fujimori, las victimas de esterilización forzada siguen exigiendo justicia," *La Izquierda Diario*, April 5, 2023, https://www.laizquierdadiario.com/A-31-anos-de-autogolpe-de-Fujimori-las-victimas-de-esterilizacion-forzada-siguen-exigiendo-justicia.

3. United Nations, "Peru: Fujimori Government's Forced Sterilization Policy Violated Women's Rights, UN Committee Says in Landmark Ruling," October 30, 2024, https://www.ohchr.org/en/press-releases/2024/10/peru-fujimori-governments-forced-sterilisation-policy-violated-womens-rights.

4. Bueno-Hansen, *Feminist and Human Rights Struggles in Peru.*

5. Ruti G. Teitel, "Transitional Justice Genealogy," *Harvard Human Rights Journal* 16 (2003): 77.

6. Priscilla B. Hayner, *Unspeakable Truths: Transitional Justice and the Challenge of Truth Commissions*, 2nd ed. (Routledge, 2011).

7. Carranza Ko, *Truth, Justice, and Reparations in Peru, Uruguay, and South Korea* (Palgrave Macmillan, 2021), 43.

8. Hun Joon Kim, *The Massacres at Mt. Halla: Sixty Years of Truth Seeking in South Korea* (Cornell University Press, 2014).

9. Salomón Febres Lerner, "Tareas de la Comisión de la Verdad y Reconciliación: Fundamentos Teológicos y Éticos," in *Verdad y Reconciliación: Reflexiones Éticas*, ed. Salomón Lerner, José Burneo, Guillermo Kerber, et al. (Centro de Estudios y Publicaciones, 2002), 30.

10. For more information about these types of cases, see Carranza Ko, *Truth, Justice, and Reparations in Peru, Uruguay, and South Korea.*

BIBLIOGRAPHY

"Acerca de PetroPeru" [About PetroPeru]. PetroPeru. February 1, 2023. https://www.petroperu.com.pe/acerca-de-petroperu/-que-hacemos-/.

Ailwood, Sarah, Rachel Loney-Howes, Nan Seuffert, and Cassandra Sharp. "Beyond Women's Voices: Towards a Victim-Survivor-Centered Theory of Listening in Law Reform on Violence Against Women." *Feminist Legal Studies* 31 (2023): 217–241. https://doi.org/10.1007/s10691-022-09499-1.

"Alberto Fujimori declarará por esterilizaciones forzadas con miras a ampliar su extradición desde Chile" [Alberto Fujimori will declare on forced sterilizations with outlook to expand the extradition from Chile]. *Infobae.* May 12, 2023. https://www.infobae.com/peru/2023/05/12/alberto-fujimori-declarara-por-esterilizaciones-forzadas-con-miras-a-ampliar-su-extradicion-desde-chile/.

Alcalde, M. Cristina. *The Woman in the Violence: Gender, Poverty, and Resistance in Peru.* Vanderbilt University Press, 2010.

Alderson, Priscilla, Joanna Hawthorne, and Margaret Killen. "Are Premature Babies Citizens with Rights? Provision Rights and the Edges of Citizenship." *Journal of Social Sciences* 9 (2005): 71–81.

Alderson, Priscilla. Margaret Killen, and Joanna Hawthorne. "The Participation Rights of Premature Babies." *International Journal of Children's Rights* 13, nos. 1–2 (2005). https://doi.org/10.1163/1571818054545231.

Als, Heidelise. "Reading the Premature Infant." In *Development Interventions in the Neonatal Intensive Care Nursery,* edited by Edward Goldson. Oxford University Press, 1999.

Alva-Arévalo, Amelia. "La identificación de los pueblos indígenas en el Perú ¿Qué está sucediendo con el criterio de autoidentificación?" [The identification of Indigenous peoples in Peru: What is happening with the criteria of auto identification?]. *CUHSO (Temuco)* 30, no. 2 (2020): 60–77. https://dx .doi.org/10.7770/2452-610x.2020.cuhso.01.a05.

Alvites Sosa, Lucía. "Sistema patriarcal, articulo de importación colonial en los Andes" [Patriarchal system, imported colonial article in the Andes]. *Revista de Sociología* 26 (2016). https://doi.org/10.15381/rsoc.v0i26.18992.

Ames, Patricia ."Niños y niñas andinos en el Perú: crecer en un mundo de relaciones y responsabilidades" [Andean boys and girls in Peru: Growing in a world of relations and responsibilities]. *Bulletin de l'Institut français d'études andines* 42, no. 3 (2013): 389–409.

Amnistía International. "Perú: Rechazo de Amnistía Internacional a una ley anti ONG" [Peru: Rejection of Amnesty International towards the anti-NGO law]. April 15, 2025. https://amnistia.org.ar/noticias/peru-rechazo-de -amnistia-internacional-a-una-ley-anti-ong.

Annett, Kevin. *Hidden from History: The Canadian Holocaust; The Untold Story of the Genocide of Aboriginal Peoples by Church and State in Canada.* The Truth Commission into Genocide in Canada, 2001.

Annett, Kevin. *Hidden No Longer: Genocide in Canada, Past and Present.* The International Tribunal into Crimes of Church and State and The Friends and Relatives of the Disappeared, 2010.

Archivo PSRPF. "Arte." Accessed January 1, 2022. https://1996pnsrpf2000.word press.com/arte/.

Arista Zerga, Adriana. "La importancia de llamarse indígena: Manejo y uso político del termino indígena en Lircay-Perú" [The importance of being called Indigenous: Political use of the term Indigenous in Lircay-Peru]. *Identididades, cidadanias e Estado* 7 (2010). https://doi.org/10.4000/eces.430.

Asante, M. K. *It's Bigger Than Hip Hop: The Rise of the Post-Hip-Hop Generation.* New York: St. Martin's Press, 2008.

Asociación de Mujeres Peruanas Afectadas por las Esterilizaciones Forzadas [Association of Peruvian Women Affected by Forced Sterilizations]. Facebook page. November 28, 2022. https://www.facebook.com/photo.php?fbid =553588463472961&set=pb.100064654363391.-2207520000.&type=3&locale= nl_NL.

"Autoridades de salud aseguran que no obligan a esterilizarse" [Health authorities assure that they do not obligate sterilizations]. *La Industria.* September 26,

1996. https://1996pnsrpf2000.files.wordpress.com/2012/10/la-industria-chimbote-24-de-setiembre-de-1996.pdf.

Avram, Kristine. "Courts as a Site to Tell the 'Truth': The Case of Former Prisoner Commander Alexandru Visinescu." In *The Impact of Human Rights Prosecutions*, edited by Ulrike Capdepon and Rosario Figari Layus. Leuven University Press, 2020.

Baer, G. R., and R. M. Nelson. "A Review of Ethical Issues Involved in Premature Birth." In *Institute of Medicine (US) Committee on Understanding Premature Birth and Assuring Healthy Outcomes: Preterm Birth: Causes, Consequences, and Prevention*, edited by Richard E. Behrman and Adrienne Stith Butler. National Academies Press, 2007.

Bahati Kuumba, Monica. "Perpetuating Neo-Colonialism Through Population Control: South Africa and the United States." *Africa Today* 40, no. 3 (1993). http://www.jstor.org/stable/4186924.

Baldárrago Estremadoyro, Elin Roselia. *Dinámicas Étnicas en el Perú: Hacia una caracterización y tipología para el diseño de políticas públicas* [Ethnic dynamics in Peru: Towards a characterization and typology for public policy design]. INEI, 2017.

Ballón Gutiérrez, Alejandra. "ARTE" [Art]. *Archivo PNSRPF* (blog). 2023. https://1996pnsrpf2000.wordpress.com/arte/.

Ballón Gutiérrez, Alejandra. "El caso Peruano de esterilización forzada: notas para una cartografía de resistencia" [Peruvian case of forced sterilization: Notes for a cartography of resistance]. *Aletheia* 5, no. 9 (2014). https://www.aletheia.fahce.unlp.edu.ar/article/view/ATHv5n09a12/11476.

Ballón Gutiérrez, Alejandra. "El caso peruano de esterilizaciones forzadas: Una pieza clave del conflicto armado interno." In *Perú: Las esterilizaciones forzadas, en la década del terror* [The Peruvian case of forced sterilizations: A key part of the internal armed conflict], edited by Alberto Chirif. IWGIA (International Work Group for Indigenous Affairs), 2021.

Ballón Gutiérrez, Alejandra. "Fechas" [Dates]. *Archivo PNSRPF* (blog). 2023. https://1996pnsrpf2000.wordpress.com/fechas/.

Ballón Gutiérrez, Alejandra. "PRENSA." *Archivo PNSRPF* (blog). 2023. https://1996pnsrpf2000.wordpress.com/prensa/.

Ballón Gutiérrez, Alejandra. "Una forma posible de política afectiva." *Revista Arte y Diseño A&D* 2 (2013). https://revistas.pucp.edu.pe/index.php/ayd/article/view/19669.

Barry, Kathleen. *Female Sexual Slavery*. New York University Press, 1979.

Bob, Clifford. *Rights as Weapons: Instruments of Conflict, Tools of Power.* Princeton University Press, 2019.

Boesten, Jelke. "Free Choice or Poverty Alleviation? Population Politics in Peru Under Alberto Fujimori." *European Review of Latin American and Caribbean Studies,* no. 82 (2007). http://www.jstor.org/stable/25676252.

Boesten, Jelke. *Violencia sexual en la Guerra y en la paz: Genero, poder y justicia posconflicto en el Perú* [Sexual violence in war and peace: Gender, power, and justice in postconflict Peru]. Biblioteca Nacional del Perú, 2016.

Bonacker, Thorsten. "Global Victimhood: On the Charisma of the Victim in Transitional Justice Processes." *World Political Science Review* 9, no. 1 (2013): 97–129.

Bonfil Batalla, Guillermo. "El concepto del indio en América: Una categoría de la situación colonial" [The concept of the indian in America: A category of the colonial situation]. *Revista semanal de la Asociación Latinoamericana de Antropología* (ALA) 3, no. 2 (2019): 15–37.

Brave Heart, M. Y., and L. M. DeBruyn. "American Indian Holocaust: Healing Historical Unresolved Grief." *American Indian and Alaska Native Mental Health Research* 8, no. 2 (1998): 56–78.

Brazelton, T. Berry, and J. Kevin Nugent. *Neonatal Behavioral Assessment Scale.* 3rd ed. Clinics in Developmental Medicine no. 137. MacKeith Press/Cambridge University Press, 1995.

Bronfman, Mario N., and Roberto Castro. "Discurso y practica de la planificación familiar: El caso de América Latina" [Discourse and practice in family planning: The case of Latin America]. *Saúde em Debate* 25 (1989): 61–67.

Brown, Matthew and Karen Tucker. "Esterilizaciones forzadas, narrativa participativa y contramemoria digital en el Perú" [Forced sterilizations, participant narratives, and digital counter memory in Peru]. *Conexión* 7, no. 9 (2018). https://doi.org/10.18800/conexion.201801.004.

Brysk, Alison. "From Above and Below Social Movements, the International System, and Human Rights in Argentina." *Comparative Political Studies* 26, no. 3 (1993): 59–85.

Bueno-Hansen, Pascha. *Feminist and Human Rights Struggles in Peru.* University of Illinois Press, 2015.

Burgos, Elizabeth. *Me llamo Rigoberta Menchú y así me nació la conciencia* [I am Rigoberta Menchu and this i show my conscience was born]. Siglo Veintiuno, 1985.

Burneo Labrín, José. *Justicia de Genero: Esterilización Forzada En El Perú; Delito de Lesa Humanidad* [Justice of gender: Forced sterilization in Peru; Crime against humanity]. Editorial Linea Andina, 2008.

Butler, Judith. *Gender Trouble: Feminism and the Subversion of Identity.* Routledge, 1999.

Butler, Judith. "Performative Acts and Gender Constitution: An Essay in Phenomenology and Feminist Theory." In *Performing Feminisms: Feminist Critical Theory and Theatre*, edited by Sue-Ellen Case. Johns Hopkins University Press, 1990.

Callirgos, Juan Carlos. *El racismo: La cuestión del otro (y de uno)* [Racism: The question of the other (and of oneself)]. DESCO, 1993.

Campos, Guiliana, and Ronny Condor, "La etnicidad en el Perú y su naturaleza multidimensional: Una propuesta de medición" [Ethnicity in Peru and its multidimensional nature: A proposal for mediation]. *Desde el Sur* 14, no. 1 (2002). https://doi.org/10.21142/DES-1401-2022-0012.

Canales Poma, Melania. "La justicia es inalcanzable para las mujeres indígenas" [Justice is not reachable for Indigenous women]. In *Las esterilizaciones forzadas 25 años después: Justicia y Reparación* [Forced sterilizations 25 years later: Justice and reparation], edited by Lucía Santos Peralta. Pontifica Univerisdad Católica del Perú, 2023.

Carpenter, Charli R. "Setting the Advocacy Agenda: Theorizing Issue Emergence and Nonemergence in Transitional Advocacy Networks." *International Studies Quarterly* 51, no. 1 (2007): 99–120.

Carpenter, Charli R. "Studying Issue (Non)-Adoption in Transnational Advocacy Networks." *International Organizations* 61, no. 3 (2007): 643–667.

Carranza Ko, Ñusta. "Complicating Genocide: Missing Indigenous Women's Stories." In *Oxford Research Encyclopedia of Politics.* September 29, 2021. https://doi.org/10.1093/acrefore/9780190228637.013.2008.

Carranza Ko, Ñusta. "Forcibly Sterilized: Peru's Indigenous Women and the Battle for Rights." In *Human Rights as Battlefields: Changing Practices and Contestations*, edited by Gabriel Blouin-Genest, Marie-Christine Doran, and Sylvie Paquerot. Palgrave Macmillan, 2019.

Carranza Ko, Ñusta. "Making the Case for Genocide, the Forced Sterilization of Indigenous Peoples of Peru." *Genocide Studies and Prevention: An International Journal* 14, no. 2 (2020): 90–103.

Carranza Ko, Ñusta. "Qishpikayqa Aham: The Hardships of Becoming." In *Indigenous Futures and Learnings Taking Place*, edited by Licho López López and Gioconda Coello. Routledge, 2021.

Carranza Ko, Ñusta. "Repairing and Reconciling with the Past: 'El Ojo que Llora' and Peru's Public Monuments." In *Monument Culture: International Perspectives on the Future of Monument in a Changing World*, edited by Laura A. Macaluso. Rowman & Littlefield, 2019.

Carranza Ko, Ñusta. *Truth, Justice, and Reparations in Peru, Uruguay, and South Korea*. Palgrave Macmillan, 2021.

Carranza Romero, Francisco. *Diccionario Quechua-Ancashino* [Quechua-Ancash dictionary]. Iberoamericana Vervuert, 2003.

Casas, Bartolomé de las. *A Short Account of the Destruction of the Indies*. Penguin Books, 2004.

Cedano, María Ysabel. "Deuda histórica: Esterilizaciones forzadas y derecho a reparaciones integrales" [Historical debt: Forced sterilizations and right to integral reparations]. March 20, 2021. https://www.demus.org.pe.

CEDAW. "General Recommendation Adopted by the Committee on the Elimination of Discrimination Against Women." 1992. https://www.oursplatform.org/wp-content/uploads/CEDAW-Committee-General-Recommendation-19-Violence-against-Women.pdf.

CEDAW. "Views Communication No. 4/2004." August 29, 2006. https://www.escr-net.org/sites/default/files/CEDAW_Committee_Decision_0.pdf.

CEJIL. "Caso Mamérita Mestanza Chávez." [Case of Mamérita Mestanza Chávez]. 2023. https://cejil.org/caso/caso-mamerita-mestanza-chavez/.

"Censos Nacionales 2007: XI de Población y VI de Vivienda; Resumen Ejecutivo" [National Census 2007: XI of population and VI of residence; executive summary]. INEI. 2007. https://www.inei.gob.pe/media/Menu Recursivo/publicaciones_digitales/Est/Lib0789/Libro.pdf.

Center for Reproductive Rights. "A.S. v. Hungary: Informed Consent; A Signature Is Not Enough." December 2008. https://reproductiverights.org/wp-content/uploads/2020/12/AS_v_Hungary_Informed_Consent.pdf.

Center for Reproductive Rights. "The Case of Celia Ramos: Seeking Justice for Women Forcibly Sterilized Under Peru's Fujimori Regime." May 19, 2025. https://reproductiverights.org/celia-ramos-forced-sterilization-peru/.

Chaparro-Buitrago, Julietta. "Debilitated Lifeworlds: Women's Narratives of Forced Sterilization as Delinking from Reproductive Rights." *Medical Anthropology Quarterly* 36, no. 3 (2022): 301.

Chávez, Susana, and Anna-Britt Coe. "Emergency Contraception in Peru: Shifting Government and Donor Policies and Influences." *Reproductive Health Matters* 15, no. 29 (2007). https://doi.org/10.1016/S0968-8080(07)29296-1.

Clark, Ann Marie. *Diplomacy of Conscience*. Princeton University Press, 2001.

Coe, Anna-Britt. *Health, Rights and Realities: An Analysis of the ReprodSalud Project in Peru*. Center for Health and Gender Equity, 2001.

Coello, Gioconda, and Ligia (Licho) López López. "Futures Taking Place." In *Indigenous Futures and Learnings Taking Place*, edited by Ligia (Licho) López López and Gioconda Coello. Routledge, 2021.

Cojti Ren, Avexnim. "Maya Archaeology and the Political and Cultural Identity of Contemporary Maya in Gutemala." In *Indigenous Archaeologies: A Reader on Decolonization*, edited by Margaret M. Bruchac, Siobhan M. Hart, and H. Martin Wobst. Routledge, 2016.

Comisión de la Verdad y Reconciliación. *Final Report*. 2003. Accessed August 1, 2019. http://www.cverdad.org.pe/ingles/ifinal/index.php.

Comisión de la Verdad y Reconciliación. *Informe Final: Conclusiones* [Final report: Conclusions]. 2003. https://www.cverdad.org.pe/ifinal/conclusiones.php.

Comisión Interamericana de Derechos Humanos. "Informe No. 66/00" [Report no. 66/00]. 2000. https://www.cidh.oas.org/annualrep/2000sp/CapituloIII/Admisible/Peru12.191.htm.

Comisión Interamericana de Derechos Humanos. "Solución amistosa María Mamérita Mestanza Chávez v. Perú." Accessed April 19, 2022. https://www.cidh.oas.org/women/peru.12191sp.htm.

Comité de América Latina y El Caribe Para la Defensa de los Derechos de la Mujer (CLADEM). *Nada Personal: Reporte de Derechos Humanos Sobre la Aplicación de la Anticoncepción Quirúrgica en el Perú 1996–1998* [Nothing personal: Report on human rights about the application of surgical contraception in Peru 1996–1998]. CLADEM, 1999.

Congreso de la República. "Constitución para la República del Perú (12 de Julio de 1979)" [Constitution of the Republic of Peru]. 1979. https://www.leyes.congreso.gob.pe/Documentos/constituciones_ordenado/CONSTIT_1979/Cons1979_TEXTO_CORREGIDO.pdf.

Congreso de la República. "Constitución Política del Perú: Promulgada el 29 de Diciembre de 1993" [Political constitution of Peru: Promulgated on 29 December 1993]. 2019. https://www.congreso.gob.pe/Docs/files/constitucion/constitucion2019/index.html.

Congreso de la República. "Diario de los Debates" [Notes of debates]. 1823. https://www4.congreso.gob.pe/dgp/constitucion/constituciones/Constitucion-1823.pdf.

Congreso de la República. *Diario de los debates: Segunda Legislatura Ordinaria de 1997 4ª Sesión Miércoles 18 de marzo de 1998* [Notes of debates: Second Ordinary Legislature of 1997 4th Session Wednesday 18 of March 1998].

March 18, 1998. Accessed May 1, 2019. http://www2.congreso.gob.pe/sicr/
diariodebates/Publicad.nsf/2b66b8a68552546d05256f1000575a5c/05256d6e.
0073dfe9052565d1007dcde5?OpenDocument.

Congreso de la República. *Informes de Comisión: Subcomisión Investigadora de la
Denuncia Constitucional No. 151* [Commission report: Investigative Subcomis-
sion of Constitutional Complaint No. 151]. January 30, 2003. https://www2
.congreso.gob.pe/Sicr/ApoyComisiones/informes.nsf/InformesPorComision
/C405450DEB310E6C05256CBE0076A35E.

Congreso de la República. "Ley de Comunidades Nativas y de Desarrollo
Agrario de la Selva y de Ceja de Selva" [Law of native communities and
agrarian development of the Amazon and outer edges of the Amazon (jungle areas)]. 1978. https://www2.congreso.gob.pe/sicr/cendocbib/con3_uibd
.nsf/0D41EC1170BDE30A052578F70059D913/$FILE/(1)leydecomunidades
nativasley22175.pdf.

Congreso de la República. "Nueva Reforma Agraria" [New agrarian reform].
1969. https://leyes.congreso.gob.pe/Documentos/Leyes/17716.pdf.

Congreso de la República del Perú. "Hilaria Supa Huamán." 2006. https://
www4.congreso.gob.pe/congresista/2006/hsupa/_hoja-vida.htm.

Constitución Política de 1826. "Constitución Política para la Republica
del Perú" [Political constitution of the Republic of Peru], 1826. https://
www.leyes.congreso.gob.pe/Documentos/constituciones_ordenado
/CONSTIT_1826/Cons1826_TEXTO.pdf.

Constitución Política de la República Peruana Sancionada por el Primer
Congreso Constituyente [Political constitution of the Republic of Peru
approved by the First Constituent Congress]. November 12, 1823. Accessed
August 1, 2019. http://www.leyes.congreso.gob.pe/Documentos/constituciones
_ordenado/CONSTIT_1823/Cons1823_TEXTO. pdf.

Cook, Michael. "Peru's Forced Sterilization Tragedy Drags on in the Courts."
BioEdge. January 31, 2023. https://bioedge.org/public_health/population
/perus-forced-sterilization-tragedy-drags-on-in-the-courts/.

Corte Interamericana de Derechos Humanos. "Caso Brítez Arce y Otros v.
Argentina" [Case of Brítez Arce and others vs. Argentina]. November 16,
2022. https://www.corteidh.or.cr/docs/casos/articulos/resumen_474_esp
.pdf.

Corte Superior de Justicia de Perú. "Inst. No. 2000-0785-0-2001-JR-PE-02."
2001. https://1996pnsrpf2000.wordpress.com/wp-content/uploads/2014/09
/victoriavigo_sentenciaef_autor-inmediato.pdf.

Crenshaw, Kimberle. "Mapping the Margins: Intersectionality, Identity Politics, and Violence against Women of Color." *Stanford Law Review* 43, no. 6 (1991): 1241–1299.

Cuba Corimaita, Kahty. "Huella Psicológicas de la Esterilización Forzada" [Psychological marks of forced sterilization]. *Revista Ideele* 244 (2014). https://www.verdadyreconciliacionperu.com/admin/files/articulos/2027 _digitalizacion.pdf.

Cueto, Marcos. "La vocación por volver a empezar: Las políticas de población en el Perú" [The call for starting over: Population politics in Peru]. *Revista Peruana de Medicina Experimental y Salud Publica* 23, no. 2 (2006): 123–131.

Cumes, Aura Estela. "Mujeres indígenas patriarcado y colonialismo: Un desafío a la segregación comprensiva de las formas de dominio" [Indigenous women, patriarchy, and colonialism: A challenge against comprehensive segreation of forms of dominance]. *Anuario de Hojas de Warmi* 17 (2012). https://revistas.um.es/hojasdewarmi/article/view/180291.

Davila Puño, Julio. *Perú: Gobiernos Locales y Pueblos Indígenas* [Local governments and Indigenous peoples]. Tarea Grafica Educativa, 2005.

Davis, Angela Y. *Women, Race and Class*. Vintage Books, 1983.

De Greiff, Pablo. "Justice and Reparations." In *The Handbook of Reparations*, edited by Pablo de Greiff. Oxford University Press, 2006.

De la Cadena, Marisol. "Discriminación étnica" [Ethnic discrimination]. *Cuestión del Estado* 32 (2003): 1–9.

De la Cadena, Marisol. *Indigenous Mestizos: The Politics of Race and Culture in Cuzco, Peru, 1919–1991*. Duke University Press, 2000.

De La Cruz Huamán, Rosario B. "Análisis de las Esterilizaciones Forzadas en el Perú desde una Perspectiva de Interculturalidad Critica" [Analysis of forced sterilizations in Peru from a perspective of critical interculturality]. *Tierra Nuestra* 12, no. 1 (2018). https://doi.org/10.21704/rtn.v12i1.1272.

"Decreto Legislativo No. 346" [Legislative decree no. 346]. 1985. https://faolex .fao.org/docs/pdf/per128573.pdf.

Defensoría del Pueblo. *Anticoncepción Quirúrgica Voluntaria I: Casos Investigados por la Defensoría del Pueblo* [Voluntary surgical contraception I: Cases investigated by the Human Rights Ombudsman's Office]. Defensoría del Pueblo, 1998.

Defensoría del Pueblo. *Decimonoveno Informe Anual de la Defensoría del Pueblo* [19th annual report of the Human Rights Ombudsman's Office]. Defensoría del Pueblo, 2015.

Defensoría del Pueblo. *Informe de la Defensoría del Pueblo del Peru para el cuarto ciclo del examen periódico universal* [Human Rights Ombudsman's Office report for the fourth cycle of UPR review]. Defensoría del Pueblo, 2022.

Defensoría del Pueblo. *La actuación del estado frente a la violencia sexual contra la niñez y adolescencia Indígena Awajún en la provincia de Condorcanqui* [State actions towards sexual violence against girls and Indigenous adolescents]. Defensoría del Pueblo, 2024.

Defensoría del Pueblo. *La aplicación de la anticoncepción quirúrgica y los derechos reproductivos III: Casos Investigados por la Defensoría del Pueblo* [Application of surgical contraception and reproductive rights III: Cases investigated by the Human Rights Ombudsman's Office]. Defensoría del Pueblo, 2002.

Defensoría del Pueblo. *La aplicación de la anticoncepción quirúrgica y los derechos reproductivos II: Casos investigados por La Defensoría del Pueblo* [Application of surgical contraception and reproductive rights II: Cases investigated by the Human Rights Ombudsman's Office]. Defensoría del Pueblo, 2000.

Degregori, Carlos Iván. "Identidad Étnica, Movimientos Sociales y Participación Política en el Perú" [Ethnic identity, social movements, and political participation in Peru]. In *Democracia, etnicidad y violencia política en los países andinos*, edited by Alberto Adrianzén, Jean Michel Blanquer, Ricardo Calla, and others. Instituto de Estudios Peruanos, 1993.

DEMUS. "Cédula de notificación: Resolución formalización de denuncia esterilizaciones forzadas" [Notification: Resolution that formalizes complaint of forced sterilizations]. 2018. http://www.demus.org.pe/wp-content /uploads/2019/01/12-11-18-Resoluci%C2%A6n-Formalizaci%C2%A6n -denuncia-caso-EEFF-versi%C2%A6n-comprimida.pdf.

DEMUS. "Esterilizaciones Forzadas en Perú: Luego de 18 Años de Proceso Penal se Abre Investigación Judicial Contra Alberto Fujimori y sus Exministros de Salud" [Forced sterilizations in Peru: After 18 years of the legal process opens a judicial investigation against Alberto Fujimori and his ex-ministers of health]. December 16, 2021. https://www.demus.org.pe.

DEMUS. "Poder judicial ordena al ejecutivo cumplir con reparaciones integrales a las víctimas de esterilizaciones forzadas" [Judicial branch orders executive to comply with integral reparations for victims of forced sterilizations]. December 2, 2022. https://www.demus.org.pe/noticias/poder -judicial-ordena-al-ejecutivo-cumplir-con-reparaciones-integrales-a-las -victimas-de-esterilizaciones-forzadas/.

Diakonia. "Las Esterilizaciones Forzadas—un Crimen Que Nadie Quiere Reconocer" [Forced sterilizations: A crime no one wants to recognize].

Accessed June 20, 2019. https:// www.diakonia.se/es/donde-trabajamos/peru /demus/.

"Dina Boluarte: Pedro Castillo se reunirá con las víctimas del caso esterilizaciones forzadas" [Pedro Castillo will meet with victims of forced sterilizations]. Ideele Radio. May 19, 2021. https://www.ideeleradio.pe/lo-ultimo /dina-boluarte-pedro-castillo-se-reunira-con-las-victimas-del-caso -esterilizaciones-forzadas/.

Doran, Marie-Christine. "Indigenous Peoples in Chile: Contesting Violence, Building New Meanings for Rights and Democracy." In *Human Rights as Battlefields: Changing Practices and Contestations*, edited by Gabriel Blouin-Genest, Marie-Christine Doran, and Sylvie Paquerot. Palgrave Macmillan, 2019.

Dussel, Enrique. *Invention of the Americas: Eclipse of "the Other" and the Myth of Modernity.* Continuum, 1995.

DW. "Chile amplia por tercera vez extradicion de Alberto Fujimori" [Chile expands for the third time the extradition of Alberto Fujimori]. June 25, 2024. https://www.dw.com/es/chile-ampl%C3%ADa-por-tercera-vez -extradici%C3%B3n-de-alberto-fujimori/a-69461905.

El Comercio. "Estado le debe mas de S/100 millones a clínicas privadas por atender asegurados del SIS y EsSalud, según ACP" [The state owes more than S/100 millions to private clinics for attending those insured with SIS and EsSalud, according to ACP]. June 16, 2022. https://elcomercio .pe/economia/peru/estado-le-debe-mas-de-s-100-millones-a-clinicas -privadas-por-atender-asegurados-del-sis-y-essalud-segun-acp-rmmn -noticia/?ref=ecr.

El Peruano. "Ley No. 31119" [Law no. 31119]. Accessed October 9, 2021. https:// busquedas.elperuano.pe.

El Peruano. "Ministerio de Cultura: 38.5% de la población indígena vive en situación de pobreza" [Ministry of Culture: 38.5% of Indigenous population lives in poverty]. June 24, 2022. https://elperuano.pe/noticia/162238 -ministerio-de-cultura-385-de-la-poblacion-indigena-vive-en-situacion -de-pobreza.

El Peruano. "Normas Legales" [Legal norms]. February 6, 2021. https://busquedas .elperuano.pe/download/url/ley-que-modifica-los-articulos-3-y-6-de-la -ley-28592-ley-qu-ley-n-31119-1926075-2.

El Peruano. "Normas Legales" [Legal norms]. July 29, 2005. https://www.mimp .gob.pe/homemimp/direcciones/ddcp/normas/4_5_Ley_28592_Crea_el _PIR.pdf.

El Tiempo. "Por Programa de Planificación Familiar Enfrentamiento Fujimori-Iglesia" [Due to the family planning program confrontation Fujimori-Church]. November 2, 1990. https://www.eltiempo.com/archivo /documento/MAM-2438.

Elinghaus, Katherine. "Biological Absorption and Genocide: A Comparison of Indigenous Assimilation Policies in the United States and Australia." *Genocide Studies and Prevention: An International Journal* 4, no. 1 (2009): 59–79.

Estermann, Josef. *Filosofía Andina* [Andean philosophy]. Instituto Superior Ecuménico Andino de Teología, 2006.

Ewig, Christina. "La Economía Política de Esterilización Forzada en el Perú" [The political economy of forced sterilization in Peru]. In *Memorias del Caso Peruano de Esterilización Forzada*, edited Alejandra Ballón. Biblioteca Nacional del Perú, 2014.

Ewig, Christina. "Hijacking Global Feminism: Feminists, the Catholic Church, and the Family Planning Debacle in Peru." *Feminist Studies* 32, no. 3 (2006), 632–659.

Flores Galindo, Alberto. *Buscando un Inca* [Finding an Inca]. Editorial Horizonte, 1988.

Fontaine, Theodore. Foreword to *Colonial Genocide in Indigenous North America*, edited by Andrew Woolford, Jeff Benvenuto, and Alexander Hinton. Duke University Press, 2014.

Fujimori, Alberto. "Before the IV World Conference on Women, September 15, 1995, Beijing, China." Speech presented at the Beijing Conference on Women, United Nations, September 15, 1995. Traducción no oficial del español. Accessed May 1, 2019. https://www.un.org/esa/gopher-data/conf /fwcw/conf/gov/950915131946.txt.

Galeano, Eduardo. *Open Veins of Latin America*. Monthly Press, 1997.

Gap Min, Pyong. *Korean "Comfort Women": Military Brothels, Brutality, and the Redress Movement*. Rutgers University Press, 2021.

Gestión. "Elegir entre Keiko Fujimori y Humala, es como optar por el cáncer o el sida" [Choosing between Keiko Fujimori and Humala is like opting for cancer or AIDS]. 2011. https://archivo.gestion.pe/noticia/290532/elegir -entre-keiko-fujimori-humala-como-optar-cancer-sida.

Gestión. "Pedro Castillo y Keiko Fujimori polemizan sobre el caso de las esterilizaciones forzadas" [Pedro Castillo and Keiko Fujimori polemize over the case of forced sterilizations]. May 30, 2021. https://gestion.pe/peru/politica /debate-presidencial-del-jne-pedro-castillo-y-keiko-fujimori-polemizan

-sobre-el-caso-de-las-esterilizaciones-forzadas-elecciones-2021-peru
-libre-fuerza-popular-nndc-noticia/.

Gestión. "TC Vera Mañana Habeas Corpus Que Busca Liberar a Alberto Fujimori" [TC will see tomorrow habeas corpus that seeks to liberate Alberto Fujimori]. February 22, 2022. https://gestion.pe.

Getgen, Jocelyn E. "Untold Truths: The Exclusion of Enforced Sterilizations from the Peruvian Truth Commission's Final Report." *Boston College Third World Law Journal* 29, no. 1 (2009). https://scholarship.law.cornell.edu/facpub/1087.

Gómez Vega, Renzo. "Más de 500 estudiantes de la Amazonía peruana fueron abusadas por sus profesores de manera sistemática" [More than 500 students of the Peruvian Amazon were abused systematically by their professors]. *El País.* June 24, 2024. https://elpais.com/america/2024-06-24/mas
-de-500-estudiantes-de-la-amazonia-peruana-fueron-abusadas-por-sus
-profesores-de-manera-sistematica.html?event_log=oklogin.

González Casanova, Pablo. *Sociología de la explotación* [Sociology of exploitation]. Siglo del Hombre Editores, CLACSO, 2009.

Greeley, Robin Adéle, Michael R. Orwicz, José Luis Falconi, Ana María Reyes, Fernando J. Roseberg, and Lisa J. Laplante. "Repairing Symbolic Reparations: Assessing the Effectiveness of Memorialization in the Inter-American System of Human Rights." *International Journal of Transitional Justice* 14 (2020). https://doi.org/10.1093/ijtj/ijaa002.

Green, Shane. "Incas, Indios, and Indigenism in Peru." NACLA. 2007. https://nacla.org/article/incas-indios-and-indigenism-peru#2.

Grupo de Trabajo sobre Justicia Transicional y el ODS16+. "Hacia un cambio centrado en las victimas [Towards a change centered on victims]." ICTJ. June 2024. https://www.ictj.org/sites/default/files/2024-06/jac_report_wg
-tj-sdg16_2023_sp.pdf.

Guaman Poma de Ayala, Felipe. *Nueva corónica y buen gobierno* [New chronicle and good government]. Edited by Franklin Pease. Biblioteca Ayacucho, 1980.

Gugelberger, Georg M. *The Real Thing: Testimonial Discourse and Latin America.* Duke University Press, 1996.

Haas, Megan. "Fujimori Extraditable! Chilean Supreme Court Sets International Precedent for Human Rights Violations." *University of Miami Inter-American Law Review* 39, no. 2 (2008): 373–407.

Hamber, Brandon. *Transforming Societies after Political Violence: Truth, Reconciliation, and Mental Health.* Springer, 2009.

Hayner, Priscilla B. *Unspeakable Truths: Transitional Justice and the Challenge of Truth Commissions*. 2nd ed. Routledge, 2011.

Hirsch, Susan F. "The Victim Deserving of Global Justice: Power, Caution, and Recovering Individuals." In *Mirrors of Justice. Law and Power in the Post-Cold War Era*, edited by Kamari Maxine Clarke and Mark Goodale. Cambridge University Press, 2010.

Human Rights Committee. "General Comment No. 36." September 3, 2019. https://documents-dds-ny.un.org/doc/UNDOC/GEN/G19/261/15/PDF/G1926115.pdf?OpenElement.

Iglesia, Cristina, and Julio Schvarztman. *Cautivas y misioneros: Mitos blancos de la Conquista* [Captives and missionaries: White myths of the Conquest]. Catálogos Editora, 1987.

Ilizarbe Pizarro, Carmen. *La Democracia y la Calle: Protestas y contrahegemónicas en el Perú* [Democracy and the streets: Protests and counterhegemony in Peru]. Instituto de Estudios Peruanos, 2022.

Infobae. "Corte Suprema anula proceso de esterilizaciones forzadas cometidas en el régimen de Alberto Fujimori." December 7, 2023, https://www.infobae.com/peru/2023/12/07/alberto-fujimori-corte-suprema-anula-proceso-judicial-sobre-esterilizaciones-forzadas/.

Instituto Nacional de Desarrollo de Pueblos Andinos, Amazónicos y Afro-peruanos (INDEPA). "Mapa Etnolingüístico del Perú" [Ethnolinguistic map of Peru]. *Revista Peruana de Medicina Experimental y Salud Pública* 27, no. 2 (2010). https://www.redalyc.org/articulo.oa?id=36319368019.

Instituto Nacional de Estadística e Informática (INEI). *Perú: Resultados Definitivos* [Peru: Definitive results]. INEI, 2018.

Instituto Nacional de Estadística e Informática (INEI). *Perú: Síntesis Estadística 2015* [Perú: Statistical overview]. INEI, 2015. https://www.inei.gob.pe/media/MenuRecursivo/publicaciones_digitales/Est/Lib1292/libro.pdf.

Inter-American Commission on Human Rights. "IACHR Expresses Its Deep Concern over the Claim of Sterilizations Against Indigenous Women in Canada." OAS. January 18, 2019. http://www.oas.org/en/iachr/media_center/PReleases/2019/010.asp.

Inter-American Commission on Human Rights. "IACHR Files Case Concerning Peru with IA Court on Sterilization Without Consent." OAS. August 18, 2023. https://www.oas.org/en/iachr/jsForm/?File=/en/iachr/media_center/preleases/2023/186.asp.

Inter-American Commission on Human Rights (IACHR). Report No. 71/03. Petition 12.191. *Friendly Settlement María Mamérita Mestanza-Chávez.* IACHR, 2003. http://cidh.org/annualrep/2003eng/ Peru.12191.htm.

Inter-American Court of Human Rights. "Caso Eduardo Nicolás Cruz Sánchez y otros (Chavín de Huántar) v. Perú" [Case Eduardo Nicolás Cruz Sánchez and others (Chavín de Huántar) v. Peru]. 2012. https://www .corteidh.or.cr/docs/casos/cruz-sanchez/esap.pdf.

International Center for Transitional Justice. *Reparations in Peru: From Recommendations to Implementations.* ICTJ, 2013.

International Criminal Court. "Rome Statute of the International Criminal Court." 2002. https://www.icccpi.int/nr/rdonlyres/ea9aeff7-5752-4f84 -be94-0a655eb30e16/0/rome_statute_english.pdf.

International Federation of Gynecology and Obstetrics. "Executive Board Meeting: Female Contraceptive Sterilization." June 2011. https://www .womenenabled.org.

Jacob, Margaret D. "The Habit of Elimination: Indigenous Child Removal in Settler Colonial Nations in the Twentieth Century." In *Colonial Genocide in Indigenous North America*, edited by Andrew Woolford, Jeff Benvenuto, and Alexander Hinton. Duke University Press, 2014.

Janoff, Abby F. "Rights of the Pregnant Child vs. Rights of the Unborn Under the Convention on the Rights of the Child." *Boston University International Law Journal* 22 (2004): 163–188.

Jiménez, Beatriz. "Miles de peruanos marchan en Lima para pedir: Dignidad, Fujimori nunca más" [Thousands of peruvians march in Lima to demand: Dignity, Fujimori never again]. *El Mundo.* May 27, 2011. https://www.elmundo .es/america/2011/05/27/noticias/1306459260.html.

Jung, Jae-wook. "위안부 피해자 할머니 "내 소원은 한국과 일본이 원수 지지 않는 것" [Comfort women victim grandmother: "My wish is that South Korea and Japan do not become enemies"]. *Future Korea Weekly.* June 24, 2015. http://www.futurekorea.co.kr/news/articleView.html?idxno=28466.

Keck, Margaret E., and Kathryn Sikkink. *Activists Beyond Borders: Advocacy Networks in International Politics.* Cornell University Press, 1998.

Kelly, Liz, Sheila Burton, and Linda Regan. "Beyond Victim or Survivor: Sexual Violence, Identity and Feminist Theory and Practice." In *Sexualizing the Social*, edited by Lisa Adkins and Vicki Merchant. Palgrave Macmillan, 1996.

Khan, Asher. "Reivindicar la cercanía entre los feminismos poscoloniales y decoloniales con base en Spivak y Rivera Cusicanqui" [Reclaiming the closeness between postcolonial and decolonial feminisms based in Spivak and Rivera Cusicanqui]. *Tabula Rasa* 30 (2019): 13–25.

Kim, Hun Joon. *The Massacres at Mt. Halla: Sixty Years of Truth Seeking in South Korea*. Cornell University Press, 2014.

La República. "Denuncia de Esterilizaciones Forzadas Fue Archivada por la Fiscalía" [Complaint of forced sterilizations put aside by Prosecutor's Office]. July 27, 2016. http://larepublica.pe/sociedad/789156-denuncia-de -esterilizaciones-forzadas-fue-archivada-porla-fiscalia.

LeBlanc, Lawrence J. *The Convention the Rights of the Child: United Nations Law- making on Human Rights*. University of Nebraska Press, 1995.

Leinaweaver, Jessaca B. *The Circulation of Children: Kindship, Adoption, and Moral- ity in Andean Peru*. Duke University Press, 2008.

Lerner, Salomón Febres. *La Rebelión de la Memoria: Selección de Discursos 2001– 2003* [The rebellion of memory: Selected discourses 2001–2003]. Centro de Estudios y Publicaciones, 2004.

Lerner, Salomón Febres. "Tareas de la Comisión de la Verdad y Reconcilia- ción: Fundamentos Teológicos y Éticos" [Work of Truth and Reconciliation Commission: Theological and ethical elements]. In *Verdad y Reconciliación: Reflexiones Éticas* [Truth and reconciliation: Ethical reflections], edited by Salomón Lerner, José Burneo, Guillermo Kerber et al. Centro de Estudios y Publicaciones, 2002.

Letschert, Rianne, and Jan van Dijk. "New Faces of Victimhood: Reflections on the Unjust Sides of Globalization." In *The New Faces of Victimhood: Glo- balization, Transnational Crimes and Victim Rights*, edited by Rianne Letschert and Jan van Dijk. Springer, 2011.

Libertad, Lisandro, and Eduardo Brenis Pita. "Entrevista: A 31 años de auto- golpe de Fujimori, las victimas de esterilización forzada siguen exigiendo justicia" [31 years since the autocoup of Fujimori, victims of forced ster- ilization continue demanding justice]. *La Izquierda Diario*. April 5, 2023. https://www.laizquierdadiario.com/A-31-anos-de-autogolpe-de-Fujimori -las-victimas-de-esterilizacion-forzada-siguen-exigiendo-justicia.

Lopez, Iris, *Masters of Choice: Puerto Rico Women's Struggle for Reproductive Freedom*. Rutgers University Press, 2008.

Lugones, María. "Colonialidad y género" [Coloniality and gender]. *Tabula Rasa* 9 (2008): 73–101.

Luna, Zakiya. *Reproductive Rights as Human Rights*. New York University Press, 2020.

Luttrell-Rowland, Mikaela. *Political Children: Violence, Labor, and Rights in Peru*. Stanford University Press, 2023.

Madrid, Raul. "Ethnic Proximity and Ethnic Voting in Peru." *Journal of Latin American Studies* 43, no. 2 (2011). https://doi.org/10.1017/S0022216X11000034.

Mantilla Falcón, Julissa. "El Caso de las Esterilizaciones Forzadas en el Perú Como una Violación de los Derechos Humanos" [The case of forced sterilizations in Peru as a violation of human rights]. *Ius et Veritas* 23 (2016). https://revistas.pucp.edu.pe/index.php/iusetveritas/article/view/16014.

Martín Beristain, Carlos. *Manual sobre perspectiva psicosocial en la investigación de derechos humanos* [Manual on the psychosocial perspective in the investigation of human rights]. Center for Justice and International Law (CEJIL), 2015.

McDermott, Mairi. "Mo(ve)ments of affect: Towards an Embodied Pedagogy for Anti-Racism Education." In *Politics of Anti-Racism Education: In Search of Strategies for Transformative Learning*, edited by G. J. S. Dei and M. McDermott. Springer, 2013.

[startMcEnvoy, Kieran, and Kirsten McConnachie. "Victimology in Transitional Justice: Victimhood, Innocence, and Hierarchy." *European Journal of Criminology* 9, no. 5 (2012). https://doi.org/10.1177/1477370812454204.

Méndez, Juan. "Significance of the Fujimori Trial." *American University International Law Review* 25 (2010): 649–656.

Mignolo, Walter D. *La Idea de América Latina* [The idea of Latin America]. Gedisa, 2005.

Millán Moncayo, Márgara. "Feminismos, postcolonialidad, descolonización: ¿Del centro a los márgenes? *Andamios* 8, no. 17 (2011): 11–36.

Ministerio de Cultura. "Lista de lenguas indígenas originarias" [List of Indigenous languages]. Accessed April 18, 2022. https://bdpi.cultura.gob.pe/lenguas.

Ministerio de Justicia y Derechos Humanos. Decreto Legislativo No. 635 Código Penal. 2016. http://spij.minjus.gob.pe/content/publicaciones_oficiales/img/CODIGOPENAL.pdf.

Ministerio de la Mujer y Poblaciones Vulnerables. "Conociendo el Servicio de la Defensoría del Niño y del Adolescente" [Getting to know the service in the defense of children and adolescents]. Accessed October 2, 2021. https://www.mimp.gob.pe/files/direcciones/dgnna/conociendo_servicio_dna.pdf.

Ministerio de la Mujer y Poblaciones Vulnerables. "Ley No. 27337—Aprueba el nuevo código de los niños y adolescentes" [Law No. 27337: Approves the new code on children and adolescents]. 2000. Accessed October 1, 2021. https://www.mimp.gob.pe/files/direcciones/dga/nuevo-codigoninos-adolescentes.pdf.

Ministerio de la Mujer y Poblaciones Vulnerables. "Ministra Anahí Durand Se Reúne con Mujeres Víctimas de Esterilizaciones Forzadas" [Minister

Anahí Durand meets with women victims of forced sterilizations]. Gobierno del Perú. October 19, 2021. https://www.gob.pe.

Ministerio de la Mujer y Poblaciones Vulnerables. *Resumen Estadístico Victimas de Esterilizaciones Forzadas 2016.* [Summary statistics victims of forced sterilizations 2016]. Ministerio de la Mujer y Poblaciones Vulnerables, 2016.

Ministerio de la Mujer y Poblaciones Vulnerables. *Resumen Estadístico Victimas de Esterilizaciones Forzadas 2017* [Statistical summary of victims of forced sterilization 2017]. Ministerio de la Mujer y Poblaciones Vulnerables, 2017.

Ministerio de la Mujer y Poblaciones Vulnerables. *Resumen Estadístico Victimas de Esterilizaciones Forzadas 2018* [Summary statistics victims of forced sterilizations 2018]. Ministerio de la Mujer y Poblaciones Vulnerables, 2018.

Ministerio de la Mujer y Poblaciones Vulnerables. *Resumen Estadístico Victimas de Esterilizaciones Forzadas 2019* [Summary statistics victims of forced sterilizations 2019]. Ministerio de la Mujer y Poblaciones Vulnerables, 2019.

Ministerio de Salud. *Programa de Salud Reproductiva y Planificación Familiar 1996–2000* [Program of reproductive health and family planning 1996–2000]. Ministerio de Salud, 1996.

Ministerio de Salud (MINSA) and USAID. *Los primeros años del Proyecto 2000* [The first years of Project 2000]. Ministerio de Salud, 1997.

Ministerio Público. *Resolución Fiscal No. 16* [Fiscal resolution no. 16]. Ministerio Publico Fiscalía de la Nación, 2016.

Ministerio Público. "Resolución Formalización Denuncia Caso EEFF Versión Comprimida" [Resolution of formalization of complaint case EEFF shortened version]. Ministerio Público Fiscalía de la Nación. October 31, 2018. http://www.demus.org.pe/wpcontent/uploads/2019/01/12-1118-Resoluci%C2%A6n-Formalizaci%C2%A6n-denuncia-caso-EEFFversi%C2%A6n-comprimida.pdf, 1.

Moon, Claire. "'Who'll Pay Reparations on My Soul?' Compensation, Social Control and Social Suffering." *Social & Legal Studies* 21, no. 2 (2012): 187–199.

Morgan, Jennifer L. "Partus Sequitur Ventrem: Law, Race, and Reproduction in Colonial Slavery." *Small Axe* 22, no. 1 (2018): 1–17.

Municipalidad de Lima. "Realizan Tribunal De Conciencia Por Justicia Para Las Mujeres Víctimas Del Conflicto Armado Interno" [Justice tribunal of conscience held for female victims of the internal armed conflict]. November 8, 2013. https://www.youtube.com/watch?v=54gYcGyF03I.

"No hay campaña de esterilización" [There is no campaign of sterilizations]. *El Sol.* January 6, 1998. https://1996pnsrpf2000.files.wordpress.com/2012/10/el-sol-6-de-enero-de-1998.pdf.

O'Donnell, Norah, and Alicia Hastey. "The 4 Highest-Ranking Women in the U.S. Military Speak About the Obstacles They Overcame." *CBS News*. March 7, 2023. https://www.cbsnews.com/news/4-highest-ranking-women -u-s-military-speak-about-obstacles-challenges/.

Orentlicher, Diane F. "'Settling Accounts' Revisited: Reconciling Global Norms with Local Agency." *International Journal of Transitional Justice* 1, no. 1 (2007): 10–22.

Organización Nacional de Mujeres Indígenas Andinas y Amazónicas del Perú (ONAMIAP). "Testimony from Dionicia Calderón Arellano (Campesina)." Presented at ONAMIAP Public Forum and Hearing on Forced Sterilizations-Lima, 1st session, 2017.

Organización Nacional de Mujeres Indígenas Andinas y Amazónicas del Perú (ONAMIAP). "Testimony from Luisa Pinedo Rango (Campesina)." Presented at ONAMIAP Public Forum and Hearing on Forced Sterilizations-Lima, 1st session, 2017.

Organization of American States. "Inter-American Convention on the Prevention, Punishment, and Eradication of Violence Against Women (Convention of Belém do Pará)." 2023. https://www.oas.org/en/mesecvi/docs /BelemDoPara-ENGLISH.pdf.

Ossio, Juan M. "Existen las poblaciones indígenas andinas en el Perú" [There exist Indigenous Andean populations in Peru]. In *Indianismo e Indigenismo* [Indianism and indigenism], edited by José Alcina Franch. Alianza Universidad, 1990.

Paredes, Julieta. "Entronque patriarcal: La situación de las mujeres de los pueblos originarios de Abya Yala después de la invasión colonial de 1492" [Patriarchal convergence: The situation of native women in Abya Yala after the colonial invasion of 1492]. Tesis de Maestría. FLACSO, Buenos Aires, 2018. http://hdl.handle.net/10469/17739.

Patel, Priti. "Forced Sterilization of Women as Discrimination." *Public Health Reviews* 38 (2017). https://doi.org/10.1186/s40985-017-0060-9.

Pegoraro, Leonardo. "Second-Rate Victims: The Forced Sterilization of Indigenous Peoples in the USA and Canada." *Settler Colonial Studies* 5, no. 2 (2015). https://doi.org/10.1080/2201473X.2014.955947.

Peru21, "Informe.21." January 13, 2018. https://www.inei.gob.pe/media/inei_en _los_medios/13_ene_Peru-21_14-y-15-a.pdf.

Pine, Emilie. "Digital Campaigns, Forums, and Archives." In *Routledge Handbook of Memory Activism*, edited by Yifat Gutman and Jenny Wustenberg. Routledge, 2023.

Poma, Melania Canales. "La Justicia es Incansable para las Mujeres Indígenas." In *Las esterilizaciones forzadas 25 años después: Justicia y reparación*, edited by Lucía Santos Peralta. Pontifica Univerisdad Católica del Perú, 2023.

"Por Programa de Planificación Familiar Enfrentamiento Fujimori-Iglesia" [Due to family planning program, tension Fujimori-Church]. *El Tiempo*. November 2, 1990. Accessed November 1, 2018. https://www.eltiempo.com /archivo/documento/MAM-2438.

Premo, Bianca. "Pena Y Protección: Delincuencia Juvenil Y Minoridad Legal En Lima Virreinal, Siglo XVIII" [Penalty and protection: Juvenile crime and legal minority in viceroyalty of Lima, XVIII century]. *Histórica* 24, no. 1 (2000): 85–120. https://doi.org/10.18800/historica.200001.004.

Prosecutor v. Goran Jelisic. International Criminal Tribunal for the former Yugoslavia (ICTY). IT-95-10-A. Accessed February 1, 2020. https://www.icty.org /x/cases/jelisic/ind/en/jel-ii950721e.pdf.

Quijano, Aníbal. "Colonialidad del Poder, Eurocentrismo y América Latina." In *La Colonialidad del Saber: Eurocentrismo y Ciencias Sociales*, edited by Edgardo Lander. Consejo Latinoamericano de Ciencias Sociales (CLACSO), 2000.

Quipu Project. "The Quipu Project." 2017. https://interactive.quipu-project .com/#/en/quipu/listen/intronode?currentTime=0&view=thread.

Republic of Perú. "Título II Del Estado y la Nación" [Title II of the state and nation]. 1993. http://www4.congreso.gob.pe/comisiones/1996/constitucion /cons_t2.htm.

República del Perú. "D.L. No. 26102—Aprueba código de los niños y adolescentes" [D.L. no. 26102: Approves code on children and adolescents]. 1992. Accessed October 2, 2021. https://docs.peru.justia.com/federales/decretos -leyes/26102-dec-28-1992.pdf.

Resistencia. "El 'Plan Verde': Historia de un traición." 2001. http://www .resistencia.org/documentos/el_plan_verde/historia_de_una_traicion.pdf.

Rivera Casanovas, Claudia. "Las mujeres en Tiwanku: Aproximaciones a los roles de género y aspectos de poder en una sociedad prehispánica" [The women in Tiwanku: Approximations of gender roles and aspects of power in a prehispanic society]. In *Otras miradas, presencias femeninas en una historia de larga duración*, edited by. Walter Sánchez Canedo and Claudia Rivera Casanovas. Instituto de Investigaciones Antropológicas y Museo Arqueológico de la Universidad Mayor de San Simón, 2016.

Rivera Cusicanqui, Silvia. "Ch'ixinakax utxiwa: A Reflection on the Practices and Discourses of Decolonization." *South Atlantic Quarterly* III, no. 1 (2012). https://doi.org/10.1215/00382876-1472612.

Rivera Cusicanqui, Silvia. *Ch'ixinakax utxiwa: Una reflexión sobre prácticas y discursos descolonizadores.* Tinta Limón, 2010.

Rivera Cusicanqui, Silvia. "La noción de 'derecho' o las paradojas de la modernidad postcolonial: Indígenas y mujeres en Bolivia" [The nation of "rights" or the paradoxes of postcolonial modernity: Indigenous and women in Bolivia]. *Aportes Andinos* 11 (2004). https://revistas.uasb.edu.ec/index.php/aa/article/view/3685.

Rivera Cusicanqui, Silvia. *Violencias (re) encubiertas en Bolivia* [Violence (un)covered in Bolivia]. Editorial Piedra Rota, 2010.

Robins, Nicholas. *Genocide and Millennialism in Upper Peru: The Great Rebellion of 1780–1782.* Praeger, 2002.

Rogobete, Ileana Carmen. *Reconstructing Trauma and Meaning: Life Narratives of Survivors of Political Violence During Apartheid in South Africa.* Cambridge Scholars Publishing, 2015.

Roht-Arriaza, Naomi. "Measures of Non-Repetition in Transitional Justice: The Missing Link?" In *From Transitional to Transformative Justice,* edited by Paul Gready and Simon Robins. Cambridge University Press, 2019.

Rostworowski, María. *Historia del Tahuantinsuyu* [History of Tahuantinsuyu]. Instituto de Estudios Peruanos, 1999.

Rostworowski, María. *La mujer en el Perú prehispánico* [The woman in prehispanic Peru]. Instituto de Estudios Peruanos, 1995.

Rostworowski, María. *Los Incas: Economía, Sociedad y Estado en la Era del Tahuantinsuyo* [The Incas: Economy, society, and the state in the era of Tahuantinsuyo]. Ediciones Inkamaru, 2012.

Ruiz Molleda, Juan Carlos. "Análisis de la Constitucionalidad de la Nueva Ley Anti-ONG aprobada por el Congreso" [Analysis of the constitutionality of the new anti-NGO law approved by Congress]. March 14, 2025. https://www.idl.org.pe/analisis-de-la-constitucionalidad-de-la-nueva-ley-anti-ong-aprobada-por-el-congreso/.

Santa Cruz, Nicomedes. *La décima en el Perú.* [The décima in Peru]. Instituto de Estudios Peruanos, 1982.

Santa Cruz, Victoria. "El importante rol que cumple el obstáculo" [The important role of the "obstacle"]. In *El Perú en los albores del siglo XXI-4: Ciclo de conferencias 1999–2000* [Peru at the dawn of the century XXI–4: Cycle of conferences 1999–2000], edited by Fondo Editorial del Congreso del Perú. Fondo Editorial del Congreso del Perú, 1999.

Sanz Romero, Estefanía. "La mujer en el sistema sociopolítico Inca" [The woman in the Incan sociopolitical system]. Publicaciones Didácticas, 2016. https://core.ac.uk/download/pdf/235858099.pdf.

Schabas, William A. *Genocide in International Law: The Crime of Crimes.* Cambridge University Press, 2009.

"Schenone: Gobierno no impone esterilización de mujeres" [Schenone: Government does not impose sterilizations on women]. *Expreso.* December 9, 1997. https://1996pnsrpf2000.files.wordpress.com/2012/10/expreso-9-de -diciembre-de-1997.pdf.

Schoen, Johanna. *Choice and Coercion: Birth Control, Sterilization, and Abortion in Public Health and Welfare.* University of North Carolina Press, 2005.

Serra, Ainhoa Molina. "Esterilizaciones (forzadas) en Perú: Poder y Configuraciones Narrativas" [Forced sterilizations in Peru: Power and narrative configurations]. *Revista de Antropología Iberoamericana* 12, no. 1 (2017). https:// doi.org/10.11156/aibr.120103e.

Silva Santisteban, Rocío. "Esterilizaciones forzadas: Biopolítica, patriarcado y genocidio" [Forced sterilizations: Biopolitics, patriarchy, and genocide]. In *Perú: Las esterilizaciones forzadas, en la década del terror* [Peru: Forced sterilizations in the decade of terror], edited by Alberto Chirif. IWGIA (International Work Group for Indigenous Affairs), 2021.

SisterSong. "Mission." 2022. https://www.sistersong.net/mission.

Smith, Andrea. *Conquest-Sexual Violence and American Indian Genocide.* Duke University Press, 2005.

Son, Angella. "Translator's Preface." In *Stories That Make History: The Experience and Memories of the Japanese Military Comfort Girls-Women*, edited by The Research Team of the War & Women's Human Rights Center and The Korean Council for the Women Drafted for Military Sexual Slavery by Japan. De Gruyter, 2020.

Starn, Orin. "Antropología Andina, 'andinismo' Y Sendero Luminoso" [Andean anthropology, "andeanism' and Shining Path]. *Allpanchis* 24, no. 39 (1992): 15–71. https://doi.org/10.36901/allpanchis.v24i39.803.

Stavig, Lucía. "Unwittingly Agreed: Fujimori, Neoliberal Governmentality, and the Inclusive Exclusion of Indigenous Women." *Latin American and Caribbean Ethnic Studies*, 17, no. 1 (2021): 34–57.

Stetz, Margaret D. "Making Girl Victims Visible: A Survey of Representations That Have Circulated in the West." In *Japanese Military Sexual Slavery:*

The Transnational Redress Movement for the Victims, edited by Pyong Gap Min, Thomas Chung, and Sejung Sage Yim. De Gruyter, 2020.

Stote, Karen. *An Act of Genocide: Colonialism and the Sterilization of Aboriginal Women*. Fernwood, 2015.

Stote, Karen. "The Coercive Sterilization of Aboriginal Women in Canada." *American Indian Culture and Research Journal* 36, no. 3 (2012): 117–150.

Stover, Eric. *The Witness: War Crimes and the Promise in The Hague*. University of Pennsylvania Press, 2011.

Supa, Hilaria. "Esterilizaciones: ¡Hasta dónde puede llegar un ser humano con el menosprecio y el racismo!" [*Sterilizations: Until which point can a human being be undermined and be subject to racism!*]. In *Perú: Las esterilizaciones forzadas, en la década del terror* [Peru: Forced sterilizations in the decade of terror], edited by Alberto Chirif. IWGIA (International Work Group for Indigenous Affairs), 2021.

Supa, Hilaria. *Hilos de Mi Vida* [Threads of my life]. Ediciones del Congreso del Perú, 2010.

Supreme Court of Justice of Piura. "Sentencia." [Sentence]. July 5, 2001. https://1996pnsrpf2000.files.wordpress.com/2014/09/victoriavigo_sentenciaef_autor-inmediato.pdf.

Taft, Jessica. *The Kids Are in Charge*. New York University Press, 2019.

Tamayo, Giulia. *Derechos sexuales: Bajo la piel*. Centro de la Mujer Peruana Flora Tristán, 2001.

Tamayo, Giulia. *Nada Personal*. CLADEM, 1999.

Taylor, Lucy, and Geraldine Lublin. "Settler Colonial Studies and Latin America." *Settler Colonial Studies* 11, no. 3 (2021): 259–270.

Teitel, Ruti G. "Transitional Justice Genealogy." *Harvard Human Rights Journal* 16 (2003): 69–94.

"Testimonios" [Testimonies]. Archivo PSRPF. Accessed October 2, 2021. https://1996pnsrpf2000.wordpress.com/testimonios-2/testimonios/.

Thambinathan, Vievetha, and Elizabeth Anne Kinsella. "Decolonizing Methodologies in Qualitative Research: Creating Space for Transformative Praxis." *International Journal of Qualitative Methods* 20 (2021): 1–9.

Theidon, Kimberly. "First Do No Harm: Enforced Sterilizations and Gender Justice in Peru." *Open Democracy*. April 29, 2015. https://www.opendemocracy.net/en/opensecurity/first-do-no-harm-enforced-sterilizations-and-gender-justice-in-peru/.

Theidon, Kimberly. "Guerra Reproductiva: Esterilizaciones Forzadas en Perú" [Reproductive war: Forced sterilizations in Peru], in *Las esterilizaciones forzadas 25 años después: Justicia y reparación*, edited by Lucía Santos Peralta. Pontifica Univerisdad Católica del Perú, 2023.

Theobald, Brianna. *Reproduction on the Reservation: Pregnancy, Childbirth, and Colonialism in the Long Twentieth Century.* University of North Carolina Press, 2019.

Torpy, Sally J. "Native American Women and Coerced Sterilization: On the Trails of Tears in the 1970s." *American Indian Culture and Research Journal* 24, no. 2 (2000): 1–22.

Transfer Commission of the Truth and Reconciliation Commission of Peru. *Hatun Willakuy: Abbreviated Version of the Final Report of the Truth and Reconciliation Commission.* Transfer Commission of the Truth and Reconciliation Commission of Peru, 2014.

Tuhiwai Smith, Linda. *Decolonizing Methodologies: Research and Indigenous Peoples.* Zed Books, 2021.

Tzul Tzul, Gladys. "Forma Comunal de la Resistencia" [Communal form of resistance]. Dossier, Revista de la Universidad de México, 2019.

Ulfe, María Eugenia. "Desaparición Feminicida En Perú." NACLA. June 25, 2024. https://nacla.org/desaparicion-feminicida-en-peru.

United Nations. "Basic Principles and Guidelines on the Right to a Remedy and Reparation for Victims of Gross Violations of International Human Rights Law and Serious Violations of International Humanitarian Law." December 2005. https://www.ohchr.org/en/professionalinterest/pages/remedyandreparation.aspx.

United Nations. "Convention Against Torture and Other Cruel, Inhuman or Degrading Treatment or Punishment." December 10, 1984. https://www.ohchr.org/en/professionalinterest/pages/cat.aspx.

United Nations. "Convention on the Prevention and Punishment of the Crime of Genocide." December 9, 1948. https://www.un.org/en/genocideprevention/documents/atrocity-crimes/Doc.1_Convention%20on%20the%20Prevention%20and%20Punishment%20of%20the%20Crime%20of%20Genocide.pdf.

United Nations. "Convention on the Rights of the Child." November 20, 1989. https://www.ohchr.org/en/professionalinterest/pages/crc.aspx.

United Nations. "Declaration of Basic Principles of Justice for Victims of Crime and Abuse of Power." 1985. https://www.un.org/en/ga/search/view_doc.asp?symbol=A/RES/40/34.

United Nations. "Declaration on the Elimination of Violence against Women." December 20, 1993. https://www.ohchr.org/en/instruments-mechanisms/instruments/declaration-elimination-violence-against-women.

United Nations. "Geneva Declaration of the Rights of the Child." September 26, 1924. http://www.undocuments.net/gdrc1924.htm.

United Nations. "International Covenant on Civil and Political Rights." December 16, 1966. https://www.ohchr.org/en/professionalinterest/pages/ccpr.aspx.

United Nations. "International Covenant on Economic, Social and Cultural Rights." December 16, 1966. https://www.ohchr.org/en/professionalinterest/pages/cescr.aspx.

United Nations. "Peru: Fujimori Government's Forced Sterilization Policy Violated Women's Rights, UN Committee Says in Landmark Ruling." October 30, 2024. https://www.ohchr.org/en/press-releases/2024/10/peru-fujimori-governments-forced-sterilisation-policy-violated-womens-rights.

United Nations. "Report of the Special Rapporteur on Torture and other Cruel, Inhuman or Degrading Treatment or Punishment, Juan E. Méndez." February 1, 2013. https://www.ohchr.org/documents/hrbodies/hrcouncil/regularsession/session22/a.hrc.22.53_english.pdf.

United Nations. "Sexual and Reproductive Health and Rights." Accessed January 1, 2022. https://www.ohchr.org/en/issues/women/wrgs/pages/healthrights.aspx.

United Nations. "Technical Note on the Implementation of the United Nations Protocol on the Provision of Assistance to Victims of Sexual Exploitation and Abuse." 2021. https://www.un.org/preventing-sexual-exploitation-and-abuse/sites/www.un.org.preventing-sexual-exploitation-and-abuse/files/technical_note_on_the_implementation_of_the_un_protocol_on_the_provision_of_assistance_to_victims_of_sea_eng.pdf.

United Nations. "Twenty-Second Session, Geneva, 25 April–12 May 2000, Agenda Item 3." August 11, 2000. https://docs.un.org/en/E/C.12/2000/4#:~:text=In%20conformity%20with%20articles%2022,of%20the%20right%20to%20health.

United Nations. "Universal Declaration of Human Rights." 1949. https://www.un.org/en/udhrbook/pdf/udhr_booklet_en_web.pdf.

United Nations Committee on the Elimination of Discrimination Against Women. "CEDAW General Recommendation No. 24: Article 12 of the Convention (Women and Health)." 1999. https://www.refworld.org/docid/453882a73.html.

United Nations Office of the High Commissioner. "Basic Principles and Guidelines on the Right to a Remedy and Reparation for Victims of Gross Violations of International Human Rights Law and Serious Violations of International Humanitarian Law." 2005. https://www.ohchr.org/en

/instruments-mechanisms/instruments/basic-principles-and-guidelines
-right-remedy-and-reparation.

US Congress, House of Representatives. Committee on International Relations. *The Peruvian Population Control Program: Hearing Before the Subcommittee on International Operations and Human Rights.* 105th Cong., 2nd sess. (1998).

Valladolid, Orelia. "El infierno de las violaciones de niñas en comunidades awajún de Perú no es 'una práctica cultural'" [The hellish violations against girls in awajún communities in Peru is not a "cultural practice"]. *El País.* August 13, 2024. https://elpais.com/planeta-futuro/red-de-expertos/2024-08-14/el-infierno-de-las-ninas-en-comunidades-awajun-de-peru-no-es-una-practica-cultural.html.

van Krieken, Robert. "Rethinking Cultural Genocide: Aboriginal Child Removal and Settler-Colonial State." *Oceania* 75, no. 2 (2004): 125–151.

Van Vleet, Krisa E. *Hierarchies of Care.* University of Illinois Press, 2019.

Vasquez del Aguila, Ernesto. "Invisible Women: Forced Sterilization, Reproductive Rights, and Structural Inequalities in Peru of Fujimori and Toledo." *Estudos e Pesquisas em Psicología UERJ RJ* 6, no. 1 (2006). http://pepsic.bvsalud.org/pdf/epp/v6n1/v6n1a10.pdf.

Velásquez Nimatuj, Irma Alicia. "Acceso de las mujeres indígenas a la tierra, el territorio y los recursos naturales en América Latina y el Caribe" [Access of Indigenous women to earth, territory, and natural resources in Latin America and the Caribbean]. ONU Mujeres. October 2018. https://genderandsecurity.org/sites/default/files/Velasquez_Nimatuj_-_Acceso_de_m_indigenas_a_la_tierra.pdf.

Vicenti Carpio, Myla. "The Lost Generation: American Indian Women and Sterilization Abuse." *Social Justice* 31, no. 4 (2004): 40–53.

"Víctimas de esterilizaciones forzadas en Perú siguen luchando por la justicia" [Victims of forced sterilizations in Peru continue fighting for justice]. *France24.* January 30, 2023. https://www.france24.com/es/programas/boleto-de-vuelta/20230130-v%C3%ADctimas-de-esterilizaciones-forzadas-en-per%C3%BA-siguen-luchando-por-justicia.

Vicuña, Cecilia. "An Introduction to Mestizo Poetics." In *The Oxford Book of Latin American Poetry: A Bilingual Anthology*, edited by Cecilia Vicuna and Ernesto Livon-Grosman. Oxford University Press, 2009.

Vidal, Ana María. "Por el solo hecho de ser mujeres: La impunidad y el desamparo de miles de victimas frente al crimen de lesa humanidad de las esterilizaciones forzadas" [Just because one is a woman: Impunity and helplessness of thousands of victims in the face of crimes against humanity of forced sterilizations]. In *Perú: Las esterilizaciones forzadas, en la década del terror* [Peru: Forced sterilizations in the decade of terror], edited by Alberto Chirif. IWGIA (International Work Group for Indigenous Affairs), 2021.

Wesley-Esquimaux, Cynthia C., and Magdalena Smolewski. *Historic Trauma and Aboriginal Healing.* Aboriginal Healing Foundation, 2004.

Wilson, Shawn. *Research Is Ceremony: Indigenous Research Methods.* Fernwood Publishing, 2008.

Wobst, H. Martin. "Indigenous Archaeologies: A Worldwide Perspective on Human Materialities and Human Rights." In *Indigenous Archaeologies: A Reader on Decolonization*, edited by Margaret M. Bruchac, Siobhan M. Hart, and H. Martin Wobst. Routledge, 2016.

WOLA (Washington Office on Latin America). "Why I Will Vote for Humala." May 31, 2011. https://www.wola.org/analysis/why-i-will-vote-for-humala/.

World Health Organization. "The Prevention and Elimination of Disrespect and Abuse During Facility-Based Childbirth." 2015. http://www.who.int/reproductivehealth/topics/maternal_perinatal/statement-childbirth/en/.

Wulff, Dan. "Unquestioned Answers: A Review of Research Is Ceremony: Indigenous Research Methods." *Qualitative Report* 15, no. 5 (2010):1290–1295.

Younging, Gregory. *Elements of Indigenous Style: A Guide for Writing by and about Indigenous Peoples.* Brush Education, 2018.

INDEX

Founded in 1893,
UNIVERSITY OF CALIFORNIA PRESS
publishes bold, progressive books and journals
on topics in the arts, humanities, social sciences,
and natural sciences—with a focus on social
justice issues—that inspire thought and action
among readers worldwide.

The UC PRESS FOUNDATION
raises funds to uphold the press's vital role
as an independent, nonprofit publisher, and
receives philanthropic support from a wide
range of individuals and institutions—and from
committed readers like you. To learn more, visit
ucpress.edu/supportus.

www.ingramcontent.com/pod-product-compliance
Lightning Source LLC
Chambersburg PA
CBHW032345280326
41935CB00008B/454